CELEBRATING THE WORD

J. D. Crichton

Celebrating the Word

HOMILIES FOR THE SUNDAYS OF THE YEAR,
CYCLES A, B, AND C, WITH INTRODUCTIONS
ON THE NATURE OF THE LITURGICAL HOMILY,
ITS PREPARATION, AND ITS DELIVERY

the columba press

First published in 1995 by
ᴄHE ᴄoᴌᴜᴍBᴀ PRᴇSS
93 The Rise, Mount Merrion, Blackrock, Co Dublin, Ireland

Cover by Bill Bolger
Origination by The Columba Press
Printed in Ireland by Colour Books, Ltd, Dublin

ISBN 1 85607 123 5

Contents

References

Vatican Council II: The Conciliar and Post-Conciliar Documents, Edited by Austin Flannery OP, revised edition, 1988 (Dominican Publications, Dublin).

Lectionary I: Proper of Seasons, Sundays in Ordinary Time. 2nd revised edition. Introduction to this edition, pp xvii-xlvii.

Abbreviation: CL: *The Constitution on the Liturgy.*

The Biblical texts, as in the Lectionary, are from the *Jerusalem Bible.*

The psalms are from the *Grail Psalter.*

The Importance of the Word of God

After more than twenty-five years since the ending of the Second Vatican Council, it is possible that many do not realise how great a change was made in its emphasis on the scriptures in the Church's worship. In the pre-conciliar Mass the selection of scripture readings was haphazard and very meagre. There was an 'epistle' which, if you examined the context, sometimes began in the middle of a sentence; this was followed by a 'gradual', a few verses of scripture which often had no relevance to what had gone before, and the Alleluias with verse or verses which, if sung (and that was rare in parish churches), often took longer than the epistle and the gospel put together. The liturgy or ministry of the word was brought to an end with the proclamation of the gospel. Only at the principal Mass of the morning was there supposed to be a sermon (other Masses may or may not have an 'instruction' according to local diocesan rules) and its subject matter usually was not that of the liturgical texts. In some places the celebrant took off the chasuble before preaching as if to say, 'What follows has got nothing to do with what has gone before or indeed with what will come after.' In other sacramental celebrations, infant baptism, confirmation, penance, the anointing of the sick, there was no scripture reading and of course no homily. All was in Latin. At weddings there was often, though not always, a homily that may or may not have unfolded the rich meaning of Christian marriage.

For some years, however, before Vatican II there had been an ever increasing desire and pressure for a reform of the liturgy that, among other things, would allow of a much better use of the scriptures in its celebration. In this the Liturgical Movement was moving hand-in-hand with the Biblical Movement which was actively promoting the study and reading of the scriptures at home and at what came to be called Bible Services in church. What was desired (and required) was a radical reform of the Mass lectionary which would draw on the riches of the Old as well as the New Testament, and that, of course, the readings should be proclaimed in the language of the people. As we know, this all came to pass and the revision of the ministry of the word surpassed anything that most of us expected, at least in this respect. Not only did we have an entirely new lectionary, but we were given a ministry of the word that had a comprehensible pattern. Gone were the irrelevant graduals, and on the other hand there now appeared readings from the Old Testament. The graduals were replaced with a responsorial psalm, the oldest form of singing psalms, which enables the people to take their part in singing it. The Alleluia, with its verse from the gospel of the day and its lights and procession, is visibly a welcoming of Christ the Lord 'who is still proclaiming his gospel' (CL 33).

But that is not the end of the ministry of the word. After saying that the 'treasures of the Bible' are to be opened up more lavishly for the spiritual nourishment of the people, the Constitution on the Liturgy goes on to speak of the homily: 'By means of the homily the mysteries of faith and the guiding principles of the Christian life are expounded *from the sacred text* during the course of the liturgical year. The homily therefore, is to be *highly esteemed as part of the liturgy itself.*' It may not be omitted on Sundays, feasts of obligation or whenever there is a large assembly of people. For the council the homily was not an optional extra: 'The two parts which in a sense go to make up the Mass, viz. the liturgy of the word and the eucharistic liturgy, are so closely connected with each other that *they form but one single act of worship*' (CL 56). Nor is this teaching confined to the Mass. In the document on the Ministry and Life of Priests (4) we find this: ' ... the preaching of the word is required for the sacramental ministry itself, since the sacraments are sacraments of faith, drawing their origin and nourishment from the word.' This is but a repetition of the teaching of the Constitution on the Liturgy (59). Again, if we consider the Prayer of the Church, also called the Divine Office, which is made up so largely of the singing of the psalms and the reading of holy scripture, we find that Christ is present 'when the church prays and sings, for he promised: "When two or three are gathered together in my name, there I am in the midst of them" (Matthew 18:20)'.

We are familiar with the saying, 'The word of God is living and active, sharper than any two-edged sword, piercing to the division of soul and spirit, of joint and marrow, and discerning the thoughts and intentions of the heart' (Heb 4:12), and we should not be surprised to find the same teaching in the council document on Divine Revelation. There we are told that the holy scriptures are 'constantly actualised' by being read in church and 'God who spoke in the past, continues to converse with the spouse of his beloved Son. And the Holy Spirit, through whom the living voice of the gospel rings out in the church – and through her in the world – leads believers to the full truth and makes the word of Christ dwell in them in all its richness' (8, pp 754-5).

Furthermore, echoing words of Origen who said that we must take care not to neglect the word of God any more than we would let a part of the Body of Christ fall to the ground, the council stated that 'the church has *always venerated the divine scriptures* as she (has) *venerated the Body of the Lord* in so far as she never ceases, particularly in the sacred liturgy, to partake of the bread of life and to offer it to the faithful from the one table of the word of God and the Body of Christ' (21, p 762).

Lastly, the council applied all its teaching on the importance of the word of God to the homily: 'The ministry of the word too – *pastoral preaching*, catechetics and all forms of Christian instruction, *among which the homily holds pride of place* – is healthily nourished and thrives in holiness through the word of scripture' (24, p 764).

When we come to consider the place of preaching and teaching in the life and vocation of the pastoral clergy, we find clear and emphatic statements in the council documents. Preaching and teaching are 'among the principal duties of bishops' and preaching is a 'primary duty' of the pastoral clergy: 'The People of God

is formed into one *in the first place* by the word of the living God
which is quite rightly sought from the mouth of priests. For
since nobody can be saved who has not first believed, it is the
first task ('primary duty') of priests as co-workers of the bishops
to preach the gospel of God to all. In this way they carry out the
Lord's command: "Go into all the world and preach the gospel
to every creature" (Mark 16:15) and thus set up and increase the
People of God.' How this comes about is explained in the following words: 'By the saving word of God faith is aroused in the
hearts of unbelievers and is nourished in the heart of believers.
By this faith then the congregation of the faithful begins and
grows, according to the saying of the apostle: "Faith comes from
what is heard, and what is heard comes by the preaching of
Christ" (Rom 10:17).'

Preaching however is necessary not only to bring the non–be-
liever to Christ and his church. The faith of people within the
church needs enlightening, strengthening and nourishing: 'In
the Christian community itself … especially for those who seem
to have little understanding or belief underlying their practice,
the preaching of the word is required *for the sacramental ministry
itself,* since the sacraments are sacraments of faith, drawing their
origin and nourishment from the word. This is of *paramount importance* in the case of *the liturgy of the word within the celebration of
Mass* where there is an inseparable union of the proclamation of
the Lord's death and resurrection, the response of its hearers
and the offering itself by which Christ confirmed the new
covenant in his blood. In this offering the faithful share both by
their sacrificial sentiments and by the reception of the sacraments.'[1]

Finally, to bring this consideration on the importance of the
word of God to an end, and to set it in the context of the eucharist
itself, we can quote from the same document on the Ministry
and Life of Priests: 'Since in their own measure priests partici-
pate in the office of the apostles, God gives them the grace to be
ministers of Christ Jesus among the people. They shoulder the
sacred task of the gospel so that the offering of the people can be
made acceptable through the sanctifying power of the Holy
Spirit. For through the proclamation of the gospel, the People of

God is called together and assembled so that when all who belong to the People have been sanctified by the Holy Spirit, they can offer themselves as "a sacrifice, living, holy, pleasing to God' (Rom 12:1).'[2]

Notes:

1. The above quotations are taken from *The Decree on the Ministry and Life of Priests* (4) 869-870. See *Vatican Council II*, ed. Austin Flannery, OP, 1988, revised edition (New York, 1987). An alternative translation of the last sentence can be found in the Abbott and Gallagher, *Documents of Vatican II*: 'The faithful share in this offering by their prayers and by their recognition of the sacrament for what it is' (p 540).

2. *Decree on Ministry and Life of Priests* (2), *The Documents of Vatican II*, ed. Walter M. Abbott and Joseph Gallagher (London, 1966), 535, which seems better than the translation in *Vatican II* (cited above), 865.

The Nature of the Liturgical Homily

There are several kinds of sermon, ranging from a great discourse on a grand or important occasion to the humble discourse of a Sunday evening in a country parish church. Likewise, there are different sorts of homily. There is the brief and familiar talk at an infant baptism, the often delicate and difficult homily at a wedding when many not of our faith are present. There is the homily to be delivered at a Funeral Mass which is not to be a eulogy of the deceased but one based on the paschal mystery of Christ's passion, death and resurrection. But, as the Decree of the Ministry and Life of Priests observes, such discourses must not 'expound the word of God in a merely abstract and general way' but must apply the eternal truths about life and death (in this case) to the circumstances of persons, time and place. Here we are concerned primarily with the homily that is preached at the eucharist Sunday by Sunday. It too has its difficulties, as we shall see, but it has a unique importance for it is on this occasion that the preacher deepens faith, arouses devotion and leads the people into a prayerful act of thanksgiving with Christ in the eucharist.

There however seems to be some obscurity about its nature and purpose. One hears pleas for a form of catechetical teaching which would be arranged as a course so that the people would 'know their faith'. What in effect such schemes meant in the past was dry as dust discourses which told the people what they already knew and sometimes, since they paid no regard for the liturgical year, it was possible to be required to preach on adultery on Easter Sunday. Then there are those who have been asking for 'theme' Masses. It is not clear whether they have worked out the enormity of their proposition. First, someone (who?)

would have to think up the themes and then search the scriptures to find texts to fit their ideas. And one has to assume that the authors of these schemes would have to work out their system every year or lay down one for two or three years. If that were not done everyone would perish of boredom. The holy scriptures have their own way of presenting the content of what we believe. To the over–rationalistic mind it may seem very untidy; it needs to be put into a catechism or a manual of theology. But it is a matter of experience that most people have not very tidy minds and pastoral priests know that not everyone comes to Mass in their churches every Sunday, or anyone else's church for that matter. One of the great illusions of the clerical mind is that we can 'instruct' people on Sundays during the celebration of the eucharist. It has been tried for centuries; it did not work in the past and now, with very mobile congregations, it will not work in the present. That 'instruction' needs to be given is undeniable but one reflects that we have an educational system (very expensive to keep going) and at least the beginnings of a Christian Adult Education system, and for young children the Brusselmans' family–sacramental scheme which can be done quite apart from the school system in those places (which are numerous) where Catholic schools do not exist.

What then can we do on Sundays and indeed on some other days in church? This raises the question of the nature and, in the end, the literary form of the liturgical homily. As an approach to understanding what it is, it will be useful to set out schematically what the documents of the church say:

1) The homily is part of the liturgy (not a disposal extra); that is, it is a liturgical act.

2) In the eucharistic word (including homily) and sacraments form one single act of worship.

3) The delivery of the liturgical homily is a ministry, a duty 'to be fulfilled with exactitude and fidelity'.

4) Its content is to be taken from the scriptures (primarily those of the day) and the texts of the liturgy itself.

5) 'Its character should be that of a proclamation of God's wonderful works in the history of salvation, that is the mystery of Christ ever made present and active within us, especially in the celebration of the liturgy' (CL 35/2).

6) Preaching homilies has its difficulties in our own time when people have a short listening ability (or so it seems). That is one reason why they should not be generalised or abstract discourses but should speak to the people in the condition in which they live and with an awareness of their needs and problems (cf Decree on Ministry or Priests, (4), *Vatican II*, 869).

If we reflect on 1) we see that it has certain implications. The homily is part of the liturgy and therefore a liturgical act, 'The homily is to be highly esteemed as part of the liturgy itself'. One consequence that can be drawn from this is that 'just as the celebrant or president acts *in persona Christi*, so he does in the homily', and just as in the eucharist he has a part – and a principally active part – in making present the mystery of Christ by consecration, so in his preaching he is performing a sacramental role in making Christ present by his word.'[1] Or we can put it like this: present in preaching is the action of Christ who is teacher as well as priest and, just as any other action of Christ, if received with love and faith, is fruitful in grace, so is the liturgical homily.

But just as the action of Christ in his church is a mediated action, limited and partially obscured by the material symbol of the sacrament, so it is with the homily. All sacramental signs are at once revealing (of the presence of Christ) and opaque, i.e. they are inevitably inadequate to their purpose. In preaching there is the added opacity of the human person. Personal quirks, style of speech, general character, can get in the way of the word of God and there must be few preachers who are not aware of this. Yet just as Christ chose humble water to be the instrument of new life and bread to be the vehicle of his presence, so he chooses weak and imperfect human beings to be the bearers of his word. The preacher then has all the greater need to ensure that it is the word of God that he is delivering to the people and not his own prejudices and whimsies. If he is aware of his vocation, namely that, however unworthy, he is the mouthpiece of Christ, his words will carry the message of the word of God for the day. For he will be fulfilling the words of the Constitution on the Liturgy (33): 'In the liturgy God speaks to his people and Christ is still proclaiming his gospel'.

'Proclaiming', 'proclamation' are terms used in the church documents. Of the homily the Constitution says, 'Its character should be that of a proclamation of God's wonderful works in the history of salvation, that is the mystery of Christ ever made present and active within us, especially in the celebration of the liturgy.' At the root of the word 'proclamation' is the Latin *clamare* 'to cry out or shout' and *proclamare* could be translated 'to tell forth' (the greatness of the Lord). It is as if it suggests that the word of God is so active, so compelling in the mind and heart of the preacher that he can hardly choose not to proclaim the mighty saving works of God throughout history. But the word has another and deeper meaning that takes us to the New Testament itself. The word for the proclamation of the Good News is *kerygma*, precisely a 'proclamation', the announcement that the herald of a king (*keryx*), would make. This is what the apostles were doing in the first decades of the church's life, it was what Jesus himself was doing when he announced the coming of the kingdom of God and showed by his life and work that it was come.

From this we can draw two conclusions. The first is that the homily is the prolongation in its own way of the proclamation of the word of God that is found in the scriptures. As then Christ is present when the scriptures are read in church, as he is present in his word, so it can be said that he is present in the homilist when he is breaking the bread of God's word to the people.[2] This seems to be a large claim to make but it is completely consequential. As has been said above, the priest celebrant acts *in persona Christi* not only when he is offering the eucharist but also when he is preaching the word of God.

From another viewpoint he is working within the tradition. Tradition does not mean verbally repeating what has been said a thousand times before. Tradition is dynamic, it is in the process of being handed-on (tradition) that the word of God becomes alive and active, piercing to the inmost parts of the human being. It is a frightening thought for the preacher; it is nonetheless true that he is an instrument of God whereby his word may live and penetrate the hearts of the hearers. The priest is a minister of the church and a minister of the word, and through the centuries the church has been reflecting on the word of God, has penetrated

more deeply into its meaning and so has enriched the understanding of Christians since the beginning. In his first Letter to
the Corinthians (15:1-57) St Paul hands on to his converts what
he has received about the resurrection of Christ: 'I deliver to you
... what I also received' and then through a long chapter draws
out the deeper meaning of the resurrection and the vast implications of it for the faith and life of his people. At an infinitely
lower level, the parish priest on Sunday is doing the same. With
the church, and enlightened by the church, he ponders on the
tradition, on the word of God in the Bible, on the understanding
of it that has been achieved by the church, by theologians and by
scripture experts, and he, guided by the Holy Spirit, finds an in-
sight that will help his people to understand the word of God
more deeply, but also to see its relevance to their lives.

The second conclusion is that the homily has the character or, as
the Latin has it, *is* the proclamation of God's wonderful works of
salvation and, since it should draw its content from the scriptures and liturgical sources, it will be a renewed announcement
of the good news first proclaimed by Jesus himself. If the
homilist does indeed draw on the scriptures, then his discourses
will have some likeness to the scriptures in their literary form.
The Hebrew language, somewhat like English, uses concrete
words, it goes for images rather than concepts, it conveys its
truths by narrative, poetry and gnomic sayings. It is pre-
Scholastic and even pre-catechismal, for catechisms are too often
digests of theological manuals with a topping up of scripture
texts and definitions from councils. The poetic, image-like and
narrative style of the Bible appeals to the modern mind which
now, through TV, is operating much more by images than by a
reasoned thesis. There is of course a place and an important
place for reasoned discourse, there is an indispensable place for
theology, and the Sunday homily cannot be just an untidy mass
of words, however image-full or stuffed with stories.

So far then we have seen that the homily is proclamation that
usually involves narrative for it is so largely through narrative
that the Bible communicates its message or, to be exact, its many
messages. In the historical books, the redeeming works of God
are first recounted and then the word gives the explanation. Even

the historical books have a theological substructure and intent. The prophets proclaimed their message but recalled the experience of the people of Israel and the events they had known so that they could insert their 'word' in those lived contexts. In the Old Testament especially, 'event' and 'word' go together; *dabar* can mean both event and word. The same is true of the New Testament to a large extent. Jesus taught so much and so often through the parable precisely to make people stop, think and consider. And the evangelists teach through their four narratives the meaning of the life, passion, death and resurrection of Jesus Christ.

Proclamation and narrative then are closely connected and with the latter some element of explanation or, to use a New Testament word, *didaché*, which means teaching, exposition. This is precisely what we find in Acts 2:42. After Peter had proclaimed the good news and many had been converted, they met together, they listened to the apostles' teaching, who expounded to them the deeper meaning of the word of God.

Finally, as we can also gather from that first 'sermon' of Peter, he exhorted them to repent and be baptised. They responded and, prompted by the proclaimed word, they turned to God, were baptised and celebrated their first eucharist. As modern writers say, the word of God in the liturgy and the word of the homily that follows are not simply informative (as a lecture is) but *performative*. The word in the liturgy enables action and prompts it. In the Acts of the Apostles we find exhortation and initiation into baptism and the eucharist very closely associated. This introduces the notion of mystagogy, the introduction into a deeper understanding of the 'mysteries', the holy sacraments that have been celebrated.

The main elements then of the homily can be summed up as proclamation (*kerygma*), teaching or exposition (*didaché*), exhortation (*parainesis*) leading to mystagogy. This may seem a formidable array of technical terms but any homilist who is constructing and preaching his homilies Sunday by Sunday is doing much of it pretty well by instinct. If we turn again to Acts 2 we find St Peter (or Luke!) unconsciously following the pattern set out above. Peter, drawing on the Old Testament (Joel) proclaims that the Day of the Lord has come. Salvation history has reached its climax in the passion, death and resurrection of Jesus, the descendant of David. Crucified and dead, God his Father has raised him to life 'and all of us are witnesses to that. Now raised to the heights by God's right hand, he has received from the Father the Holy Spirit'. All this is proclamation and in a way teaching, but it was teaching of the kind that penetrated people's minds and hearts. 'What shall we do?' they cried and Peter replied: 'Repent and be baptised.' Here is what the proclamation, the teaching and the exhortation led to. The word was performative.[3]

The great exponents of the art of the homily were the Fathers of the Church, both east and west, especially during the fourth and the fifth centuries. St Augustine of Hippo (died 430) was, as most people know, a theologian with a penetrating mind but he also preached to his people tirelessly for more than thirty years. What, from our point of view here, is interesting and important is that his sermons to the people were almost always simpler in style than anything he ever wrote for a more learned audience. This is particularly clear in his sermons to the 'neophytes', the newly-baptised, during and after the Easter Vigil. In doing so he was, knowingly or unknowingly, illustrating another feature of the homily. Homily in Greek means a 'familiar discourse', a 'talk' rather than a grand oration such as Bossuet preached in seventeenth century France on certain important occasions. But if we are to take Augustine for a model, it does not mean that the homily should be slackly put together or that it should be a 'matey chat' (which seems to be the fashion in some places). Augustine was obviously speaking to his people but his discourse was, we can see, as carefully thought out as his more learned writings. Still, what he did, great orator that he was, suggests to us that the parish clergy, not necessarily being orators, can address their people in terms and in a way that makes the word of God live.

Among the homilists of the church in the west St Leo the Great, who was pope from 440 to 461, is outstanding as a preacher on Lent, Passiontide-Easter and on the Ascension and Pentecost. In

his homilies time and again we can see the underlying pattern
which can be described as classical. If we take the first of his
Christmas homilies (that is read in the Office of Readings) we
find this verified. He proclaims in one short sentence the mys-
tery-event that is being celebrated: 'Today our Saviour was
born, let us rejoice.' It is a joyful event for saint and sinner who
are called to grace and the renewal of grace. Then he expounds
the mystery of the incarnation: it was God's plan seen from before time began; the Invisible became visible, the Immortal took
on mortal nature so that he who was the Son of God might van-
quish the enemy and gain for all salvation. Then in his conclusion he mingles exhortation with what one might call reflective
mystagogy: 'Let us give thanks for the great mercy and love God
shows to us in this event; by the birth of Christ it has been made
possible for us to be re-born; by the generation in time of the Son
of God we are made sons and daughters of God, sharers in the
divine nature. That is your dignity, Christian; remember the
body of which you are a member, remember that Christ is its
head and do not forget that in baptism you have been made a
temple of the Holy Spirit, so you must not return to the wicked
ways that were yours before you were initiated into the Body of
Christ.'

If what has been said above makes the homily look unduly com-
plicated, it must be said that the 'mix' of its four features can be
and should be different on different occasions and at different
times of the liturgical year. This is divided into two main parts,
the Proper of Time, from the First Sunday in Advent to Pentecost
or Whitsunday after Easter, and Ordinary Time with its 33 or 34
Sundays. These suggest and usually require different treatment
and even within the Proper of Time there are the great moments
when the element of proclamation suggests emphasis. For the
Fathers of the Church these moments were made present
through the word and the eucharistic celebration. Thus Origen
in the third century could say: 'It was not simply then that the
birth, growth, maturity, death and resurrection of Jesus took
place, it is now.' Speaking directly to the people, he said, 'Now,
if you wish, in this assembly your eyes can see the Saviour' and
'if you wish to grasp Jesus and hold him in your arms, make

every effort to have the Spirit for your guide' (*Homilies on Luke* 24, 32, 15).

St Leo too made good use of the proclamatory element in announcing the presence of the mystery being celebrated. Thus preaching at Christmas he proclaims:

> We do not only *remember* the words of Gabriel to Mary; we, as it were, witness with our eyes the conception by the Holy Spirit and her faith, as marvellous as the proclamation itself.

> For *today* the Creator of the world is born of Mary ... *Today* the Word of God appeared in the flesh and what before had never been visible to human eyes we could now begin to touch with our hands.

> Today's festival *renews for us* the coming of Jesus, born of the Virgin ... We are celebrating our own origins for the birth of Christ is the origin of the Christian people and the birthday of the Head is the birthday of the body' (*De Nativitate* VI).

Here in this last paragraph we see proclamation merging into exposition and even application to life. The feast of Christ renews us in the here and now because it was the beginning of what we are, members of Christ's body, and so we must live accordingly.

It needs to be said, it seems, that the homily can contain exposition or teaching (*didaché*) and people complain sometimes that it does not. It is woolly, they say, or unduly exhortatory (though they don't use that word!). But the teaching should not be that of the lecture hall or the classroom. What is needed is a brief recall of the meaning of the event being celebrated. For instance, Christmas or the Christmas season does not call for a disquisition on the hypostatic union as defined at the Council of Chalcedon. But the preacher may well remind his hearers of the fact that it was the eternal Son of God who became a man for us, really united our human nature with his divine nature, and he did this 'for us and for our salvation' as we say in the Creed. Or during the Sundays of the year when we are reading from St Mark's gospel and come to the sending out of the Twelve who preached repentance but also 'anointed with oil many that were sick and healed them', there is no reason why the preacher should not refer to the anointing of the sick which the church still practises. If that were made the point of the homily it would be a sort of mystagogy, a leading of the people into a deeper understanding of the holy 'mystery' that is the sacrament of anointing.

Some books say that the homilist should always lead his hearers towards the celebration of the eucharist with explicit reference to it. I object to the 'always'! Sometimes it can be done and rightly done; at other times one would have to force the conclusion of one's homily in that direction. If the homilist has stimulated and perhaps deepened the faith of the assembly, it is with that faith they will go on to celebrate the eucharist.

As for 'application to life', or the exhortatory part of the homily, the theme of what people should do should emerge from the body of the homily. If people are brought closer to God by a renewed faith and love they will be ready and encouraged to do those things they already know they should do. Heavy moralisings are a wasting asset; the more they are indulged in the less effective they become.

Again we can learn from the scriptures. In the First Letter of St Peter, which has been described as a Paschal Homily, we find in chapter 2:1-10 what is very much like an address to the neophytes who have just been baptised and received their first eucharist and this is followed by an exhortation. This however emerges from what they are: 'Come to him, that living stone, rejected by men' ...; be 'like living stones built into the spiritual house, to be a holy priesthood' offering spiritual sacrifices to God through Jesus Christ ...' They are to be part of the structure of the temple of which Christ is the cornerstone. And finally the apostle reminds them of what they are: 'You are a chosen race, a royal priesthood, a holy nation, God's own people, *that you may declare the wonderful deeds* (mission) of him who called you out of darkness into his marvellous light. Once you were no people but now you are God's people; once you had not received mercy but now you have received mercy.' Then, because of what they are, St Peter can urge then to live Christian lives.

To sum up, on the great days of the Proper of Time the homily should have something of the nature of a proclamation or an announcement of the mystery being celebrated though, as we have seen, this does not exclude exposition, exhortation (i.e. application to life) and mystagogy, leading people into a deeper understanding of the mystery or leading them towards the celebration of the eucharist. On the Sundays of the Year the treatment can be more flexible though even then the homily is the proclamation of the mystery of Christ as he lived his earthly life. But here exposition (*didaché*) can and should have a greater part, but always leading to a deepening of faith and not just the giving of information.

Notes:

1. See the present writer's essay in *The Ministry of the Word*, ed. Paulinus Milner (1967), 'The Nature of the Liturgical Homily', 29.

2. In the first draft of the Constitution on the Liturgy after the words, 'It is Christ who is present when the scriptures are read in church' there were the words 'and are explained'. For some reason they were deleted but they evidently expressed the mind of some in the council.

3. Other examples can of course be found in Acts: e.g. 3:11-26, 10:34-48 (the conversion of Cornelius); 13:17-41 (St Paul in Cyprus).

The Preparation of the Homily

No doubt it is asking a good deal of one man to deliver a homily every Sunday and perhaps others during the week as well. But that is what the priest is ordained for, it is an essential part of his vocation, and church documents from the Council of Trent in the sixteenth century to the Second Vatican Council have said just that in various ways. As said above in Chapter 1, the proclamation of the word of God is a ministry, a service of the people committed to one's charge and, if one may put it this way, it is a service to God whose people one is trying to lead nearer to him. As in the Decree on the Ministry and Life of Priests puts it, 'Of all spiritual helps (which the clergy can offer the people) those acts are outstanding by which the faithful receive nourishment from God's word at the twofold table of sacred scripture and the eucharist' (18).

The aim and purpose of the homily is stated in the Introduction to the Lectionary (2nd edition, 1982): 'The one presiding (at the eucharist) exercises his proper office and the ministry of the word of God … as he preaches the homily. In this way he leads his brothers and sisters to an affective knowledge of holy scripture. He opens their souls to gratitude for the wonderful works of God. He strengthens their faith in the word that in the celebration becomes a sacrament through the Holy Spirit. Finally, he prepares them for a fruitful reception of communion and invites them to embrace the demands of the Christian life' (41).

Such statements can be seen as part of the preparation that a man makes before even beginning to think about a homily. He can say to himself: 'This is what I am, a minister of God's word, and this is what by vocation and ordination I must do. For this I need God's help' and so his thoughts can move into prayer. As we shall see, homily making and delivering is a mode of prayer. And this prayer emerges from a certain use of the Bible. The lectionary contains a very large part of the Bible, both Old and New Testaments, but the appointed passages for this or that day need to be put in perspective. In short, continual reading and study of the Bible is the remote preparation for the making of a homily. For this the best single instrument known to me is the *New Jerusalem Bible* with introduction and full notes (1985). The long notes that, as it were, punctuate the text often supply material for homilies even if it would not be wise to use the whole content of these notes on a single occasion. Secondly, one often needs recourse to commentaries to make clear to oneself what the scriptures of the day really mean and to eliminate difficulties if they occur. It is an illusion, and can be a dangerous illusion, to think that we always know what the scriptures are saying. They were written down over the space of some 2,000 years and the traditions incorporated in the Hebrew Bible are older than that. The scriptures were also written in languages that most do not know, Hebrew and Greek, and they came from cultures that were very different from ours. We owe it to ourselves and to the people we speak to to 'search the scriptures' and to understand them to the best of our ability.

Does this mean that the pastoral clergy have to become experts? No harm if they did! What is possible and necessary is a constant reading of the Bible, for it has been said over and over again that the Bible is its own best interpreter. Through constant reading one gets the 'mind' of the Bible and in this way comes to an understanding of particular passages, those set for the day. To assist in an understanding of the word of God as it is arranged and used in the liturgy it is necessary to read the whole of the introduction to the second edition of the lectionary (1-25). For it must be realised that the church in the liturgy uses the scriptures in a particular way. The Old Testament is seen as foreshadowing and anticipation of the events of the New Testament.

Or, in other words, the New Testament often gives the fuller or Christian meaning of passages in the Old Testament. Even when considering the gospel passages in the Mass we need to be aware of their liturgical use. This is particularly important for the greater seasons and feasts. Thus on Good Friday when we have the figure of the Suffering Servant put before us, the church, from the beginning, has seen in him the suffering Christ of the gospels. Yet for the professsional scripture scholar he is a puzzling figure. Is he an individual sufferer? Does he represent suffering Israel? And who was he? These an other questions can be asked but the church is not concerned with them on Good Friday. Something of the sort needs to be said about the great gospels of Lent, Year A, when we have the great passages about the Samaritan woman, the man born blind and the raising of Lazarus. These were originally used to mark certain stages of the catechumenate. They are oriented to life (the gift of God), to light (Christ is the light of the world) and to resurrection (of which Lazarus' raising was a 'sign' or symbol). This is how they are to be interpreted and used to lead us even now to an inner renewal which is the basic meaning of Lent. Instances could be multiplied, notably in the liturgy of the Easter Vigil where the whole series of readings, psalms and prayers is based on the fuller or Christian sense of the Old Testament passages.[1]

Even the gospel passages for the long series of Sundays of the Year are not to be treated as a professional exegete would handle them. They too are set in certain liturgical context, as we shall see lower down, and attention needs to paid to that context. For instance, John 2:1-11, 2nd Sunday, Year C, which is about the marriage feast of Cana, is often treated by the homilist as if it were about Christian marriage. It has a wider and a deeper message. It is about the supersession of the old law by the new, symbolised by the changing of water into wine in generous quantities. A secondary sense may well have a reference to the eucharist.

Even if some explanation of a text is called for to clarify its meaning, it remains true that it is not the homilist's business to do exegesis at the lectern. He needs to do the exegesis in the course of *preparing* his homily. The gospel accounts read every Sunday may seem plain enough but there are at once difficulties and depths of meaning that only study and reflection will reveal and, since one has to go on preaching year after year, it is as well that we should realise that there are these depths of meaning which can be gradually dispensed at different times and on different occasions. The gospels can come to seem banal if we do not do some work on them as we come to them year after year. Sound commentaries can help, but in the study and not in church.

As we read the Bible *in ecclesia*, that is with due regard to the living tradition, so we preach within the tradition which is the result of the church's reflection on the scriptures through the centuries from the beginning. No more than a theologian is the preacher a freelancer who makes up his 'theology' as he goes along. But this does not mean that he just goes on saying without reflection what has been said a thousand times before, nor does it mean that he must have an anxious eye on authority for fear of committing 'heresy'. As Karl Rahner wrote somewhere, we are all unwittingly *heterodox* in one matter or another or at one time or another. But heterodoxy, excusable, is different from heresy, which is culpable. What the preacher then needs to do is to know well the teaching of the church and himself to reflect on it so as to deepen his understanding of it. In this sense and in his own way, he too is a theologian, His reflections will of course affect his preaching but he will *use* them, he will not be giving theological lectures.

One example that presents considerable difficulties is the Feast of the Holy Trinity which most priests find difficult to handle. It is what has been called a 'feast of idea' and that does not make it any more acceptable. Yet it presents the central doctrine of the Christian Church and to baulk at it seems unworthy of a Christian preacher, whatever the difficulties. The truth of the matter is that in the theological schools the Holy Trinity was taught in a highly abstract and metaphysical manner. It was all about distinctions that are not divisions and a network of relationships that are very difficult to keep in mind. Yet it is a doctrine that can be found in the New Testament and it is a doctrine the apostles gradually learned not only from the scattered words of Jesus but from their experience. Like all Jews, they were convinced monotheists, from their youth they had been brought up to recite the *Shema* daily: 'Hear, O Israel, the Lord our God is one Lord; and you shall love the Lord your God...'

(Deuteronomy 6:4-7). But for two or three years they had followed Jesus, they had listened to him, their faith in him was
growng all the time and after the resurrection they came to full
faith in Jesus as the only Son of God. Finally, they experienced
the reality of the Holy Spirit in the extraordinary event of
Pentecost. This seems to me to be the basis of a Trinity Sunday
homily that is within the understanding of everyone.

Or, one might to see Trinity Sunday as the conclusion of the
Liturgical Year from Christmas to Pentecost. The Father sends
the Son into this world as human being (Christmas), he lives,
moves among the people, teaching and healing (Sunday
gospels), he offers himself on the cross and is raised by his
Father for us and for our salvation (Holy Week and Easter) and
he sends the Holy Spirit on the apostles (Pentecost). Again, I
would submit that here are the elements of a homily that is comprehensible to all. Of course, neither homily will be a complete
theological statement of the doctrine of the Trinity but is eucharist the time to attempt such an impossible task?

To Bible study and theology in the sense stated above one could
add general knowledge. It was Karl Barth, I think, who said that
the preacher should have the Bible in one hand and the newspaper in the other. If we are going to preach to the 'world' we must
know what is happening in the world and able to welcome the
good things (on which newspapers are sparing) and criticise the
bad things, but above all so that the preacher can, as it were, incarnate Christ's word in life as experienced by the men and
women of our time. The word, whether that of the scriptures or
the word of the preacher, needs to be inserted into the experience of the people one is speaking to, if it is to be meaningful and
help to them in their daily living.

There is however another source of 'knowledge'. Constant contact with people, being close to them in their joys and sorrows,
an ability to listen to them, are all invaluable sources that enable
us to speak out of experience, the experience of those we know,
a word that meets their need and enters into their living. As the
number of priests decreases this may get more difficult, but such
knowledge of people is essential if the word of God is to be alive
for them.

Another source that can be useful in different ways is a continued acquaintance with English literature. No doubt, in the
course of their education, priests will have read a good deal of
literature and, although they may be only half aware of it, it has
affected their speaking and their writing. In our day there has
been a vast increase of jargon, political jargon, economic jargon,
sociological jargon, there is a great deal of slang, sloppy English
and even an apparent abandonment of grammar. A continued
reading of the English classics, not excluding modern writers,
can do much to remind of us what good English is. Poetry in
particular suggests to us the sort of imaged and concrete language that will correct any tendency to the academic or the
scholastic. Reading also helps to keep one's English fresh and
free from the deplorable clichés that affect the talk of modern
politicians, journalists and publicity merchants and make their
utterances so boring.

Since we are concerned here with the homily preached during a
liturgy, and since, as has been said above, the church uses the
scriptures in this context in a special way, it is obvious that the
homilist will pay attention to the liturgical year.

The distinction between the two parts of it are well enough
known: there is the period from Advent to Pentecost and secondly there is the long period of the Sundays of the Year during
which certain feasts like that of the Holy Trinity, Corpus Christi
and the Assumption of the Blessed Virgin Mary have their place.
In the first part, the Proper of Time, the church celebrates the
mystery of Christ in the work of redemption (*opus redemptionis*)
in its various phases. As the Constitution on the Liturgy puts it:
'As each year passes by, she (the church) *unfolds the whole mystery of Christ* from the incarnation and birth until the ascension,
the day of Pentecost and the expectation of the blessed hope of
the coming of the Lord (cf Titus 2:13)' (102). During this time the
church, reflecting on the *mysteries* of redemption, 'opens to the
faithful the riches of her Lord's powers and merits, so that these
are in some way *made present* for all time and the faithful are enabled to lay hold upon them and become filled with saving
grace' (ibid). These two statements indicate what is the structure
of the Proper of Time and they are the basis of what has been

carried out in the Missal and the Divine Office. Through the proclamation of God's word and the homily, the mystery of the redeeming Christ is made present to the people. But this mystery has many facets (hence the use of the plural) which become the subject-matter of the homily on different days and feasts.

Preaching about the mystery of these occasions is facilitated by the arrangement of the readings and the provision of other texts. The ministry of the word forms a pattern and the first reading, the psalm, the second reading and the gospel deliver the one message about the feast. Thus at the Night Mass of Christmas, we have the prophecy of Isaiah 9:1-7, 'A child is born for us … the Wonder-Counsellor … the Prince of Peace'; the responsorial psalm takes up these thoughts: 'Today a Saviour has been born for us, He is Christ the Lord.' The reading from the Letter to Titus speaks of 'salvation' now brought to the human race; to God's grace we must respond with a good life to be ready for the second coming of Christ, 'the appearing of the glory of our great God and Saviour Jesus Christ.' The gospel is announced with Alleluias echoed by the words 'I bring you news of great joy…' which we hear immediately in the gospel as it is proclaimed. In the Opening Prayer we pray on these lines and the Preface, attributed to St Gregory the Great, deepens our understanding of the mystery: 'The eyes of faith rest on a new and radiant vision of God's glory for in his Son made man we see our God made visible and so are caught up in the love of the God we cannot see.'

This is all too much for one homily, especially at a night Mass, but year by year some of the riches of the liturgy can be offered to the people. In practice, it is the pattern of each great day that we need to look for and it is in that searching that we shall find both the main theme of the feast and material for a homily.

The ordinary Sundays of the Year present a slightly different pattern. The principal text is, of course, the gospel which is preceded by an Old Testament reading (except in the Easter Season) which is chosen to correspond to the gospel passage 'to bring out the unity between the Old and the New Testament' (Lectionary, Introduction, 106). The link between the two is usually the psalm and the homilist needs to consider all three texts in the preparation of his homily. But it needs to be said that he is not obliged to *comment* on all three. He will use what contributes to the theme that, by reflection, he has found for the day. The second reading, usually from the Letters of St Paul, St Peter etc, is intended to be a semi-continuous reading of these texts but they do not form, and are not intended to form, part of the pattern of the day. They were included in the lectionary so that this important part of the New Testament might be kept before the minds of the Christian people. Sometimes a phrase or two can reinforce a point drawn from the other texts and sometimes it is possible and permissible to take the second reading for one's homily. Thus it seems indicated at least for one year out of others to take for one's homily the magnificent hymn-like text of Colossians 1:15-20, 'Christ Jesus is the image of the unseen God ... he made peace by his death on the cross', which resumes much of the history of salvation (cf Fifteenth Sunday of the Year, C).

The forgoing remarks are made because one has heard priests, even young priests, trying to include all three texts as well as the psalm in their homilies. The result: a somewhat shapeless discourse, without centre, that takes far too long, some twenty minutes.

As a general directive, it is as well to keep in mind some statements of the church's documents. The homily should be a 'proclamation of God's wonderful works in the history of salvation' (Cl, 35/2). Through the scripture readings and the homily is unfolded 'the whole mystery of Christ' during the course of the year, especially from Advent to Pentecost. But even during the Sundays of the Year it is possible to discern the 'mystery of Christ' in his earthly ministry: 'On the Second Sunday of Ordinary Time the gospel continues to centre on the manifestation of the Lord ... The distribution (of the gospels) also provides a certain coordination between the meaning of each gospel and the liturgical year. Thus after Epiphany the readings on are on the beginning of the Lord's preaching and they fit in well with Christ's baptism and the first events in which he manifests himself. The liturgical year leads quite naturally to a termination in the eschatological theme proper to the last Sundays, since the chapters of the synoptics that precede the account of the passion treat this eschatological theme rather extensively' (Lectionary, 105).

If the homily however should be at least in part a 'proclamation', it is not sufficient for it to remain just that. One has heard homilies which could be said to be 'correct' in that their subject-matter was the scripture and the saving works of God. But the discourse was, so to say, dis-incarnated. It was not embedded in life, it had nothing particular to say to the people to whom it was directed. As we have seen above, the message of the scriptures must be applied to the life of those to whom one is speaking. This does not concern simply the last bit, exhorting people to do something. It conditions the whole presentation from beginning to end. In preparation, one has constantly to think of the people one is going to address. What is their range of reference in Bible matters, for instance? Does it make sense to refer briefly to a biblical personage or event if one cannot be sure the people will know it? This is even more important if one wishes to use an historical event as an illustration. History is a subject that is less and less known, alas. One has continually to watch one's words, one's vocabulary which, again, is generally beginning to shrink. In writing out a homily it is necessary to keep this in mind and again and again to replace a 'learned' word or an academic word with something more concrete, something closer to an image perhaps. Most people do not take in abstract language. Finally, one has to think of the situation of the people one is speaking to. A homily in a Brazilian base community *must*, in the nature of the case, be very different from a homily delivered to well-heeled people in a leafy suburb. *They* are as much in need of the saving word as the poor of the base community, but the homilist has to be find ways and means of inserting the word of God into their situation. It may not be easy and the gospel message must not be diluted. What is called for is a certain 'diplomatic' way of presenting the truth of the gospel as it is relevant to those people. Harsh denunciations of the wickedness of wealth are hardly likely to persuade people to use it responsibly as stewards for God. General statements about morals can be dangerous, for such statements may apply to people who are in a difficult moral situation. As one can see from the press, statements by priests, bishops and even the pope on moral matters can seem to condemn whole classes of people and also to ignore the delicate claims of conscience.

As one gets nearer to the composition of a homily, there are some immediate tasks to be undertaken. The first of these is an investigation of the texts of the day in their context in the Bible and in their liturgical context. For this, some personal exegesis is necessary. If there are difficulties in a scriptural passage, like that curious one Genesis 15:5-18 about the sacrifice of beasts and birds Abraham is told to make, described as 'an ancient coven-antal ritual',[2] the people are owed a word of explanation, to be given in a few words of written commentary read before the reading. But in addition to that one needs to ponder on the texts and ask oneself: what are they really saying? What are they say-ing to *me*? And what, in the light of the people I am going to ad-dress, have these words to say to them?

Such cogitation may take time. 'Lights' do not always suddenly appear, and to give oneself time it is wise to look at the readings for the following Sunday early in the week. As we go about our business, they remain in our minds, we may recur to them in prayer, or some event in the week may spark off a train of thought that brings the texts to life for this occasion. If there is a liturgy group in the parish that meets say on a Thursday evening, the readings can be discussed and out of such discus-sions comes a theme that is rooted in *their* life and provides ma-terial for the homily. Or as we visit people in their homes during the week and hear a conversation, a phrase or a remark may strike us that sets off a train of thought that is consonant with the scriptures one has been pondering and so becomes the material for the homily. All this is a long way of saying that experience, our experience of life as we live it, can be the material or jump-ing-off point for a homily. However, such experiences must be not be forced into the theme that the readings of the day put be-fore us. In the past there have been exercises in what one can only call pulpit gymnastics. The preacher seized on a phrase from, say, the gospel, an unimportant phrase but suitable to what the preacher had determined to say, regardless of the real meaning of the scriptures of the day. This is not honest; such preachers are selling the people short and are distorting the meaning of God's word. Indeed, we have to remind ourselves again and again that it is not our word we have to deliver, it is the word of God, the bread of the word that we have to break for God's people. The bread of the word is no more ours than the bread of the eucharist, the body of Christ, is.

Notes:

1. This does not mean that the Old Testament has not a validity of its own. That is not in question. One would add that a deeper exploration of the Old Testament can throw light on how it is used in the liturgy.

2. *New Jerusalem Bible,* in loc. note f.

The Delivery of the Homily

One does not 'preach' nowadays. Preaching has been identified with moralising and even scolding. One 'gives' a homily or an 'address', for 'sermon' too has a bad name. It is regarded as a synomym for 'sermonising' like 'preaching'. 'Sermon' has lost its connection with *sermo*, a word, since we all stopped learning Latin. But 'preach' too has an honourable ancestry. Via the French it comes from *praedicare* which means precisely to 'proclaim'. 'Deliver' I suppose is connected with postages or parcels but it has a decently long history in English and is better than 'give' and will be used here.

Let us suppose that the homily has been well prepared. The homilist has reflected on the scriptures, he has faced up to difficulties, if any, he has shaped his discourse conveying the message of the scriptures for the day and then he comes to deliver it. Its effect can be weakened or even spoilt by bad presentation and sloppy articulation.

To take the second first: Quite a number of people nowadays, whatever their education, do not seem to realise that they are speaking badly. Consonants seem to be the first casualties; 'ds' and 'ts' (especiallv) seem to be disappearing from ordinary speech. Words are run together and in conversation I have noticed that noises are taken for words, especially among the young, who in addition talk far too fast and sometimes, when they are asked to be readers in church, they have to be slowed down again and again. Such habits can affect the delivery of homilies as well. Sometimes the homilist speaks too fast as if he must get whatever he has to say in as few minutes as possible. There is no understanding that his material may be (ought to be) divided at least mentally by paragraphs. There is no pause to indicate that and perhaps no pause at all. The whole effort seems breathless. This renders the homily futile One cannot take in such a discourse.

The pace within a homily can be varied. If one is resuming part of, say, the gospel to get to one's point, that can be done fairly quickly since the people will have heard the gospel, but whatever the point is it should be announced with a certain deliberation and consequently at a slower pace. Indeed if homilies approximated more to prayerful contempletion they would do the people more good than a rapid discourse in telegraphese. As the pace can be varied, so can the tones of the voice. A ten-minute monotone is calculated to put everyone to sleep. In fact, both in public reading and in the delivery of homilies, people do not seem to realise that in their voice they have a musical instrument, or one that could be if only they would play it. In reading, one has to look at the nature of the text. If it is narrative it can be read in a level tone but with the emphases that the text requires. If it is proclamation, as Luke 3:1-6 (2 Advent, Year C), the tone can be heightened to suggest that the passage is a proclamation of considerable importance.

If the scripture passage contains dialogue, as in the account of the man born blind (John 9), some effort should be made to show that it is dialogue with varying tones of voice. It is the same with the homily. One needs to pose questions from time to time to stimulate the assembly to think. If one should choose to tell a story, it must be carefully thought out, unnecessary words eliminated and 'loopings back' to try and retrieve what has been forgotten must be removed. Telling stories is not as easy as some seem to think it is. If the occasion is a sad one, e.g. the funeral of a much loved member of the parish, this should be reflected in the mood of the homilist, concerned, sympathetic, which can be conveyed by one's tone of voice, by one's whole bearing, by one's evident sense of mourning with the bereaved. These are subtle matters and there must be no question of play-acting. The truth of the matter is that if our inner sentiments are right they will appear in what we say, without any pretence at all.

Secondly, there is the question of presentation. A man may have done all that is necessary by way of reading the scriptures, studying them, reflecting on them and so discovering the theme of the day. But what he has prepared needs to be presented in such form that the people can understand what the homilist is driving at and be drawn to listen. In other words, the homily needs to have coherence, a structure that can be discerned, but not as it were skeletonically. There is no need for the bones to stick out. *Ars est celare artem* (artistry is concealed in good art) is applicable to the homily because it is an art which requires skill and imagination, the qualities artists bring to their work. That, the reader may think, is enough to put off anyone from ever opening his mouth in church. But there is 'high art' and 'low art'. There are the sculptures of Michelangelo and there are the carvings on the misericords under the medieval choir stalls. Both are genuine art, both valid and both to be admired for what they are. The parish clergy are not called to high rhetorical discourses but they are called to deliver coherent well-presented and attractive homilies that will lead the people to God and the things of God.

Having said that, it must also be said that the level nowadays is low. There seems to be a notion about that the homily should be a sort of 'chat-show'. The preacher leans on the lectern, talks in what he believes is a familiar voice, using slang expressions and trying to give the impression that he is 'one of them', i.e. the people sitting in front of him. It is all bogus and does not deceive anyone. This style also means that sentences may have no verbs or that they are broken off before being finished and in the end the general impression is one of incoherence. What those who do this do not realise is that talk of the 'chat-show' kind is the result of careful rehearsal by people who are skilled public speakers even if it is a particular genre. Even so, it does not always come off. One has noticed that increasingly in TV discussions, for instance, one speaker will cut off another or try to do so and the hearer can hardly make out what is being said by whom. As far as the homilist is concerned, it is true that his general attitude should be easy and unpompous. He will show by his manner, by his vocabulary, by his understanding of the people in front of him, that he is 'one *with* them', and from time to time he may well remark when he is urging people to do something that he is including himself in his remarks. A smile, a mild joke can sometimes work wonders in warming a congregation to the homilist. This is very different from what I have called the chat-show style. In any case there is a specific difference between it and the Christian homily. The homilist is breaking the bread of God's vord for the people, it is *God's* word, as said above, and not his own. It has come through human minds and human characters, it has to come through the homilist's mind and character, but if it is to have effect in the lives of people, it must be allowed to be God's word. Hence there must be a sense of the seriousness of what one is doing, what one has been authorised to do, without being *over*-solemn about the matter. Once again it is the inner attitude, respect and love of the word of God, that will show in the ways in which we handle it in the homily.

The beginning and the end of the homily are important because one wants, in the first place, to engage the attention and the goodwill of the assembly and, in the second, one wants briefly and neatly to end showing what is the main point (renewed faith, deeper understanding, service of others ...) of all one has been saying. Nothing is more devastating of attention, goodwill and the very nature of the homily itself than an 'ending' that goes on and on. It has been said, wisely I think, that even if one does not write out the whole homily, it is necessary to write out the introduction and the end.

How then to begin? Beginnings depend on circumstances and on the time of the Liturgical Year. To take this last first: On the great feasts it seems right that one should begin with proclamation, that is a recalling, quite briefly, of what is being celebrated. This moves into narrative – exposition which again need be neither detailed nor prolonged. From this should come the message for the day which, as suggested above, may bear on renewing faith or leading people to a deeper understanding of the mystery celebrated, or of exhortation which should emerge from the exposition that has gone before.

St Paul's discourse, as set down by Luke in the Acts of the Apostles (13:16-41), gives one some clues. Paul is in Cyprus, he goes to the synagogue on the Sabbath, he listens to the readings from the Law (the Pentateuch) and the prophets and then, as was the custom, he is invited as a visitor, to address the assembly. He is talking to fellow Jews and in his first sentence he seeks to engage their attention and goodwill: 'Men of Israel, and you that fear God, listen. The God of this people Israel chose our fathers and made the people great during their stay in the land of Egypt'; he reminds them of their dignity. Then he resumes salvation history in the Old Testament until the coming of Jesus, 'Israel's Saviour', whose passion, death and resurrection he proclaims, and then he draws his conclusion: 'Let it be known to you, therefore, that through this man (Jesus) forgiveness of sins is proclaimed to you, and by him everyone that believes is freed from everything from which you could not be freed by the law of Moses.' The last sentence is a warning not to be 'scoffers' but, it is suggested, they should turn to Christ.

That might be described as a 'special occasion' sermon, and the pastoral priest has to preach every Sunday and here the approach must be a little different. It is true that the scriptures of the three-year lectionary set out the broad lines of the history of salvation, and of the public ministry in word and deed of Jesus, but this is and has to be broken up into manageable sections. Always, however, we need to be aware of both elements, the history of God's approach to the human race in the Old Testament and the revelation of God through and in the life and ministry of Jesus. The readings from the synoptic gospels do this each in their own individual way and according to the tradition they have received, and this too needs to be understood and the individuality of each evangelist respected. Furthermore, the homilist needs to refer both to the context of the appointed passages in the Bible and to the context of the gospel passages of the Sundays of the Year, that is, it is necessary to see what lies ahead and sometime link up with what has gone in the past. The gospel readings are a *lectio continua* although there are some omissions so that there shall not be unnecessary duplications of the same passage from year to year. In Year 2 we have a special arrangement because Mark is too short to provide readings for the 33/34 Sundays. From the seventeenth Sunday to the twenty-first we have readings from John 6. To avoid tedious repetition, it is necessary to plan the homilies for the whole six Sundays and speak about the many aspects of the eucharist that will give a true catechesis within the context of the liturgy. Such homilies would satisfy those who from time to time want 'instruction' during the Mass.

There are two difficulties about the Sundays of the Year. The first is that, although the present lectionary is almost infinitely better than the meagre thing of the former missal, yet both preacher and people become very familiar with the texts and especially with the gospel texts. Here the preacher has a special obligation. The gospels superficially are very simple, their message is usually clear – or so it seems – but in fact their meaning is very deep and, if the homilist is going to keep his discourses alive, he needs to study the gospels, to reflect on them and, like the householder in Matthew's gospel, draw out of them things *new* and old. Commentaries help at this point but each man has to do his own work, In clerical periodicals *suggestions* are given but these too need working on and adapting to the people one is going to speak to.

The second difficulty has more to do with presentation. How is one to engage attention? How is one to sustain it? It is said, and has been said for a long time, that it is good to begin a homily with a story, a real live account or one read or even one made up. Sometimes such a device is useful but not always. The nature of the scriptures may not allow of it. They may call for some exposition or explanation before their message can be delivered. If a story is to be effective, it must be appropriate to the subject-matter of the homily. (One has occsionally heard stories that seem to have been stuck in for their own sake!) It is a good thing to write out the story and then one can be sure that it is succinct, that there are no useless words and that its narrative-line is quite clear.

It would seem that others think it is a good thing to start one's own experience. Well and good, if it is relevant to the texts and if the experience has anything to say to anyone else! The same rules apply to this as to the story however. An experience must be delivered economically, there must be no 'splurging', and it must have point, something that can be shared by others. What is better is to speak of preaching out of one's experience, that means, out of one's knowledge of human nature, out of what one has learned from life, and that does not need spelling out in details or at all. Such knowledge will appear in the homilies even if the preacher never thinks of his own exprience of human beings and life. People soon come to know whether a preacher does understand them, whether he is in touch with the sort of life that they and millions of others have to live. All this serves to emphasise what has been said above, that the pastoral priest must know the people he is appointed to serve and it is out of that knowledge/experience that will come material for his homilies.

Another way of catching attention is to use a striking first sentence. For example, I read some time ago a homily that starts like this: 'Who dares, wins!' Because the first reading was about King David, later the homilist speaks again about him and remarks, 'David both dared and won.' It is not difficult to guess how the homily captured the attention of the people and especially of the young.[2]

The body of the homily will consist of the development of the theme that has emerged from a reflection on the texts and may be illustrated in one way or another, by the use of similes or a *brief* story so that the attention of the hearers is maintained. It is here that catechesis comes in, for a homily need not be a spineless wonder with no 'instruction' which, as in the homilies in the Acts of the Apostles, consists of reminding people of what they have forgotten or undervalued. Thus by reflection on Luke 5:1-11 (5th Sunday, Year C) we can see that this is about the mission of the Church: the catch of fish is the symbol of the disciples' work later on, for Jesus says, 'Do not be afraid; from now on it is men you will catch' (or 'You will be fishers of men'). This is supported by the first reading (Isaiah 6:1-8) when the prophet was sent: 'Whom shall I send? Who will be our messenger? I answered, "Here I am, send me".' Indeed we can see that the gospel is about the *nature* of the Church which is essentially missionary, involving all its members. Other examples of Sundays of the Year would not be difficult to find when the texts suggest a reference or a paragraph in a homily to some truth of faith of some matter of practice. The style of such passages should not be 'catechismic', over didactic, but should flow out of the language of the biblical text.

Finally, there is the question of the application to the life of the people. There was a time when 'sermons' were almost wholly exhortatory and I remember a journalist saying to me after listening to a sermon by a bishop, 'He (or 'The Catholic Ciurch...' I can't remember which ... it was very many years ago) seems to be demanding an awful lot of the people', as indeed he was. He had lost himself in his exhortatory enthusiasm. As has been suggested in the previous chapter, the exhortatory part should emerge from the subject-matter of the honily. That is, material should be so presented as to make peeple want to act. The exhortation, or last and short part of the homily, will simply make a suggestion.

There is, however, yet more to be said about this part of the homily. While preparing it, one has to ask oneself what, as far as one knows, do the people stand in need of. Do they need to be encouraged? Do they need to be strengthened in faith? Do they need to be reminded that they have obligations to others who include those they live with, the parish comnunity to which they belong, the society in which they live? Without bashing such points home, the preacher needs to think such questions over in the light of his knowledge of the people. He also needs to remind himself that broadly what he is asking others to do he should be ready to do himself. In the situation in which we work nowadays, though I think it was always true, the only 'power' a pastoral priest has is that of *persuasion*. He can't *order* anyone to do anything. In the Sunday homily he is exercising his powers of persuasion which means in effect that people will *want* to listen to what he has to say and, by the time he has finished, they must have the feeling that they have been helped, encouraged, etc and are willing to act accordingly. We are not supposed to like rhetoric nowadays, though there is a good deal of it about, but it is useful to remember that rhetoric is the art of persuading and if we have nothing of that art we might as well shut up. Or at least, shut up until we have learned a sufficiency of it. It does not come naturally to many, but it can be learned without too much difficulty. In the end, if we have done what is required of us in remote and proximate preparation, and in learning how to present our material in persuasive fashion, then we can leave the effect to the Holy Spirit. It is the word of God conveyed by the Spirit that reaches into the hearts and lives of men and women, The sad thing is that we can put road-blocks on the way.

Then there is the question of the mechanics of preparation and delivery. What is to be said about the use of a script? The Catholic tradition, at least in recent centuries, has been that of extempore preaching which in fact is a very difficult art and perhaps because it is difficult the standard, at least in this country, has been low for quite a long time. It is difficult, for one thing, because if one never writes anything down thought is likely to be fuzzy and the English becomes slacker and slacker and probably cliché-ridden, whether it is the cliché of the politician or the journalist or the latest buzz words. There would then seem to be a strong case for writing out a homily before preaching. This offers some assurance that one knows what one is going to say! Indeed, during the writing of a homily, one's thought clarifies and even changes and one comes to the point sometimes when one has to say 'That will not do' or 'That is not what I really wanted to say'. Writing also does something to ensure that the language of the homily will be concrete (the concrete word instead of the abstract), direct and fresh (Clichés can be killed en route).

Next, the question arises whether to use the script in church. Some would say that this deadens the impact of what one has to say and that is true if the homilist does not know how to use a script. The reading of a script is pretty paralysing for the hearers but using the script as a sort of instrument on which one can play is altogether another matter. When being prepared for radio broadcasting years ago, one learned how to deliver a script without giving the impression that one was reading it. And preachers of considerable merit have used a script in the pulpit. Few men preached so often on such a variety of subjects in so many different places as the late Mgr Ronald Knox, yet he al-

ways used a script though most of the people listening were unaware of the fact. I am told that his scripts were scored almost
like a musical text, marking no doubt variances of pace and emphasis and so on. A pastoral priest who has to preach at least
once a week and usually oftener, acquires a certain facility with
words but if his thought is to remain fresh and challenging he
needs to write out what he is going to say, even if he makes no
further use of his script.

What I think most preachers do is to write out a series of paragraphs which they have with them as they stand at the lectern or
in the pulpit. These too will be the fruit of thought and the presence of the script will ensure that the homilist will a) not have to
practise prodigious feats of memory, and b) that he maintains
his train of thought even against howling infants or the other
distractions to which Sunday worship is prone. The least a man
can do, as said above, is that he should write out his introduction
and his conclusion. There is also another advantage. There are
some who find public speaking difficult, they are nervous about
the whole exercise and, if they have a script (and know how to
use it) or adequate notes, the nervousness will gradually disappear.

Preparing and preaching the weekly homily may seem to some
to be a boring chore and they get out of it for the slightest excuse.
This may be a hangover from the bad old days when the 'sermon' or, worse still, the 'instruction' seemed an unnecessary in-
trusion into the holy rite. If this is so, those who think that way
would do well to reflect on the statement of the Constitution on
the Liturgy (56) that 'the liturgy of the word and the eucharistic
liturgy … form but one single act of worship'. Without a homily
that act of worship is imperfect, maimed. We have to remember
also the saying of the council in more than one place that we are
saved by faith and by the sacraments of faith and that before any
council St Paul said, 'Faith comes by hearing … and how are
they (the people) to hear without a preacher?' (Rom 10:14.15).
However inadequate we may think our efforts are, the fact is
that the Christian people are largely formed, educated, instructed
(if you like) by the homilies of the pastoral priest. People are
reading less and less and religious literature least of all.[2] The

weekly homily is little enough but without it the people have nothing. And it is an illusion to suppose that faith does not need nourishing. It may be a 'gift' but it does not lie inert in the human soul like a coin in a Christmas cake. Faith is essentially dynamic and dynamos are 'fed' or they cease working.

There is one final and vexed question to be ventilated. How long should a homily last? There are those who say, 'Not more than five minutes'. But that gives neither people nor preacher time, as it were, to breathe. The preacher has not sufficient time to develop a theme based on the readings and the people can hardly take in in so short a time what he has to say. What is more reasonable is that the homily should take about ten minutes. It is undesirable and near impossible to time a homily so exactly that it lasts no more than ten minutes. Much depends on the nature of the scriptures to be expounded and the theme that comes out of them. And as said above, pace is important. In large churches (even with public address systems) and large congregations, the homily must be slower; otherwise it will come over as just a mass of words or even unintelligible noises. Whether celebrating the liturgy or delivering homilies, quite a number of the clergy do not seem to realise that when one is listening one takes things in more slowly than when one is preaching or leading people in prayer. But finally it is a matter of experience that if a homily is well constructed, if it is well presented and clearly delivered, people will listen and will not object to the homily lasting a little more than ten minutes.

There is a sense in which the homily aspires to a form of prayer. The earliest extempore eucharistic prayers were hardly different from the homily that preceded them and in the liturgy of today it is meant to lead people into prayer (the 'Bidding Prayer') first and then into the great prayer, the eucharistic prayer, when the community professes its faith with the celebrant and thanks and praises God through Jesus Christ whom he represents.

There is one different aspect of homily-preparation that may be mentioned here. It has been said for a very long time that the preacher should pray before delivering his discourse. Well and good, but it has not been said so often that the preparation of a homily is itself a form of prayer. One has to scrutinise the scriptures, it is necessary to find out what they are saying to oneself and, in the course of doing that, we are continually pondering the things of God and, with a definite turning to God while doing so, our minds are lifted up to God. As the Fathers of the Church put it, it is an *ascensus mentis ad Deum*, a lifting up of the mind to God. It is often during this process that 'lights' come as to the meaning of the scriptures and its relevance not only to one's own life but also to the lives of the people one is going to address.

If this seems to be counsel of perfection, let us realise that we can preach fruitfully only out of faith, that is out of a faith that is a commitment to God as well as a wholehearted acceptance of what he has revealed. Although it is God we have to preach we cannot avoid preaching ourselves, not our dubiously attractive personality but the word of God as we have grasped it and expressed it as best we can. It is a word that must have become our own, something we treasure, something consequently we want to commend to others. Many years ago a good Catholic man, the sort not at all given to criticism of the clergy, said to me, 'Father, some priests give the impression that they don't believe in what they are saying.' I do not know what priests he was referring to but I cannot think of a more devastating criticism of a preacher than that.

Note:

1. See *Proclaim the Word* (Kevin Mayhew Ltd, Bury St Edmunds, 1991, p. 18.

2. For example, the number of Catholic weeklies sold in parishes is, compared with the population, very small.

The Homilies

It is arguable that the task of providing homilies for the Sundays of the three years A, B, C, is the most difficult to face the preacher. The passages appointed to be read cover a great deal of the whole Bible, the Pentateuch, the prophets, Wisdom literature and nearly the whole of the New Testament. This imposes on the preacher an obligation not only to treat of the passages appointed for each Sunday but to have a general background knowledge of the Bible so that he can 'situate' the particular readings, see them in context and their relevance to each other. Yet at the same time, now that we have been using the lectionary for twenty–five years, it is possible to feel a little *ennui* as one approaches Sunday by Sunday readings that have become very familiar. On a previous page, I have suggested some ways by which one can deal with the situation. We need to ponder on the scriptures in the situation in which we and the people find ourselves; through this will come certain 'insights' that provide material for a fresh homily.

The homilies to be found in this book are the written–up versions of some of the homilies I have preached over the last few years. They are to be regarded as no more than suggestions of what might be said or indications of how the scriptures can be handled on any given Sunday. Other ways of handling them of course remain possible and these will explored in a different way by other preachers.

Generally speaking I have ignored the second readings since on the Sundays of the Year they are not connected with the first reading, the psalm or the gospel. Nor are they meant to be. They were inserted to keep before our minds the teachings of St Paul and some other New Testament writers. If, however, a preacher feels that for the time being he has exhausted all he has to say about the other two readings, there would seem to be no reason why he should not turn to the subject–matter of these readings for his homily. Homilies on the readings from 1 Corinthians would bring together the sometimes very short extracts and would enlighten the people. Both Ephesians 1:3-10 and Colossians 1:3, 15-20 occur during the year, both are very rich in doctrine and meaning and could very well form the substance of the homily of the day. They have to be worked on, however, if a clear message is to be given to the people.

In addition to the homilies for the Sundays of the Year, I have added a few more since they supersede the Sunday or may do so. Some are missing as I have provided homilies for them elsewhere. In my *The Coming of the Lord*, (1990), I have provided homilies for the whole Christmas season, including the Epiphany, the Baptism of the Lord (three in the English edition) and the Presentation of the Lord in the Temple. In *The Lord is Risen*, (1992), I have covered the whole of the church's year from Palm Sunday to Whitsunday by way of commentaries on the very numerous texts of that season. And in *Journey through Lent*, (1989), I give three homilies on the Transfiguration.

For the added feasts I have not attempted to exploit the content of all the appointed texts, for that way would spell homiletic disaster.

One last remark. The Constitution in the Liturgy says that the homily should draw on the source of holy scripture and the liturgy (34/2). This last seems to be neglected. The Prefaces (i.e. the first part of the Eucharistic Prayer) frequently give the gist of the mystery being celebrated and are very useful, indeed indispensable, for its understanding. For instance, the Preface for the Feast of the Body and Blood of Christ summarises very well all aspects of the mystery (the priesthood of Christ, the eucharistic sacrifice and holy communion). The same can be said of the Preface for Christ the King. That for the Feast of John the Baptist neatly sums up his eternal role: He was appointed 'to show the world it's Redeemer, the Lamb of sacrifice'! The Prefaces for the Immaculate Conception and for the Assumption point up Mary as the model or figure of the church: she is 'the promise of the perfection of the Bride of Christ' and so of ourselves, and she is 'the beginning of the church in its perfection' and a sign of hope for ourselves as we make our pilgrim way to God when we too (if we are faithful) will be raised body and soul.

The Opening Prayers, and those corresponding to them, also offer food for thought, and references to these, as well as to the Prefaces, during the course of a homily bring to the attention of the people texts that may otherwise pass over their heads. More importantly, these texts teach without seeming to be over didactic.

Year A

The Second Sunday of the Year

Is 49:3, 5-6; Ps 39 (in part); 1 Cor 1:1-3; Jn 1:29-34.

At first sight the gospel of today presents a difficulty. It seems to be a replica of the Baptism of Jesus which we celebrated last Sunday. To some extent it is. John does not describe the baptism, he refers to it, 'I saw the Spirit come down on him from heaven like a dove and resting on him'. We are prompted to ask then: Is St John the evangelist saying anything more than the synoptics said?

In fact there are two great images that convey a pregnant message. First, there is the familiar figure of the Lamb, 'the Lamb of God, who takes away the sin of the world'. That sets up resonances in our mind. He is the good shepherd who lays down his life for his sheep (Jn 10:15). He is the shepherd who goes out and looks for the one lost sheep and brings it home rejoicing for what was lost is found (Lk 15:3-7). This in turn evokes the shepherd of Ezekiel who tells them that the Lord himself will take charge of the flock, that he will rescue them, that he will gather those who have been scattered, that he will bind up the wounds of the injured, make the weak strong, and feed the hungry. But one day he will do this through another: 'I shall raise up one shepherd, my servant David', and here is the new David of the house and line of David, the Christ who lays down his life to take away the sin of the whole human race (Ez 34:1-24; Lk 1:32).

The shepherd has become the Lamb, as we learn from the same gospel of St John. At the very time that the paschal lambs were being slaughtered in the Temple Jesus was being sacrificed on the cross (18:28; 19:14). In fact, the image of the Shepherd-Lamb recalls to our minds the heart of salvation history which reaches from the Old Testament to the New and is now in process as it will be to the end of time. We are being saved now by the Lamb who takes away the sin of the world and the sins of everyone who repents (I Jn 2:2).

51

Then there is the second image. The Shepherd is also the Servant: 'The Lord said to me, 'You are my servant'. and the Servant is one who is sent. As we read so often in St John's gospel, Jesus speaks of himself as the One Sent, sent by his Father. In the baptism he is revealed as the chosen one, the beloved in whom the Father delights. His mission then was authenticated and now today it is beginning: 'The man on whom you see the Spirit come down and rest is the one who is going to baptise with the Holy Spirit', words that echo another Servant song, 'Here is my servant, my chosen one ... I have put my spirit on him' (Is 42:1). As is indicated by the gospel, 'He is going to baptise in the Spirit' and, as the Isaian Song continues, he is sent to open the eyes of the blind, to free captives but above all 'to be a light to the nations'. He is not to be a servant merely for his own people; as we read in our passage today, 'I will make you the light of the nations so that my salvation may reach to the ends of the earth'. All this and more we see Jesus doing in the gospel. He heals the sick, he gives sight to the blind and he proclaims the good news of salvation to the poor, those neglected and despised, the sinners and the ritually 'unclean'.

It is for this that the Spirit 'rests' on him, stays with him not simply so that he can accomplish his mission but so that he can give the Spirit as he promised to do (chapters 14 and 16) but actually did so when, as he died on the cross, he 'gave up the Spirit', gave the Spirit to those who would follow him, the church. Mission leads to and involves suffering. The servant sent by the Father to proclaim the good news of salvation became the Suffering Servant who 'was wounded for our transgressions, bruised for our iniquities' who made himself an offering for sin (Is 53:5, 10). It was in that way that he took away the sin of the world.

The lesson for us is mission and service. We too, all of us, have to proclaim the Good News by word if possible but by our life surely, and as servants of the Servant we too are likely to suffer, in our own personal lives and in the service we try to give to others. For our support however we have always the Servant who laid down his life for us, who bears us up in all our sufferings and trials.

The Third Sunday of the Year

Is 8:23-9, 3: Ps 26 (in part); I Cor 1:10-13, 17; Mt 4:12-23.

The gospel today is like the spring-time of Jesus' mission. The light promised by the prophet is breaking over the world and the light is Christ who is bringing his kingdom into existence. We see him choosing his first disciples and we see him moving among the people healing the sick and comforting the distressed. But as we follow the gospel story we find that even then there were misunderstandings and divisions among the disciples.

We remember the time when John, one of the sons of thunder, found a man casting out devils and told Jesus that he had tried to stop him 'because he was not one of us'. Jesus had to rebuke him: 'You must not stop anyone who works a miracle in my name. Anyone who is not against us is for us'. Then near the time of the Passion there was a serious disagreement among the disciples. St Luke puts the dispute in the context of the Last Supper itself. The bone of contention was who of the disciples would be the greatest in the kingdom that was coming into existence. So little did they understand Jesus or what he meant by the kingdom. He had to tell them that he, who would be the greatest among, them must be the servant of all for 'I came not to be served but to serve and give my life as a ransom for many' (Mk 10:45).

There were also divisions in the early church, as we hear from St Paul today. There were parties among them. Some were for Apollos, an eloquent preacher, some were for Cephas, i.e. St Peter, some were for Paul whom they knew well. Paul was outraged. This was all wrong. They were not baptised in the name of Paul or Cephas or Apollos. They were baptised in the name of Christ and that is what made them one. The church was not a collection of different parties agreeing to disagree and so breaking the unity.

Even worse, in their celebration of the eucharist there was separatism, a distinction of persons. Some, the better off, looked down on the poor. They misbehaved themselves, they were greedy, and St Paul suggests that some even got drunk, for there was the

meal, the *agapē*, before the eucharist. And all this during the celebration of the eucharist that is the sacrament of love and unity.

Paul had to teach them that the church is the body of Christ: 'Just
as the human body, though made up of various parts, is a single
unit because all these parts make one body, so it is with Christ.'
And he went on to show them that every member of the body
was necessary to every other member, and he concludes, 'Now
you together are one body' receiving the one loaf and the one
cup.

In this Week of Prayer for Christian Unity I thought it would be
useful to reflect on these matters.

It is true that the situation now is different from what it was
then. The churches are divided by more than internal disputes,
regrettable though they may be. There are differences of doctrine,
there are differences of worship, and for centuries one church
was opposed to another and even persecuted each other. All
that is now past and for now more than thirty years Christians of
all churches have been coming together so that, as Jesus prayed,
all may be one in him. The way is proving long and arduous but
that is not surprising since we have been separated for so many
hundreds of years. But if we are to do the will of Christ who at
the Last Supper prayed that all might be one in him, as he was
one with his Father, we must go on, whatever the difficulties.

From the scriptures today I can see certain guidelines. The disciples did not understand Jesus or what he said about the kingdom at first. It was so different from anything they expected. By
60AD those who survived must have been very surprised indeed! So, it seems to me, the first thing we have to do is to deepen
our understanding of other churches and what they teach and
do. This implies in turn that we come to see what is good in
them and we would do well to remember the words of Jesus,
'Anyone who is not against us is for us.

We have a great task on our hands. The Christian churches in
this country are faced with vast numbers of people who do not
know Christ; who are not attached to any church or seem to
have no religious affiliation of any sort whatever. Once the

churches are united they will be able to speak with one voice and with power. That is one reason why we must all be concerned about the union of the churches. Like the disciples we do not know exactly what that One Church will be like. It will be the work of God and we must go on praying and working that the Holy Spirit will guide us all into a union that will be according to God's will.

Fourth Sunday of the Year

Zeph 2:3; 3:12, 13; Ps 145, 7-10; 1 Cor 1:26-31; Mt 5:1-12.

In today's gospel we have what might be called the Charter of the New Covenant. The Beatitudes are the counterparts to and the fulfilment of the Ten Commandments of the Old Law and all that went with them, called comprehensively the *Torah*. The Torah set out the way of life for the people of Israel and was often very particular and concerned with earthly details. We, for our part, may very well treat the Beatitudes in too spiritual fashion, as if, for instance, they were rules for personal piety. So let us look a little more carefully: 'Blessed are the gentle; they shall have the *earth* for their heritage'. And if we think of the first one, 'Blessed are the poor in spirit' as speaking of only a spiritual kind of poverty, turn to the way St Luke puts it: 'Blessed are you poor, for yours is the kingdom of heaven' (6:20). Luke, whose gospel is full of compassion for the poor, meant the really poor, those who have little or nothing of this world's goods.

So the Beatitudes have to do with well-being on this earth as well as with spiritual values that, if important, do not exclude other values. Indeed, as the *Constitution on the Church in the Modern World* teaches we must be concerned with the affairs of this world, both the people in it to whom is owed justice and the very fabric of the earth which can be and is being abused and ravaged.

In 1990 Pope John Paul reinforced this message. Speaking on the subject of peace and justice, he affirmed the need for care of the planet on which we live, the skies, the seas, the rivers, the forests and all human life as well as the animal and vegetable life of this earth.

Yet I long hesitated about preaching on the matter. I wondered whether it was a specifically Christian concern but I now see more clearly that it is a matter with which all Christians must be concerned and that concern is profoundly biblical.

In the great poem about the creation of the universe in the first chapter of Genesis, we read that God looked on all he had made and saw that it was good. No doubt the biblical description of the creation is not, and is not meant to be, a scientific account. The purpose of the biblical writers was to say that God is at the origin of all that exists and that it and we, his creatures, are dependent on him.

But, as the Bible goes on to say, we have our tasks as well. When God created the first human beings he told them to 'cultivate' the earth, to take care of it, not to exploit it or ravage it for profit, to the impoverishment of millions that live on the planet.

When we turn to the gospel, we find Jesus admiring the birds of the air who ultimately are in the hands of his Father. 'Think,' he said, 'of the flowers of the field, more beautiful than Solomon in all his regal array.' Birds and flowers, beasts of the field, the very soil itself must be cared for, and who is to do that if not ourselves?

But, as we know, all is not well. There was the primeval fall of man from friendship with God into sin. That was the first and the greatest rebellion that caused disharmony in the human person, and, it would seem, disharmony in the order of nature itself.

This is what St Paul was talking about in a difficult passage of the Letter to the Romans (8:18-23). He sees the whole of creation groaning, as it were in a great act of birth or rebirth. With the human race, it is waiting for a final liberation when the original order will be restored and there will be final and complete peace and harmony. In all that process of liberation we are involved and we can and must make our contribution. As in the beginning human beings were put into the world to cultivate and care for the earth, so it is our task now. Just as our life is not our own but God's, so the world is not ours but his. It is for us to work with God in the shaping of the earth's destiny.

And there is a moral issue also. In Brazil, for instance, thousands of acres of rain forest are being destroyed; this damages the ozone and at the same time is depriving thousands of poor farmers living on those lands of their livelihood – and all incidentally for gold. That is why we should be concerned about ecology. Not only in Brazil but elsewhere the earth is being raped and millions are being deprived of the very means of existence.

The gospel today tells us that the poor, the gentle and the merciful will inherit the earth and it is our duty to see that they do. That is the only guarantee of justice, lasting peace and final harmony.

Fifth Sunday of the Year

Is 58:7-10; Ps 111 (in part); 1 Cor 2:1-5; Mt 5:13-16.

The message of the scriptures today is very clear. The prophet, the psalmist, the gospel are showing us what is our duty to others. But so clear a message does not make preaching any the easier. It becomes an underlining of the obvious. Let us, however, reflect on it in the context of our own times.

If there has been a decline in morals in some respects, it seems that people have become more sensitive to the needs of the poor, the oppressed and the homeless who sleep rough in their thousands in our towns and cities. There are numerous associations trying to find shelter for the homeless, remedial treatment for drug-addicts and food and clothing for the needy. Then there have been those spontaneous outbursts of giving for the starving in Ethiopia and other parts of the world. For this we can thank God. But there is also unfortunately an almost insolent display of wealth alongside what seems to be an ever-increasing poverty. There is so much that could be said that I will content myself with saying that charity, however great, cannot relieve all the social needs of our time. Justice, social justice, is a matter that a wealthy nation like ours cannot afford to neglect.

Let us now consider the texts.

First there is that astonishing passage from the prophet. The Old Testament is often thought to be harsh, a story filled with wars, violence and hatred. Yet here is a passage that sounds very much like gospel teaching: 'Share your bread with the hungry, and shelter the homeless poor, clothe the one you see to be naked and turn not from your own kin.' If we look at the context of those words, we find that the prophet is telling the people that religious observances, worship, and even fasting are not enough. If they are to be faithful to God's word, they must turn out from themselves and their own concerns and look at the people in need around them. Then they must serve them.

As I have said, the words of the prophet sound very much like gospel teaching and it is in this same gospel of Matthew that we find the closest parallel: Jesus said: 'Feed the hungry, give drink to the thirsty, clothe the naked, and visit the sick and the prisoner' (25:31-45). But he raises the matter to a new and higher level: 'In as far as you did it to one of the least of my people, you did it to me.' What the gospel is saying is that Christ is in the most wretched of beings, the drug-addict, the alcoholic, the rapist, the most abandoned and the most unlovable. In serving them we are serving him.

Behind this saying there is love, a self-giving love that urges us on. It is that same love coming from Jesus that supports us in all our efforts to serve those in need. And it is that same love, a self-giving love, that raises the whole matter of helping others out of the realm of mere do-gooding that can often be fussy, self-assertive and, worst of all, discriminatory. It is not only 'the deserving poor' – a horrible Victorian phrase —that should be helped. It is everyone in any kind of need. Who is my neighbour?, asked the lawyer in the gospel. And Jesus told the parable of the Good Samaritan to show him that everyone, even the hated member of another race or an enemy, is our neighbour and must be helped and loved.

When we consider the gospel of today, we see that it is the whole people of God, the followers of Christ are to bear witness – and to him. The church, that is the people, is like a city set on a hill. It is a light for all to see: 'You light must shine in the sight of men, so that seeing your good works, they may give praise to your Father in heaven.'

'Seeing your good works'. We try, rightly, to keep them hidden but if the whole Christian people are engaged (according to their ability) in feeding the hungry, housing the homeless and caring for the sick, the unwanted and the dying, like Mother Teresa in India, then the light of Christ will shine out from the church which will be seen to be the dwelling-place of love, of the unconquerable love that streams into it from the heart of God.

That is the message of today, and to help our reflections we might like to make our own the prayer after communion that shows that what we do and receive in the eucharist must have issue in our daily living: 'God our Father, by our sharing in this one bread and one cup you make us one in Christ. Help us to bring your salvation and your joy to the whole world.'

Sixth Sunday of the Year

Ecclus 15:15-20; Ps 118 (in part); 1 Cor 2:6-10; Mt 5:17-37.

It may be useful to remind you that this longish gospel is part of what we call the Sermon on the Mount, which runs from the beginning of chapter five to the end of chapter seven. In St Matthew's gospel Jesus is a second Moses; as he gave the Law (the Torah) which includes the Ten Commandments, so Jesus gives the new law or, better, the way of life that is incumbent on all those who would follow him. We shall find other extracts from the sermon in the Sundays to come and even today's passage is too long to be considered in detail. I will take only a few points.

What then is the underlying meaning of the whole text? The clue to the understanding is to be found in the verse, 'Unless your uprightness (or virtue) goes deeper than that of the scribes and Pharisees, you will not be able to enter the kingdom of heaven'. What does 'deeper' mean?

The scribes and Pharisees were good men according to their lights. The scribes discussed endlessly details of what was commanded or forbidden by the law that had been handed down from the time of Moses. But as Jesus said later, by doing so they were missing the greater things of the law, justice, mercy and love. They and the Pharisees, who always took the stricter view, were much concerned with externals, with ritual impurity. Thus, when they came back from market, they felt they must wash their hands or at least sprinkle them and, if they touched a corpse even by accident, they became ritually impure and cut off from worship.

What Jesus is saying throughout the sermon, and in many other places, is that right behaviour must first and above all be a response from the heart to what God is asking of us. External observance of the law, even his law, is not sufficient, for his law was (and is) a law of love: 'Love God and love your neighbour' and if we do that we fulfil all the law and the prophets. And the reason? The one who does the will of Jesus' Father in heaven will enter it, because we are giving a response from the depths of our heart.

To make his teaching concrete, Jesus gives a number of examples of what he means.

'You must not kill', said the old law and it remains valid to this day but it is not enough. Jesus says, 'Do not be angry with your brother', or anyone else for that matter. There are times when it is difficult not to be angry, but we must dispel angry or revengeful thoughts for they too are sinful and can lead to murder, as sometimes happens.

Connected with this is the message of reconciliation. If there is something between ourselves and another, some disagreement or quarrel, this is a barrier to love of neighbour and according to the gospel, a barrier to sincere worship. We must seek reconciliation first, we must come to terms with the other, we must restore good relationships. Though the gospel does not say it here, we know from elsewhere that reconciliation is the fruit of love, the love that God puts in our hearts, a share of his love whereby he redeemed the world.

The old law said, 'You must not commit adultery'. Jesus says, 'If anyone looks on another lustfully he has already committed adultery in his heart.' Lustful thoughts and desires, if deliberately indulged, are sinful and that is why they, as well as adultery itself, are forbidden.

With this Jesus connects divorce. Divorce and (re) marriage with another is adultery. This is one of the hard sayings of the gospel but Christians must try and live up to it to the best of their ability; if people did try, the world would be a better place, as we are learning painfully in our own time.

Perhaps the exceptive clause (only in Matthew's gospel) needs a word of explanation: 'Unless for fornication' which might be better translated 'except in the case of illicit marriages', that is marriage within certain degrees of kindred, like the marriage of a nephew to an aunt. Matthew was writing for a convert Jewish community which, it seems, still observed (or wanted to observe) part of the old law where the rules about kinship and marriage were very closely drawn. There seems to have been trouble about this.

What Jesus is saying today is that unchastity within or outside marriage is sinful, always to be avoided, always to be resisted. Some people seem to think that the church has gone soft on sin but the church cannot go soft on sin without being unfaithful to the gospel and unfaithful to Christ. And we must add, the whole church, pope, bishop, priests and people, are called to live by the gospel and the word of Christ our Lord. The Sermon on the Mount is at once a programme by which, as Christians, we must live and an ideal towards which we must strive throughout our life. The impetus and the power whereby we can do this is love, the love that is poured into our hearts by the Holy Spirit. Jesus ends this section with the words: 'You must set no bounds to your love, just as you heavenly Father sets none to his'.[1] Our love, the response to God's love for us, is the keeping of the whole law, and if we love God sincerely, from the heart, and others as he would have us love them, then there will be no sin in our lives.

1. This is the bold translation in the *New Jerusalem Bible*, 1985. It puts very positively the *meaning* of the phrase.

Seventh Sunday of the Year

Lev 19:1-2, 17-18; Ps 102 (in part); 1 Cor 3:16-23; Mt 5:38-48.

I begin with two sentences: 'Be holy, for I, the Lord your God am holy' and 'You must be perfect just as your heavenly Father is perfect'. I daresay that you, like me, have felt that those words set up an ideal too difficult for us ever to achieve. And some books on the spiritual life once gave the impression that if we tried hard enough we could somehow become perfect. This impression was confirmed by certain old-fashioned lives of the saints that would have us believe that they were perfect, even sometimes from their infancy. Other writers unwittingly presented saints as carefully calculating, practising one virtue after another to gain merit and so be fit candidates for eternal bliss. In more recent years, writers of saints' lives have been more honest (and more interesting) and have shown us that even saints were not perfect. As Jesus said to the rich young man, 'One alone is good, God', and he is wholly good. As the first reading has it, 'The Lord your God is holy'.

If we put the saying 'Be perfect ...' in context, we can perhaps begin to see its meaning. Jesus is speaking about loving enemies, loving those who persecute us, and at times the love he is asking of us does indeed seem to go beyond our human powers. Like some of you, I have lived through the Second World War and the years before when Stalin was slaughtering millions of his own people in Gulags and through trumped up trials. In Germany, Hitler killed millions of Jews and Poles in the gas-chambers; he wanted to exterminate them. It was very difficult to love Stalin and Hitler and all their minions, but what we and Christians throughout the world did was to pray (as well as fight) that their evil reign would come to an end and the death of innumerable people would stop. Yes, in those circumstances it was easy to hate and we had to struggle not to do so.

In those or similar circumstances, we have to make a super-human effort and to realise that the love that is required can come only from God. In the New Testament, especially in the Letters of St Paul, we are often told to 'imitate God, to imitate Jesus Christ'. That is not just 'copying'. It suggests a sharing in the love of God which is communicated to us by the Holy Spirit. It is this love that is as strong as death, a love that many waters cannot quench (Song of Solomon 8:6, 7). That comes near the meaning of 'Be perfect ...', and the command is more under-standable if we accept the translation, 'You must set no bounds to your love, just as your heavenly Father sets no bounds to his.' That is difficult enough but more within the bounds of possibili-ty. We are loving with a love that comes from God.

The same considerations apply to the first part of the gospel about an eye for an eye and a tooth for a tooth. It seems pretty horrible to us, but this Old Testament saying is often misunder-stood. What it meant was that people in conflict, or dispute of one kind or another, must not demand *more* than an eye for an eye or a tooth for a tooth. It was an attempt by the old law to limit revenge. But Jesus goes far beyond that: 'Love your enemy, do good to those who hate you', you must return love for evil, a love that, so to say, cancels out the evil. Once again, and this time we turn to the psalm, we must have the compassion of God 'who does not treat us according to our sins nor repay us accord-ing to our faults'. But above all we must be like Christ who, as he was being nailed to the cross, prayed, 'Father, forgive them, they do not know what they are doing.' Love and forgiveness of that kind is redemptive.

So then, there must be no revenge, no tit for tat, no wanting to get your own back. Rather, we must try and go along with those who offend us, however difficult it may be, we must try and reach out to them. If that comes to nothing, if any approach seems impossible, then we must pray for them. In answer to our

prayers God will renew his love within us and enable us to forgive as we pray in the prayer that Jesus gave us, 'Forgive us our
trespasses as we forgive those who trespass against us.' Then
gradually, and no doubt with difficulty, we shall come somewhere near the command of Jesus, 'You must therefore set no
bounds to your love, just as your heavenly Father sets no bounds
to his'.

Eighth Sunday of the Year

Is 49:14-15; Ps 61 (in part); 1 Cor 4:1-5; Mt 6:24-34.

The second and longer part of today's gospel has an attraction
all of its own. It reveals to us, or seems to do so, the delight Jesus
had in the birds of the air and the flowers of the field, all the creation that was around him. It reveals also his understanding of
his Father's watchful care over all his creatures: 'Your heavenly
Father feeds them.'

Yet when we look at the world we live in, there is a dreadful
irony in all this. There will be many who will hear this gospel
today who are so worried about what they are to eat that they do
not know where their next meal is going to come from. These
and others like them are worried about the old, ragged and
smelly clothes they must wear because they have no others. I am
not talking simply about the Third World where millions are living at or under the subsistence line. I am thinking of this country, which is still rich, where, for whatever reason, there are
thousands sleeping on the streets and something like two and a
half million who are trying to live on the 'dole', and yet others
on what is called 'benefit'. No doubt they are not starving, but
they have to 'make do' with whatever comes to hand. As has
been often said in recent years, the rich are getting richer and the
poor poorer.

It is then very painful to speak on the theme of today's gospel.
Yet we must do so to see if we are to snatch any comfort from it.

As we reflect, we see that the over-arching message is that God is in control. In the beginning God made all things, the world we live in is his world and all of us are stewards of goods that are not ultimately our own. In using them wisely, human beings who administer them can, if they are so minded, become the providence of God to the needy. In a simpler society this is what happened; no one starved; and in regions of the world where food is scarce it is shared as long as it lasts. It is for the peoples and countries with plenty to supply what is wanting; it is an obligation. What is more they have an obligation to restore and support local economies so that the ravages of destitution and natural calamities can be reversed and the people enabled to produce what is necessary for their life.

In our world numerous agencies, both Christian and others, have been doing this for many years and they are acting as a 'providence' to those they aid. It seems that some nations, often the richer ones, are less inclined to do what is their plain duty – and ultimate self-interest! There is a bigger problem into which I cannot go now. It is that industry, commerce, whole economies, are organised solely for profit and while that is so, there will always be great numbers of people who suffer. They will become unemployed, they will be dismissed at the age of fifty-five or even earlier as 'too old', which means they 'cost' too much for 'profitable' employment, and women are employed instead of men because they are 'cheaper'. So long as this system (if such it can be called) lasts, it will be difficult for the preacher and perhaps cruel to urge his hearers to put their trust in 'providence' which, through its underlings, is proving to be such a harsh master.

Is there anything to be said? If we look at the gospel message carefully we see it is warning all of us against *undue* anxiety: 'Do not worry about tomorrow; tomorrow will take care of itself'; 'Do not be over-anxious about your life ...' And the remedy for anxiety is trust. It may then be possible for you to make your own the words of the prophet who was writing to people in exile, living among strangers. The people were inclined to say, 'The Lord has abandoned me' and then comes the reply: 'Does a woman forget her baby at the breast or fail to cherish the son of her womb?' No, 'Even if these forget I will never forget you' and then comes a sentence that follows immediately, though is not included in our text: 'I have engraved you on the palms of my hand.' If no one else cares for us, he does. It may be too that in this spirit we can pray with the psalmist:

> In God is my safety and glory,
> the rock of my strength.
> Take refuge in God all you people.
> Trust him at all times.
> Pour out your hearts before him.

Ninth Sunday of the Year

Deut 11:18, 26-28, 32; Ps 30 (in part); Rom 3:21-25, 28; Mt 7:21-27.

It is helpful to realise that the long Sermon on the Mount is made up of a number of sayings of Jesus that are gathered here together (though found in other places in other gospels) and are not necessarily connected. Today there is the passage about doing the will of God, which has a separate message from the little parable about building on rock. In Matthew's text they are joined by a 'Therefore'. Presumably the evangelist meant us to see that they are connected and we will take them in that way.

'It is not those who say, "Lord, Lord" who will enter the kingdom of heaven but the one who does the will of my Father in heaven.' As we all know, saying is not doing and our world seems to be drowning in words whether uttered through 'the modern means of communication', the media, or by politicians who promise much but often produce little. And then there is all the paper that is in circulation both in church and secular life that makes life burdensome to us. There are also those who will talk much about religion but do not put it into practice. It is these the gospel seems to have in mind, people who pray long and loud saying, 'Lord, Lord' or invoking other holy names. There were those too who had, or thought they had, special gifts of prophesying, of exorcising and of miracle-working. All admirable in themselves and in the right time and place, but they are no substitute for the fundamental thing, the doing of the Father's will.

This injunction sometimes troubles people. What is God's will for me, they ask. In particular cases it is not always easy to say but generally living the life that is ours is doing God's will. Married people who live their life as well as they can are doing God's will and if one felt called to religious life one could say that is not God's will for them. The daily work, sometimes an awful grind of man or woman in factory or office, done as well as possible, is to live according to God's will. To worship God publicly on Sundays and to pray at home in private is to do God's will. If these and all the normal duties of daily life are lived in that spirit, we can be sure enough that we are doing God's will.

So we see that praying and doing go together, but praying without doing, and doing without praying, are likely to be sterile.

If such a view seems Pelagian ('we do it all by our own strength') let us remember that Jesus taught us to pray, 'Thy will be done,' and that in this matter he is our model and help. In St John's gospel there is that always impressive saying, 'My food is to do the will of the one who sent me' (4:34). His whole life, his teaching, his suffering, his very death were the doing of his Father's will: 'Father, let this cup (of suffering) pass me by. But not my will but yours be done.' We were redeemed by the dedication of Jesus' will to his Father's will and, day by day, we are supported by that will that holds us up.

So we come to the parable: 'Everyone who listens to these words of mine and acts on them, is like the man who built his house on rock.' In this sense Jesus is the Rock on whom we can depend utterly when we try to do his will. In the terms of the psalm, as so often in the psalter, God is our rock and our stronghold, he is a rock of refuge for us, and we can be confident that when we seek and do his will he will support us, hold us up and lead and guide us to the vision of himself: 'Let your face shine on your servant. Save me in your love.'

As we pray, then, that we may do God's will, let us remember that such prayer is prompted and assisted by the Holy Spirit: 'No one can say "Jesus is Lord" unless he is under the influence of the Holy Spirit' (1 Cor 2:3). To God the Father, through Jesus Christ his Son and by the inspiration of the Holy Spirit is the prayer of the Christian and such prayer is always pleasing to God. As St Paul makes clear in another place: 'The Spirit comes to help us in our weakness. For when we cannot choose words in order to pray properly, the Spirit himself expresses our plea in a way that could never be put into words.' Because of this, God knows what he (the Spirit) means and such prayers are always pleasing to him (Rom 8:26, 27).

Tenth Sunday of the Year

Hos 6:3-6; Ps 49 (in part); Rom 4:18-25; Mt 9:9-13.

In all organised religions that have rites and liturgies, there is a danger of emphasising the rites and of forgetting that of which they are expressions. The externals become, or seem to become, more important than the content. If regrettable, it is understandable. Rites are repeated and there seems to be an inerradicable tendency to attach oneself to what is done over and over again. Any change, any variation, causes distress and is often regarded as an outrage. Prophets and saints through the ages have been aware of the danger and have warned against ritual sacrifices or indeed any kind of ritualistic worship where the emphasis was rather on the rite than on its meaning and content.

In the grand Temple of Solomon there was the elaborate liturgy of the twice-daily sacrifices. There were the priests and levites, there was the slaughtering of animals and clouds of incense rising to the skies. This was accompanied by the singing of psalms and the sound of trumpets and the clashing of cymbals and the blowing of horns. The prophets were perfectly familiar with all this and severely condemned a worship that, in their view, had become so formal as to leave the heart untouched. Among these prophets was Hosea who rebuked the people and their leaders for their insincere worship and uttered the words that have rung down the centuries and were repeated by Jesus himself: 'What I want is love, not sacrifice; knowledge of God, not holocausts.' What was Hosea saying? What indeed did Jesus mean?

It is possible to misunderstand these words. The Hebrew language does not easily admit of degrees of comparison; all is positive or negative, black or white. 'Love not sacrifice', 'Mercy not sacrifice' means that mercy is preferable to sacrifice, that mercy is more important than sacrifice, and here that sacrifice without mercy, sacrifice that does not engage the heart, is false. Sacrifice that is not reflected in life, in mercy towards others, is rejected by God. This is the message of the psalm: 'I find no fault with your sacrifice, your offerings are always before me.' What then is wrong? We learn this from the rest of the psalm that is not sung today:

> You make friends with a thief as soon as you see one,
> you feel at home with adulterers,
> your conversation is devoted to wickedness,
> and your tongue is inventing lies ...

What God, through the psalmist, is objecting to is the intolerable discrepancy between the offering of sacrifices and the disreputable lives of some who were involved in the offering. If these people can put their lives in order then they can 'Pay your thanksgiving sacrifice, you can fulfil your promises' and, if they call on God in their distress, he will free them and then they will honour him.

'I would have mercy rather than sacrifice ... I did not come to call the virtuous but sinners', to repentance. Mercy, usually translated 'steadfast' or 'faithful love', is one of the great words of the Hebrew Bible and here today we see Jesus, the fulfilment in word and life of the Bible, calling the 'sinner' Matthew, ostracised because an agent of the Roman occupying power, and sitting down with sinners at table. These were the people to whom he was sent and he would let saving mercy flow from his heart to those who were marginalised from 'respectable' society. He is the model and exemplar of the divine mercy, the mercy of his Father. One is reminded of the verse of the hymn 'Sower and seed of man's reprieving':

> What sovereign pity earthward drew thee,
> our load of sins thy charge to make,
> Slain, that the guilty race that slew thee
> Life from thy guiltless death might take.[1]

That saving mercy is still available to us through repentance of our sins, through the Sacrament of Reconciliation and through the Holy Eucharist when the merciful Saviour offers himself to us, as we pray in the *Agnus Dei*, still taking away our sins.

But he is also our model and exemplar. Our world is filled with people, old and young, who feel abandoned, marginalised, not wanted by society, and it is the task and the duty of every Christian to help them in whatever way is open to them. In this way we shall combine both mercy and sacrifice and our offerings will be pleasing to God.

1. Westminster Hymnal (1940), number 60. Trans. R. A. Knox.

Eleventh Sunday of the Year

Ex 19:2-6; Ps 99 (in part); Rom 5:6-11; Mt 9:36–10:8.

It may seem surprising to us that Jesus should tell his disciples to go only to 'the lost sheep of the house of Israel'. It is best seen as their *first* mission. As the opening verses of today's gospel shows, Jesus had compassion on his own people. They were harassed and dejected, they were like sheep without a shepherd. Many of the Jewish leaders had no care for ordinary people; the scribes and Pharisees imposed on them the full rigor of the law and the human traditions attached to it, and as we learn from St Luke's gospel, in the parable of the Pharisee and the tax-gatherer, some of them despised those they called sinners. Moreover, the scribes and Pharisees had no word of life to offer them.

It was not to be so with the followers of Jesus. They, as we shall see, had a word of life, they had power to heal the sick, cleanse lepers, cast out devils and even raise the dead (as we read of Peter doing in the Acts of the Apostles). Then, as the next part of the gospel shows, the disciples were to go out to the people, they were to live with the people and live like them, and, like their Master, they were to seek out those who were lost.

We know that they did this in the life-time of Jesus but it was not until after the resurrection that they received their second and final mission to go out to the whole world: 'Going therefore,

make disciples of all nations, baptise them in the name of the
Father, the Son and the Holy Spirit.' Servants of the Servant,
they became a light to the nations so that his salvation could
reach the ends of the earth (Is 49:6). This we see them doing in
the Acts of the Apostles, though it was not until St Paul made his
impact on the first Christian community that everyone realised
that *in fact* the whole world was their mission field.

As we reflect on the texts, we ask ourselves in what exactly did
their mission consist. The apostles and those who were their
helpers (Timothy, Titus and the rest) had two things. First, they
had the word which was not their own but the word of God that
Jesus had made known to them. And because it was the word of
God it had power, a power that is revealed to us in the gospel of
St John. When some of Jesus' disciples said of his teaching on the
eucharist, 'This is a hard saying and who can take it?' they
walked away. Jesus turned to the rest and asked, 'Will you also
go away?' and Peter answering for them replied, 'Lord, to whom
shall we go? You have the words of eternal life.' In the same
place we read that the words of Jesus are 'Spirit and life'. In
God's word there is the power of the Holy Spirit that generates
the Christ-life within us and gives us a share in his divine life.

The apostles had something else. This was the word combined
with the sacred actions we call sacraments. Jesus said not only
'Go and make disciples' but also 'Baptise', by which we are
made sons and daughters of God, filled with the life of Christ
that flows through the church and the sacraments into ourselves.

They were also to heal the sick, anointing them with oil (Mk
6:13) and this the church still does by anointing with oil combined
with word and prayer (Jas 5:14-16) which is the instrument of
Christ's healing power.

Then at the Last Supper Jesus said over the bread, 'Take and eat.
This is my body which is given for you. Take and drink, This is my
blood which is shed for you. Do this in remembrance of me', for
'anyone who eats my flesh and drinks my blood has eternal life.'
Here word reaches its highest potential; we are enabled to live in
Christ and by his strength given through word and sacrament.

All this is familiar to you, but it is well to remember it when we talk of mission. It is not just a saying a lot of words, even holy words. The whole purpose of the mission of the church is that through word and sacrament people should accept Christ by faith and so be incorporated into the church to be nourished by his body and blood and become living members of his body.

There is one last thing to be said. The apostles not only had the word of God, they not only had the sacraments, they had themselves to give, and many of them, with their fellow-Christians, gave their lives even to death for Jesus Christ and his mission. If we are not called to martyrdom and death (and some in our own time have been), we are called to make known the word of God. No doubt we cannot do what the apostles did, nor are we all preachers, but we can be like the apostles and martyrs at least in this: we can try and live close to Christ and his gospel and then our lives will be the means of drawing others to him.

Twelfth Sunday of the Year

Jer 20:10-13; Ps 68 (in part); Rom 5:12-15; Mt 10:26-33.

The word of God does not always convey a comfortable message and the proclamation of that word is often difficult and sometimes dangerous. This was true both in Old Testament and New Testament times.

Today we have set before us the figure of Jeremiah, who, as he tells us himself, impelled by the word of God, denounced the Israelites because they refused to listen to the word of God. He was insulted, abused, put in the stocks, and later the Temple police would try to murder him. Even so, he confesses that the Lord is with him, 'The Lord is at my side, a mighty hero.' In spite of everything, God's cause will win, though in Jeremiah's case it did not seem to do so. War and exile came and he himself seems to have been swept off to Egypt, there to die.

In the New Testament, the apostle James was put to death by King Herod about 44 AD, Stephen was stoned to death, and

Peter and Paul suffered violence, imprisonment and finally martyrdom in Rome.

All this seems to have happened in the long distant past but it has gone on through the centuries. In our own country we remember two of our English martyrs among many others: St John Fisher, Bishop of Rochester, who faithful to God's word, denounced the divorce of Henry VIII from his wife Catherine of Aragon and died on the scaffold praying the word of God from Psalm 33. There was the great layman, St Thomas More, one of the most attractive men who have ever lived, who refused to accept that Henry was the (earthly) head of the Church in England and who was beheaded on the Tower Hill in London.

More recently (1980) there was the murder of Archbishop Romero who was shot dead at the altar for defending Christ's poor and oppressed. In the same country, El Salvador, nine years later there was the murder of six Jesuits in their own home for resisting and showing up an unjust regime. These and many others heeded the words of Jesus: 'Do not be afraid of those who kill the body but cannot kill the soul', and the witness of their death endures to this day.

These words are part of the gospel today, but they would be easier to understand if the previous passage, vv. 17-24, had been included. In all the first part of this chapter Jesus is seen sending out his disciples and preparing them for their mission. In this passage (which was probably influenced by the post-resurrection experiences of the apostles) he warns them: 'Beware of men; they will hand you over to sanhedrins and scourge you in their synagogues. You will be dragged before governors and kings for my sake ... but do not worry about how to speak or what to say; what you are to say will be given to you when the time comes ... It is not you who are speaking; the Spirit of your Father will be speaking in you.' That was the strength of the apostles and that is the strength of all who have borne witness to Christ and his church throughout the ages. Their witness is inspired and authenticated by the Holy Spirit, and Jesus himself bears witness to them and grants them their reward: 'Anyone who declares himself for me in the presence of men, I will declare myself for him in the presence of my Father in heaven.'

Where are we in all this? What is our situation and what, if anything, can we do about it?

We know that we live in a world that is largely indifferent to religion and it is a world that seems to have become increasingly immoral. For the most part, the majority of people live as if God did not exist, that Jesus Christ never existed and that the church or the churches are disposable extras which the world could very well do without. There is enormous pressure on people to live according to the values of the world, and this is especially true of the young. There is little or no sense of right and wrong, and one feature of our moral atmosphere is that people not only commit crimes – sometimes quite horrific ones – but do not seem to think they have done anything wrong. That is what I mean when I say that our world has become immoral or amoral. It is this that is very frightening and it will take a very long time to remedy.

As for ourselves, the first thing to realise is that our world is, as I have briefly described it, a pagan world, worse than some pagan civilisations and cultures of the past, and we can be affected, almost one would say infected, by the non-belief and non-morality of our world. We can, without hardly knowing it, accept this world uncritically and by consequence we may be in danger of going along with its values. There are signs that this is happening.

What then are we to do? The first thing, as I have already hinted, is to recognise our world for what it is and to decide to resist it in all that is evil. Survival in such a world requires, I believe, an ever deeper faith in Jesus Christ and in his words in the gospels which we 'listen' to every Sunday but perhaps do not take into ourselves. We should also be clear about the moral principles of the Christian life, set out in the New Testament and handed down to us by the church. To this we need to add, according to possibilities, some time of interior, private prayer either at home or in church, for this strengthens faith and enables us to make it part of our daily living.

If we do this, it will give us the strength to do what is right and of crucial importance for our lives as Christians. We shall begin to be the sort of Christian we ought to be and we shall be able to resist the immoral trends of the society in which we live. Then, without 'preaching', our daily living will be 'declaring Christ' before the world, we shall be living in continuity with the apostles and martyrs and continuing the work of Jesus Christ himself.

Thirteenth Sunday of the Year

Kings II, 11:14-16; Ps 88 (in part); Rom 6:3, 4, 8-15; Mt 10:37-42.

Sometimes the word of God is addressed to our personal living and at other times it turns our minds to the world in which we live. So first in the gospel of today there are those 'hard sayings' of Jesus about abandoning ourselves wholly to him. 'Anyone who finds his life will lose it; anyone who loses his life for my sake will find it.' But if we take the first reading with the gospel we see that the message of today is about welcome, about our attitude to others, to all others whoever they may be.

Welcome seems a very ordinary and natural thing. We are happy to welcome friends to our homes, we are glad to welcome people to our parties and so on. But as we ponder on the gospel we find that there is a much deeper meaning to welcome: 'Anyone who welcomes you welcomes me,' says Jesus, 'and those who welcome me welcome the one who sent me,' that is his Father. To welcome another is to welcome Christ. That is the great truth put before us. And it is this that St Benedict enjoins in his Rule: 'Let all guests that come be received like Christ, for he will say "I was a stranger and you took me in."' He goes even further: 'So let Christ be worshipped in them, for indeed he is received in their persons.' And that is precisely the meaning of the gospel saying. However natural and ordinary welcoming of others is, we are welcoming Christ in them and Benedict goes on to say that this is particularly true of the poor, 'because in them Christ is more truly welcomed.' If we remember those other words of Jesus, 'In as far as you did it to one of the least of my people you did it to me,' we can see they are.

Even so there are difficulties, difficulties in some people's minds and, worse still, prejudices. In an address, (originally broadcast) by Colin Morris, I have read this week he speaks of 'mind-forged manacles' that we make for ourselves about certain categories of people. If a murder or an act of violence has been committed by a black man, we say (or are inclined to say), 'Of course they are all like that.' If we see or hear of a person of another race, skin or colour, doing something wrong we may say, 'What can you expect of such people?' If we have stereotyped people of other nations or races, stereotypes that are born of ignorance, fear or prejudice, we are shackling our minds and doing the very opposite of what Jesus told us to do. With such a mentality, and even if we never come into personal contact with them, we are refusing to welcome them.

These considerations are, I believe, important as we read and hear of increasing racial discrimination against various kinds of ethnic groups. Not all of them, of course, are angels but then neither are the British. We have only to think of the appalling football hooligans of recent years who have earned for this country so bad a name abroad. But just as it is wrong to condemn all British people for this, so is it wrong to condemn whole ethnic groups for the wrong-doing of some of them.

'Anyone who welcomes you welcomes me'. Underlying this simple statement is a profound and fundamental Christian truth which was voiced by St Paul, 'There is no room for distinctions between barbarian and Scythian, slave and free man. There is only one Christ: he is all in all' (Col 3:11). Every human being of whatever race, nation or colour is a creature of God, loved by God, loved by his Son, Jesus Christ, for 'In as far as you did it to one of the least of my people you did it (and are doing it) to me'. We have to extend our welcome, our love and our service to all, and especially to the needy. The one who gives so little as a cup of water to 'one of these little ones' is the true disciple of Christ.

Welcoming, in the terms of the gospel, can be difficult and at times very demanding but, as I have suggested, the difficulty begins often enough in our own minds. So on the one hand we have to get rid of prejudices about different races and peoples, and on the other we have to realise that we are bound by the great law of Christ, 'Love your neighbour as yourself', and that we have to practice it even when our neighbour is far removed from us in his way of acting and living, and even when we find some aspects of his religion repulsive. Whether we like it or not, we live now in a multi-cultural and multi-religious society and Christ's message that we must love others extends to all. If we offer them understanding (a form of love) and are willing to help in times of need, then we shall be true disciples of him who loves all and came to save them all.

Fourteenth Sunday of the Year

Zech 9:1-10; Ps 144 (in part); Rom 8:9, 11-13; Mt 11:25-30.

I must confess that this gospel is one of my favourite passages in all the first three gospels. It is almost unique in giving us a glimpse of the inner life of Jesus and his relationship with his Father. 'I bless you (give thanks to you), Father, for hiding these things from the learned and the clever and revealing them to mere children.' The saying comes out of the blue, nothing before or after it in the gospel text is related to it. For me it is the spont-aneous and almost ecstatic prayer of the Son of God.

I think we take the term 'Son of God' too easily. It is so much more than a theological statement, so much more than a piece of apologetics. Here in this passage we see something of what it means.

The Son of God existed before all time with his Father in a union of total love, joy and exultation. By taking up our human nature he became a man, fully human like ourselves, but this gospel shows us that the union of love and joy continued while he is here on earth. It is a union so close and so precious to him that he cannot stop himself bursting out and proclaiming it, professing it and thanking his Father for it: the Father who 'is Lord of heaven and earth'. He is totally one with him and, reflecting on his rela-tionship with him, he, as it were, enters into an ecstasy, the only parallels to which are the experiences of the greatest mystical

saints who were granted a glimpse of God and were overwhelmed by it.

To understand the relationship of Jesus with his Father a little
more deeply, we need to turn to the gospel according to St John
where we find Jesus saying, 'I came to do the will of him who
sent me' and again, 'My food (my very life) is to do the will of
my Father who sent me.' 'Doing the will' of his Father was his
response to his Father's love, it was the expression of the indescribable love he had for his Father and a realisation of the love
his Father had for him.

It was this that underlay and supported all his work on earth, his
teaching, his forgiving of sinners, his compassion for the poor
and lowly, his passion, his death and his resurrection. All is the
expression of his love, all is the manifestation of God's love for
us, 'who so loved the world as to give his only son' to us and for
us and our salvation.

This leads us to an understanding of the words, 'No one knows
the Son except the Father, just as no one knows the Father except
the Son'. In the Old Testament and in the New, especially in St
John's gospel, 'knowing' does not mean just knowing something *about* a person. It means knowing another through and
through, just as a lover knows his beloved in a way that goes far
beyond mere mental knowing. The love is combined with
knowledge and the knowledge is transfused with love. That, as
far as our understanding can take us, is true of the love of the
Father for the Son and of the Son for the Father.

But does this remain just up in the clouds? Has it anything to say
to us now, anything that will help on our way? The amazing
thing is that we are invited to share the vision of God and the life
of God as we learn from the First Letter of St John: 'We are already the children of God (through Jesus Christ) but what we
are to be in the future has not yet been revealed: all we know is
that when it is revealed we shall be like him because we shall see
him as he really is' (3:2), and seeing him we shall be filled with
joy.

If, however, that is to come to pass, we must be like 'the mere children' of whom Jesus speaks. These are not merely young children, they were his own disciples, they were the humble and the lowly, the 'poor ones' of later Old Testament times, people like Mary and Joseph and Holy Simeon who were waiting for 'the redemption of Israel'. They were open to God; they were ready to receive the word of God into their hearts and live by it; they were ready to accept Jesus and did so; and whether in this world or the next, the loving union between Jesus and his Father was revealed to them and they responded with the whole love of their hearts.

'Come to me all you who labour and are overburdened.' These words are addressed to us, are an invitation to us to enter into the love of the Lord. The love that Jesus showed to the sick, the suffering and the sinful, will be shown to us if we are 'gentle and lowly in heart' as he was. The love that Jesus had for his Father is the same love that he has for us and, with his love acting in our hearts, we can take up his yoke and carry our burdens and so find the repose, the peace that will carry us on to the end when we shall enjoy the eternal sabbath, the rest and peace that lasts forever.

Fifteenth Sunday of the Year

Is 55:10-11; Ps 64 (in part); Rom 8:18-23; Mt 13:1-23.

This parable is so familiar to us that we may let it pass without letting it have any impact on us. It has many things to say to us but I will single out just one or two.

You will have noticed that after the parable there is that long quotation from Isaiah about the people who do not listen, whose ears are dull, who shut their eyes lest they should see and understand. Jesus was referring to those who did indeed listen but only with their ears. They failed to take in, make their own and live by the word of God for fear that they might be converted and healed. These words are addressed also to us. Sunday by Sunday we hear the scriptures, three readings every time, and I wonder what we make of them? I agree that sometimes there are parts of them that are difficult to understand, especially perhaps the short extracts from St Paul. But it has been said, and I think it is true, that if we do listen we shall find at least one phrase or one saying that helps us, that goes to the heart and that turns us to Christ. In the word of the gospel, we are converted and so are healed by Christ.

For the word of God has power and St Luke makes it very clear that the seed of the parable is the word of God. In the first reading from Isaiah, we are told that the word of God is like rain or snow coming down to the earth and making the seed to grow in the ground, giving it life so that it can put out shoots and then flower and finally produce fruit. So God's word goes from his mouth and does not return without accomplishing God's will and succeeding in what it was sent to do. This links up with the last sentence of the gospel: the one who receives the seed in rich soil (with a generous heart) is the one who yields a harvest and a very abundant harvest.

The word of God has power and an enduring power. As Jesus said, the world will pass away but his words will not pass away. As if to back this up, the Second Vatican Council said of the gospel in particular, 'Christ is still proclaiming his gospel when the scriptures are read in church'. That is why we should listen and take his words to our hearts and try and live by it.

If we consider the pattern of the readings for the Sundays, we shall see that it helps us to do this. The gospel is the most important reading, but it is preceded by one from the Old Testament which foreshadows, either in word or by event, the message of the gospel. In the psalm with its response we reflect on and pray about the message which is given in its fullness in the gospel. This is preceded by the singing of the Alleluias as we welcome Christ coming to us, making himself present to us in the word of his gospel. If we keep this pattern in mind we shall perhaps not find the word of God as difficult to understand as we had imagined and, more important still, it will have penetrated our minds and hearts.

Finally, let us reflect on the different kinds of people whom the gospel addresses today. We may find ourselves among them. There are those who do not try and listen. The word bounces off them and is lost. There are those who do listen but they are so full of the cares and troubles of their life that the word is smothered. If that is so, let them hold in their minds the comforting word we heard last Sunday: 'Come to me all you who labour and are overburdened and I will give you rest.' Then, as the gospel says, there are who are choked by riches, by worldly living, by heaping up goods – and they produce nothing.

All these words are challenges to us, challenges to think about our own situation. They are warnings, for though we can and should enjoy life (which is God's gift to us), we should always remember that, according to the scriptures, this world and all that is in it will pass away, and the word of God remains forever.

Sixteenth Sunday of the Year

Wis 12:13, 16-14; Ps 85 (in part); Rom 8:26-27; Mt 13:24-43.

One of the problems that bother us at one time or another is why, in the world and even in the church, there is both good and evil. Why doesn't God punish the wicked? In our own time, and especially for one of my age, we have witnessed the most appalling crimes and cruelty. There was Stalin in the Soviet Union who 'liquidated' millions of his own people to bring about his inhumane system called Marxism. In Nazi Germany there was that evil man Hitler who had millions of Jews murdered simply because they were Jews, and millions of others all over Europe whom he got rid of because they resisted him and his abominable plans for the total domination of Europe. Those who visited the concentration camps as the war ended were filled with horror at the organised cruelty that met their eyes. There have been other exhibitions of cruelty, violence and horror in more recent years in former Yugoslavia and Angola.

The question, almost an accusation, rises to our lips: Why did God not strike down the torturers, the inhuman monsters who were responsible for these crimes? It is indeed a moral problem, the greatest of all moral problems. More, it is the mystery of evil which we can never hope fully to understand.

There are various considerations we can bring forward to alleviate our anguished questionings and one way is suggested by the scriptures today.

The parable about the wheat and the weeds seems to be about the church – it is addressed to the disciples – the kingdom that Jesus was gradually bringing into being. Here the wicked, the enemy, must be bad Christians and we remember that even among the Twelve there was Judas Iscariot, the traitor who brought Jesus to his death. In the course of history there have been many more bad Christians, high and low, important and unimportant, who among other things have tried to frustrate the saving purpose of God. The answer to the problem here then is that such people were wicked because they were bad Christians who in one way or another had rejected God and Jesus Christ and refused to live the way of life laid down for them. Yet, according to the parable they are not to be uprooted, they must be allowed to live and await the judgement of God at the end. The sense of the parable then is that sometimes evil doing must be tolerated, even in the church, lest greater evil should come. In fact there seems to be a self-correcting power in the Church. Prophets and saints rise up and, prompted by the Holy Spirit, they bring about a renewal of the church.

The last part of the gospel, which gives an interpretation of the parable, seems to change the scene and the sense of the parable itself. Now the field is the world, the punishment of the wicked will be eternal loss, and the solution will only be revealed at the end of time when 'the virtuous will shine like the sun in the kingdom of their Father'.

If we do not find either of these answers satisfying to us, let us reflect that in both parts of today's gospel what is being presented to us is the forbearance of God. So the owner of the field says, 'No, don't tear up the weeds for you might pull up the wheat and destroy the whole harvest.' This notion of forbearance is suggested in the first reading: God is 'mild in judgement and governs with great lenience'. God is just and merciful, he controls his power and he waits for the moment to act and the moment will not always be according to human calculations. By what seems to be a miracle of our times, the whole evil empire of the Soviet Union has been swept away, and yet not so many years ago that seemed utterly unpredictable.

The forbearance of God, the patience of God, even with ourselves, is more enduring than the patience of human beings. We might recall the words of St James which seem to echo the gospel: 'Think of the farmer, how patiently he waits for the precious fruit of the ground until it has had the autumn rains and the spring rains. You too have to be patient; do not lose heart, because the Lord's coming will be soon.' In the gospel, God is the farmer, good and bad times will come, not only rains and drought, but frost and snow and gales. But whatever may come, God's purpose is being worked out. We may well not see the results this side of eternity, but if we believe in God, if we trust in him, then we shall learn that all is being worked out in a world that is essentially imperfect, a world that is unfinished, a world that awaits its consummation (Rom 8:18-23), and a world where human beings, including ourselves, are imperfect and sometimes wicked. Since that is so, if the world is imperfect and we are imperfect, evil will exist and we, with God's help, must do all we can to resist and overcome it. We might take note of a writer in a secular newspaper who said, 'Suffering, which is inevitable in the lives of all mankind ... exists to be faced, challenged and overcome' (Bernard Levin, in *The Times*).

Seventeenth Sunday of the Year

I Kings 3:7-12; Ps 118 (in part); Rom 8:28-30; Mt 13:44-52.

When Pope John XXIII opened the Second Vatican Council in 1962, in his address to the council fathers he bade them read the 'signs of the times'. What did he mean by that? He meant that the church had moved into a new kind of society with new problems, a society in rapid development with good and bad features. The council, and indeed the whole church, must take account of the new situation. They must try and discern what is good and bad and find ways of promoting the good and finding remedies for what is bad. There was a tendency then, as there is now, to see nothing but the bad in our modern world, and indeed there is much that is wrong with it, but the Pope also condemned those he called 'the prophets of doom'.

All this may not seem very close to the scriptures we have heard today, and yet if we consider the prayer of Solomon we find that it contains much that is apt: 'Give your servant a heart to understand how to discern between good and evil.' In response he hears the words of God: 'You have asked for a discerning judgement ... here and now ... I give you a heart wise and shrewd ...' The gift of discernment and wise judgement, given to King Solomon 3,000 years ago, is as necessary now as it was then.

As one gets older, there is a temptation to see the modern world through dark spectacles and to think it has gone to the dogs. If we are inclined to do that, let us think for a moment of all these young people who, for the last thirty years or so, have gone out to different parts of the world through the Voluntary Service Organisation to help in Third World countries, or of others who have worked hard in Cheshire Homes whether here or in other countries. Think of the now widespread Hospice Movement that enables the old and the terminally ill to die in dignity and peace. And there has been, through the years, those extraordinary outbursts of generosity to try and feed the hungry in so many different places. There are those who may say that these efforts are mere palliatives, but the truth is that vast numbers of people of all kinds have discerned needs and have done what they could to meet them.

When we come to consider the gospel of today, we find that all this is very relevant. The third parable is about discernment. The fisherman is a skilled worker, he is wise in his own craft. When he looks into his drag-net he judges that there are fish fit to eat and sets them apart from the others. These he throws back into the sea. He chooses and he can choose because he knows.

In the first parable a man finds a treasure in a field, it seems by accident. But he sees that it is valuable and goes off and sells all he has to get it. A modern example of this might be a man who is restoring an old house. He comes across a hitherto unknown cupboard, he opens it and finds some old papers. He is going to burn them but then looks at them more carefully and he gradually realises they are the poems of a great poet. He looks and he judges.

In the second parable the merchant is seeking, looking for pearls, the most treasured jewel of the ancient world. He finds a pearl of great value, he judges that it is very valuable, and he goes off and sells everything he has to buy it.

All these are examples of different kinds of discernment. But what is the gospel telling us to be discerning about? These parables, like others, are about discerning the good news of the kingdom which Jesus is proclaiming to the people. And this kingdom or, better, the reign of God, which Jesus is bringing into existence, has to be discerned and the parables are intended to make their hearers think and judge and then accept their message. Indeed, it was a proclamation to the people then, as it is to us now, that God through his Son offers us salvation, grace and a share in the divine life which is worth more than all the treasures in fields or pearls however precious. These parables are repeating in different ways the great saying of this gospel: 'Seek first the kingdom of heaven …', to which we could add, 'Do not lay up for yourselves treasures on earth where moth and rust consume and where thieves break in and steal. For where your treasure is, there will be your heart also.' This is the discernment the gospel calls us to. If we seek we shall find, and when we have found we shall be able to judge that what we have found is the one treasure that matters, union with God that will flower into the vision of God.

If then, by the grace of God, we look towards him and then at our world, we shall see it as it really is, we shall be able to discern the good from what is evil and then we shall be in a position to act as we strive to do God's will for ourselves and for our world, which in fact is his.

Eighteenth Sunday of the Year

Is 55:1-3; Ps 144 (in part); Rom 8:35, 37-39; Mt 14:13-21.

As you will remember, today's gospel is recorded in all four gospels and was evidently very important to the early Christians. As the evangelists wrote their accounts, almost inevitably they thought of the Last Supper when Jesus prepared to give himself as a ransom for many, for the world. We too are reminded of these events as we hear the gospel.

But it can set up other trains of thought also. There is the invitation of the first reading 'to come and eat, and at no cost receive wine and milk'. There are the words of the psalm, 'The eyes of all creatures look to you, and you give them their food in due time'. As I read these words and as I hear the gospel, I cannot help thinking of the Third World where after years of effort on the part of various international organisations there are still millions living below the poverty line and others starving. 'The bread of life' of the gospel account is not only the eucharist. It is also the bread by which human beings live. This is why we who celebrate the eucharist must be untiring in our efforts to feed the hungry as best we can. And let us remember that it is in this same gospel of Matthew we read: 'I was hungry and you gave me food; I was thirsty and you gave me a drink ...' and, 'In so far as you did this to one of the least of my people you did it to me'.

The passage from Isaiah also reminds me of the account in St John's gospel where, in different places, the 'come' of the prophet is echoed. But more immediately to the point is the long conversation with the people around Jesus, as recorded in St John's gospel. Jesus is first concerned that the people should accept him as the one sent by the Father: 'You must believe in the one he has sent.' If they do, they will never hunger or thirst. Jesus in himself is the 'Bread of life' and belief, faith in Jesus Christ is indispensable if we are to accept him as present in the eucharist. It is only after his teaching about faith that Jesus comes to the subject of the eucharist: 'I tell you most solemnly, if you do not eat the flesh of the Son of Man and drink his blood you will not have life in you.'

This was so tremendous a statement that many could not take it and walked no more with Jesus. He, turning to his disciples, asked sadly, 'Will you also go away?' And Peter answered, 'Lord, to whom shall we go? You have the words of eternal life'.

It is the same with us. The presence of Jesus in the eucharist is a tremendous mystery; as we hear after the consecration, it is the 'Mystery of faith', and if we did not have the words of Jesus and the guarantee of the church's teaching, we could not believe it.

Long years ago a lady came to me one afternoon and said she was thinking of becoming a Catholic. We discussed various matters and then she as it were burst out, 'But I could never accept that Christ is present in the eucharist'. I replied, as gently as I could, 'And neither could I if I had not the word of Christ himself and the teaching of the church from the beginning.' She went away and I never saw her again.

Yes, it is a matter of faith but can we come a little nearer to understanding it? It is a hidden presence, it is a sacramental presence, under the appearances of bread and wine, which are signs of his presence which is real though existing in a special manner. What above all is important is that we receive Christ himself in holy communion. When Jesus spoke of his flesh, he meant his whole self and, when he spoke of his blood, he meant his very life, poured out for the taking away of the sins of the world. He gives himself to us, we receive him and we should give ourselves to him.

Can we go a little further? The presence is brought about by the Holy Spirit, the giver of life, as we pray in the Eucharistic Prayer: 'Let your Spirit come upon these gifts (the bread and wine), to make them holy so that they may become for us the body and blood of our Lord Jesus Christ.' And after the consecration we pray: 'Grant that we who are nourished by his body and blood, may be filled with his Holy Spirit and become one body, one spirit in Christ.'

As we think of these things we should be filled with great gratitude and a sense of reverence. As we receive holy communion we should remember that we are being united personally to

Christ, who nourishes us and strengthens us so that we can go out and do whatever is within our power to feed the hungry of the world.

Nineteenth Sunday of the Year

I Kings 19:9, 11-13; Ps 84 (in part); Rom 9:1-5; Mt 14:22-33.

At first sight, this event concerning Elijah seems to have little if any connection with the story about Peter in the gospel. But on second thoughts, we can see that both pose a question to us. Is it possible to have too much trust in God? Peter first steps out of the boat and then, filled with fear as he sees the waves, begins to sink and has to be hauled out by Jesus. He is called a 'man of little faith' but perhaps he had too much confidence in himself.

So we turn to Elijah. He has denounced the wicked King Ahab and his even worse wife Jezebel who had introduced into Israel the corrupt and immoral worship of pagan gods. She threatens to kill him. Filled with fear and almost in despair, Elijah flees and when he has put a safe distance between himself and the queen, he sits down and says to himself in a sort of a prayer, 'Lord, I have had enough ... I am no better than my ancestors.' He is no better than anyone else who had tried to uphold the pure worship of the one true God. Then he goes on further, to the mountain of Horeb where God has appeared to Moses. After storm, wind and earthquake, the conventional signs in the Old Testament of God's presence, Elijah realises that God is not in all that. Then comes a gentle breeze and he understands that God is now speaking to him and, in spite of his fears, he now receives a very difficult mission which in effect meant overturning the royal house. Sure of God's support, he sets out on his mission.

As we see then, in both the Old Testament story and the gospel there is an encounter with God, in both there is a word of God. Elijah hears the message of God and Peter hears the voice of Jesus, the Son of God: 'Courage. It is I. Do not be afraid.' Whether Peter took in fully that Jesus was declaring himself in that 'I am' it is difficult to say. A little later Peter, on behalf of the rest of the disciples, will respond, acknowledging that Jesus is the Messiah, 'the Son of the living God'.

That, as I see it, is the meaning of the scriptures set before us today. Elijah meets God, receives his word and his mission from him which he carries out, strong in his faith in God. Peter rather later realises that Jesus, who has called him, is the promised Messiah, the Son of God who will send him on his mission. He has much to learn and there are painful episodes awaiting him. He tries to turn Jesus from his mission, he denies his Lord during the Passion, and it was not until he has met his Lord risen from the dead that he was able to renew his faith and give himself in total dedication to his Master's work: 'Lord, you know that I love you.' But it was only after his faith had been confirmed at Pentecost that he was able to proclaim the good news of salvation and, later still, give his life for Christ, as he did in Rome.

This brings us back to the question about trust in God. If we are united to God by desire, prayer and intention, if we really believe in God, then we can have full confidence in him, like the little child resting in its mother's arms of the psalmist. Perhaps we should remember that Jesus told us to be like little children.

There remains the question whether we can have too much trust in God. Perhaps we need to realise, or refresh our realisation, that like Elijah and like Peter we all have a mission, which we usually call a vocation. We all have a vocation whether we are married or single, and whatever our work may be. In carrying out our vocation, God will always be with us even in times of distress, suffering or even failure. But if we had a tendency to leave it all to God, if we said to ourselves 'What will be will be', which is a sort of fatalism, then it must be said that the confidence we have in God is a false confidence. St Paul tells us that we must be co-workers of God. He seeks our collaboration in every department of human living. When, as we read in the book of Genesis, God made human beings, he set them in the world to cultivate it and to care for it. The same is true of our bodies; we must look after our health and if we become ill we must take advantage of all that medical care has to offer us. Even in our spiritual life we are co-workers with Christ: 'Work out your salvation,' said St Paul, 'with fear and trembling.' We are co-workers with God in our personal prayer, in our worship and by living our daily life as God wants us to. Then indeed we can be sure that God is with us, that his grace is always supporting us, as it will be to the end of our lives when, with Christ and through him, we surrender ourselves and our whole life to the Father.

Twentieth Sunday of the Year

Is 56:1, 6-7; Ps 66 (in part); Rom 11:13-15, 29-32; Mt 15:21-28.

The scriptures today face us fairly and squarely with a question: Can those who seem not to believe in God and Jesus Christ be saved? Is there such a thing as a faith of desire ('I would like to believe'), a faith however feeble, obscure or even distorted it may be? Is there some unexpressed and perhaps inexpressible feeling for God in the thousands of people in this country alone who seem not to believe in God? We can hardly know but I think it worthwhile to reflect on the problem in the light of the scriptures set before us today.

The Second Isaiah was certainly thinking about it. His mind goes out to the future, an unknown future. He speaks of foreigners who do not know the one true God and yet is convinced that somehow or other they will 'attach themselves to the Lord' and that they will be able to enter the covenant, and worship and pray in the Temple which will then be a 'house of prayer for all the peoples' and not just for the Jews. That entering the New Covenant, as we know, only came about with the coming of Jesus who quotes these very words (Mk 11:17).

For St Paul this situation had arrived. The Gentiles, the non-Jews, had flooded into the new Temple of God, the church, and yet he was movingly concerned for the Jews, his own flesh and blood, who continued to remain outside. Through three chapters of this Letter to the Romans he wrestles in anguish with the problem of the apparent non-salvation of his own people. So many had rejected Christ (who was also one of them, 'according to the flesh', Rom 9:5) and, as the first century drew on, the hostility of the Jews increased and unhappily the Christians repaid it with interested.

But loving Jesus Christ as St Paul did, and seeing in him the depths of wisdom and knowledge, he remains optimistic. The Jews had been given the promises, they had been made the people of God by the covenant, they were God's chosen people and 'God never takes back his gifts or revokes his choice.' Eventually, Paul does not know when, 'those who are disobedient (to Christ) will also enjoy mercy' one day.

When we come to the gospel we have a little difficulty. We naturally think of Jesus as the one who came to save the whole human race, as indeed he did. Yet here we read, 'I was sent only to the lost sheep of the house of Israel.' It may be that Matthew had either remembered the phrase uttered on another occasion or that writing, as he was, to a Jewish-convert community he wanted to remind them that they had been the first to be called and the first to be saved. This is suggested in Mark's account of this same incident where we find Jesus saying to the gentile woman, 'the children (that is, the children of Israel) should be fed first'. And this is what St Paul did. In his preaching missions he first went to the Jews in their synagogues and, when they rejected him and his message about Christ, he went to the Gentiles and converted large numbers of them in Asia Minor, in Greece and finally in Rome.

But there remains the question of the gentile woman. Did she have a kind of obscure faith of which I spoke at the beginning? In any case, how did she know about Jesus? How was it that she came to appeal to him for her daughter? True, she was living on the borders of the Holy Land and rumours of Jesus' healing powers may have reached her and the very appearance of Jesus, the attractiveness of his personality, may have drawn her to him, as he had drawn other people. However that may be, she had, immediately it seems, a confidence, (faith?) in him. Jesus at any rate in the end commends her for her faith: 'Woman, you have great faith. Let your wishes be granted.' Faith had been beginning but, through her initial obscure and perhaps distorted understanding of Jesus – she may have thought that he was some sort of benevolent magician – she came to the faith that ultimately would be a saving faith.

That then, as I see it, is the answer to the questions I posed at the beginning. We live in an apparently Godless world and the religious and moral condition of the society in which we live is bad, but all the time there crop up little incidents that seem to show that some people, few or many it is impossible to say, who admit to praying at least in times of stress, illness or calamity. From time to time there are those little shy requests from apparent unbelievers for prayer for themselves or for a sick child. What do such people believe? We don't know, but we do know that God's love and mercy are boundless. God has chosen everyone in Christ and he 'never takes back his gift or revokes his choice'. As a writer put it years ago, 'God's grace is everywhere.'[1]

1. Georges Bernanos, *The Diary of a Country Priest*.

Twenty-first Sunday of the Year

Is 22:19-23; Ps 137 (in part); Rom 11:33-36; Mt 16:13-20.

'I will build my church ...' I wonder how most of us think of the church. Do we think of it as a vast organisation spread throughout the world with a 'management' of pope, bishops and priests and with the people as shareholders? The world at any rate often seems to think of it in that way. But as the Second Vatican Council proclaimed, it is rather different and it is much more than that. Fundamentally it is the whole people of God on pilgrimage towards eternity. But in the light of today's scripture message, let us take up another image or model of the church. Taking up a long traditional theology, the Council also emphasised that the church is the body of Christ. As we read in the Letter to the Ephesians, 'There is one body and one Spirit ... there is one Lord, one faith, one baptism and one God who is Father of us all.' Of that body we, by baptism, confirmation and the eucharist, are members, living limbs of the body, who live by the life of the Head, Christ, which is infused into us by the Holy Spirit. That life within us is invisible and the essential, the all-important life of the church is invisible. Normally no one can see the working of the Holy Spirit within us and usually it is hidden in the life of the church.

But, as the Council also said, the church is like a sacrament, it is both invisible and visible. The invisible grace of God comes to us through the visible celebration of the rite which we call baptism. It is the same with the church. Its inner life demands an outward, visible expression if we are to grasp it and understand what it is. That outward aspect is an expression of its inner life. It is what we call the visible church which can be identified as existing in the world.

What then of its unity? There is one Lord, there is the one body, the one faith and, we can add, there is the one love coming from Christ that binds us all together. The church is one, it is a union, indeed a com-union of all with Christ and he is Lord of it. He is the Head of the church now invisible in heaven. But as the whole church needs visible expression, so does the Headship of Christ. He has an earthly representative, the Pope, the Vicar of Christ: 'You are Peter (the rock man) and on you I will build my church and I will give you the keys of the kingdom of heaven.' The keys, as we learn from Isaiah, are the sign of authority. He is given the power to bind and loose which is another example of authority. He can rule, but only in the name of Christ.

But the nature of the authority which is strongly affirmed in the epilogue to St John's gospel is made clear. In chapter ten of that gospel we hear Jesus saying that he himself is the shepherd of the flock, and after the resurrection we find him saying to Peter, 'Feed my lambs, feed my sheep', the whole flock. Peter is the deputy shepherd of Christ and this office is to be continued in the church for the gates of the underworld, the powers of evil, will never overcome it. The church will continue to the end of time and so will the papacy.

In the light, then, of the model of the church as the body of Christ, as union in Christ, we can see that the pope is a symbol of unity in the church. To be united with him is to be a recognisable member of the church and many accept him as the earthly head of the church as we do.

Then there is the question of the one faith. This in turn raises the question of infallibility of the pope, namely that he is preserved from error when, as shepherd and teacher of the whole church, he defines a doctrine to be held by all the members of the church. It is his role to maintain the unity of faith which is an essential mark of the church, without which the church would fall apart.

If, then, we can see that the church is the one body, invisible and visible, of Christ, with the one faith handed down by the apostles, we can also see that the office of the pope is a necessity if the unity of the church and its faith is to be maintained. The history of centuries has proved this to be so.

This then is our faith, the faith we all accept and we can thank God for it. It gives security in believing and, while we should always be trying to understand our faith more deeply, it is on the basis of that faith that we can go on living the Christian life, as we should. Faith without works, said St James, is dead, and if we express in our daily living the faith that is in our hearts then, we, the church, will be like a city set on a hill and a light that shines attracting all who will come to it.

Twenty-second Sunday of the Year

Jer 20:7-9; Ps 62 (in part); Rom 12:1-2; Mt 16:21-17.

Jeremiah, in the liturgy and according to a long tradition in the church, is often taken as a figure or type of Jesus. Like Jesus, Jeremiah proclaims the word of God, like Jesus he suffers for it and he feels it very deeply: 'I am a laughing stock, everybody's butt', violence is pressing upon him and, in a sentence unfortunately not included in today's reading, he exclaims, 'The Lord is at my side', thus like the psalmist he expresses his confidence in God.

This reading from the Old Testament suggests that we consider the first part of the gospel where Jesus foretells his death and resurrection. This saying, about what is to happen to him, he is recorded as pronouncing three times in the course of his public ministry, and we are also told that the disciples did not understand the meaning of these words, particularly those referring to resurrection. There can be little doubt that Jesus had forebodings of what awaited him, and no doubt he expressed them in rather vaguer terms than we read in the gospel accounts. But Peter understood enough to protest, he could not bear the thought that his beloved Master should have to undergo grievous suffering and be put to death. The rebuke he receives from Jesus is very severe; he is regarded as a Satan, a tempter, or even worse, an enemy standing in the way of Christ's appointed mission. For that is why the rebuke is so severe. Jesus had been sent into the world to do the will of his Father, in a word, to save the world. As we learn from John 18:19, Jesus was dedicated, in the strictest sense of that word, to the task, laid upon him by his Father, of reconciling the human race to his Father so that all could be transferred into the kingdom of marvellous light and joy. Anyone who would divert him from that course must be rejected, as for the moment Peter was. It is ironical that in this same chapter where Peter is told that he has a revelation from God when he confessed that Jesus was the Messiah and the Son of God, is now told, and has to be told, that the way he was thinking was not God's way; it was mere human thinking.

Then, as if to emphasise that not only *he* must suffer but all who would be his followers, he tells his disciples that they must deny themselves and even take up the cross – a cross on which Jesus would die, a cross which he would sanctify by his death. It was a fearful symbol but, even worse, a reality with which the disciples were perfectly familiar. It was the brutal punishment that Roman authority meted out to law-breakers and robbers; the crosses, and the execution, were open to the public gaze of everyone. It is difficult to believe that, by the time the gospels were written down, the cross had become a mere metaphor. As the words that follow show, the cross meant a total giving of self: 'Anyone who wants to save his life will lose it; but anyone who loses his life for my sake will find it', and what he will find will be worth more than everything in this world or anything that can be imagined in this world.

With the law of love, of which this saying is an expression, this is the supreme demand of the gospel and it is no wonder that it is repeated again and again in all four gospels. It is a demand to which all of us have to respond. There are two ways of doing this. As the gospel text enjoins, the follower of Christ must 're-nounce' or deny himself. Sometimes this is seen as simply nega-tive: giving up something, or doing without something. That is not without value, because we are all inclined to hang on to things or habits and we need to detach ourselves from them, at least from time to time, to show our sincerity – not to mention the therapeutic benefit of doing so! But more profoundly we 'give up' so that we may offer ourselves and our lives more gen-uinely to and for Jesus Christ who gave himself totally for us.

The second aspect of self-denial is offering, daily offering and the offering of our whole life. This is what St Paul is urging us to do today: 'Think of God's mercy ... in a way that is worthy of thinking beings, by offering your living bodies as a holy sacri-fice, truly pleasing to God.' 'Living bodies', for St Paul as for the whole of the Old Testament, meant the whole self, body, mind and spirit, and it is this, as we live our daily lives, that we are urged to offer to God through our Lord Jesus Christ who offered himself for the salvation of the human race.

No doubt this self-offering in and through Christ is a life-long task, but it is there before us every day and if we offer ourselves daily we shall be responding to the words of Jesus in the gospel, we shall be doing the will of God, we shall be doing what he wants, and, surprisingly, what is perfect.

Twenty-third Sunday of the Year

Ez 33:7-9; Ps 94 (in part); Rom 13:8-10; Mt 18:15-20.

As you will have learned for the newspapers and the other media, Pope John Paul has issued an encyclical called *Veritatis*

Splendor, The Splendour of Truth, on the principles of moral behaviour. It is about what is right and what is wrong, what is sinful and what is not. At first sight it might seem to be unnecessary, but we live in an immoral world, a world in which people have got very fuzzy about what is right and what is wrong, about what is sinful and what is not.

Are adultery and pre- and extra-marital sex sins? Is murder or unlawful killing a sin? Are stealing and coveting other people's goods (burglary) sins? Today St Paul, repeating the teaching of Christ and echoing the teaching of the whole Bible, says that they are.

There are other matters that are equally or more sinful. There is the savage fighting, the genocide and the 'ethnic cleansing' in the former Yugoslavia that has been going on for so long. But, say some, this is war and in war bad things happen, in this case sins crying to heaven for vengeance or punishment. But those evil deeds have been committed by human beings and they are responsible for their actions. They have sinned and that is what Ezekiel is telling us today: 'If a wicked man does not repent, then he shall die for his sin.'

But there is another message to be found in Ezekiel and also in the gospel. We too, according to our condition, are at least partly responsible for what others do. The prophet says that we are to warn another when he has taken to evil ways and the gospel is even more explicit: 'If your brother does something wrong, go and have it out with him alone.' The difficulty is who is to do the correcting? It is not unknown that in the past certain busybodies, oh yes, with the best of intentions, have gone about trying to correct their brother or sister in Christ. No, it is a very delicate matter and there is the danger of hypocrisy. It is easy enough to see the splinter in the eye of another and not to see the plank in our own, as Jesus said.

Then who *is* to do the correcting? It seems to me that parents have a special responsible to their own children, though I also know that the task is not easy for them. But if they see one or other of their teenage children going astray, they have the right and the duty to warn them, and according to circumstances, to tell them that what they are doing is wrong and sinful. If they can do this calmly and with affection it is likely that their warning will be successful.

It may be too that teachers, or any in charge of the young, have a similar duty and, if they know how to go about it, they can save them from actions that may ruin their lives. No doubt great tact is necessary but if we look back on our early days we may well remember the warning and the guiding word that saved us when we were young.

And what of the role of the clergy? We have been thought of for so long as moral policemen that when we warn or attempt to rebuke we are rejected. It's our job, they say, we are paid for it. Professional moralists are not liked in our society. What the priest can do is what I am doing now. He can and must point out the challenges of the gospel; he must convey to the best of his ability the moral teaching of the church; and finally, as occasion offers, he will lead those going astray or those who have gone astray back into the right way with all the gentleness and tact of which he is capable.

What I have ventured to say to you seems to me to be a modern way of putting what the gospel has to say to us today. Private correction may fail but the whole community has a responsibility. The priest represents the parish community but he is not the whole community. Others share with him that responsibility. Again, let me say, that there is difficulty here but I think there are two further things to be said.

We ourselves, who are trying to live the Christian life, must be clear about what is right and what is wrong, what is tolerable and what is not. We have a duty to resist the moral permissiveness of our own time and our own society and, if we show our disapproval of prevailing views on moral matters and try and live by what we know to be right, we shall have some chance of influencing the young. As an experienced headmistress said to me years ago, the young like to use older people, including their parents, as a grindstone. They like to disagree, they like to strike sparks if they can, but what they do not look for is parents or others who are willing to let them go their own ways, especially when they are the wrong ways.

The second consideration is this. The last part of the gospel is about prayer, the prayer of the Christian community: 'Where two or three are gathered together in my name I shall be there with them.' As we come together week by week to pray in the name of Jesus Christ, united with him, we support each other, we pray for all our brothers and sister who are not here, we pray for those who are alienated from God and the church by sin or for whatever reason. May these prayers help us to go out to those who are not with us, to help them in anyway we can and thus show that we do feel a responsibility for their well-being in the face of God who desires, not the death of the wicked, but that they should turn back to him and live.

Twenty-fourth Sunday of the Year

Ecclus 27:30, 28:7; Ps 102 (in part); Rom 14:7-9; Mt 18:21-35.

The first reading today and the gospel are about two things: mercy and forgiveness. The reason is that forgiveness is the fruit of mercy. And mercy is a very precious quality of the soul:

The quality of mercy is not strained
It droppeth as the gentle rain from heaven
upon the place beneath; it is twice blessed.
It blesseth him that gives and him that takes ...
It is an attribute of God himself.

You will recognise the words; they are Shakespeare's from *The Merchant of Venice*. They are addressed to the merchant Shylock who wanted his pound of flesh for which he had bargained and which had been agreed. Portia, who is speaking, is saying that there is something higher and better than justice. It is mercy. And she wins!

So also in the parable. The king is owed 10,000 talents, an enormous sum which in strict justice ought to have been repaid but that was an impossibility. The king's heart is moved to pity for the unhappy man and he cancels the debt. I do not know whether the king in the parable is supposed to stand for God, but for the moment we can suppose he does. Then we can see, as Shake-speare said, mercy is a Godlike quality, an 'attribute of God him-self'. When we are showing mercy we are being godlike – or to use the old-fashioned word, we are being 'godly'.

The Wise Man in the first reading and the psalm throws further light on the matter. 'Remember the covenant of the Most High and overlook the offence' as he 'overlooks' and takes away the offence. For 'The Lord is compassion and love, slow to anger and rich in mercy; as far as the east is from the west so far does he remove our sins.' Man, sin, covenant and, above all, the mer-ciful God. As we read in the Letter to the Ephesians, 'God who is rich in mercy, out of the great love with which he loves us, even when we were dead through our sins, made us alive together with Christ ... and raised us up with him' (2:4-6).

Throughout the ages God was extending his mercy to the people of old; through his prophets he was calling them to repentance and, when that seemed ineffective, he sent his own Son who, out of his infinite love and mercy for us, forgave and forgives our sins. He bound himself by a New Covenant at the Last Supper: 'This is my blood of the covenant which is poured out for many' and 'for the taking away of sins'. That covenant is renewed among us today in this eucharist so that we may continue to be forgiven, so that we may have the grace and the strength to for-give others up to seventy times seven, that is without limit. It is by the grace of God that we can have mercy and forgive and it is by showing mercy and forgiving that we become godlike.

Even so, we know it not always easy to forgive, not always easy to have mercy in our hearts. Do we not hear after some crime or offence, 'I can never forgive or forget.' Understandable as that saying and attitude may be in certain circumstances, it is pro-foundly unchristian. Or we hear another version of it, 'I can for-give but I shall never forget.' It occurs to me that many who have suffered in Northern Ireland, people whose father, brother or son have been brutally murdered and who have said that they want no reprisals, that they have no bitterness in their hearts, are showing a profoundly Christian spirit. They are peo-ple who try both to forgive and to forget.

Let us also be people who forgive and forget whatever others have done to us or against us. Let us realise that forgetting is part of the forgiving. Forgetting means letting go of the past and, as we let go, the pain of the past offence gradually fades away.

Every Sunday at Mass we pray, 'Forgive us our trespasses (sins) as we forgive those who trespass (sin) against us.' We are preparing for holy communion which makes us one with Christ and also with all our brothers and sisters around us – or not around us. We are praying to be reconciled with those who have offended us so that we and they may be made one in Christ. In this prayer, without recalling persons, times and places (forgetting), we are forgiving all who at any time may have offended us. We are letting go; we are letting ourselves go into God who, through his infinite love shown forth in his Son Jesus Christ, is filling our hearts with mercy so that hatred can be banished, so that love can replace harshness, and so that we, like him, can be filled with love and mercy for all without exception.

Twenty-fifth Sunday of the Year

Is 55:6-9; Ps 144 (in part); Phil 1:20-24, 27; Mt 20 1-16.

Two things I think have to be said about this gospel. It is not about the unemployment problem. It is not about social justice or the living wage. It is about generosity, it is about God's generosity, it is about giving and ultimately about that free and utterly undeserved gift we call grace.

If we accept that view then we can see that it is about God's call to us, and blessed are those who listen to him and 'call to him', realising that 'he is close to all who call on him, who call on him from their hearts'.

We note, however, that the landowner in the parable calls workers into his vineyard at daybreak, at the third hour, at the sixth and ninth hours and finally at the eleventh hour. If we take the parable as a kind of story or allegory, then we must come to the conclusion that it is a most peculiar way of going about things.

This leads us towards a true understanding of the parable. It is not about unemployment, it is not about wages, it is about God's dealing with the human race throughout the ages.

Jesus was speaking to his disciples who knew their Bible very well and, as he spoke to them, they remembered the call to Abraham who was called by God three times and each time he answered the call, believing, trusting in God. That same call came to Isaac, to Jacob, to Joseph, to Moses who led the people out of the captivity of Egypt into the freedom of the desert. And it is here we can begin to understand the meaning of the divine call.

It was there in the desert that God made a covenant with the people, a union that later in the Old Testament is called a love-pact, a marriage between God and the people. God gave them a way of life called the Torah, literally the law, which includes the Ten Commandments but a great deal more too. Through Moses the people were called upon to promise that they would keep the law, and God promised to bind himself to them and so they would be his people and he would be their God. This was all sealed by sacrifice when Moses sprinkled the people with the blood of the sacrificed animal saying, 'This is the blood of the covenant which the Lord has made with you.'

All seemed set fair for the future, but unhappily it was not so. As we know, in spite of repeated calls through the prophets over the centuries, in spite of the various and painful turns of fortune of the Jewish people, they failed to make an adequate response to God. So it was in the fullness of time that God sent his Son, born of a woman, Mary of Nazareth, born a subject of the old law, that he might redeem those who were under the old law. And he came and taught and called people to himself, among them the twelve disciples and all the others, men and women, of whom we read in the gospel. He called them, they responded, they followed, and they like ourselves were those who were called at the eleventh hour to experience the generosity of God. And our calling was completed by the New Covenant. At the Last Supper, on the night before he died to show us and the whole of the human race that he loved us to the uttermost, saying the prayer of blessing over some bread, Jesus said, 'Take and eat; this is my body.' And over the wine he said the prayer of thanksgiving and offered it to the twelve: 'This is my blood of the covenant. Take and drink.' This was (and is) the sacrament of the New Covenant with the new People of God, brought into existence by the shedding of Jesus' blood and the complete offering of himself to his Father. As we read in St John, greater love, (greater generosity) no one could have than that he should give his life for others. That is the generosity of today's gospel, disguised under the form of a penny.

But let us not forget that we are among the last to be called, those called at the eleventh hour, and that we have an obligation to respond to God's call by our daily living, by our lived faith, by the love which we should return for the love that Jesus has shown us. We are in a sense privileged and not privileged. Privileged in that through no merit of our own we have been called into God's church out of the infinite goodness of God, and not privileged because, if like the people of old we fail to respond to God, fail to live for him, fail to take our place in co-working with him to bring about his kingdom, his reign, then we shall have forfeited whatever may seem to have been a privileged position. The last became first but the first can also become the last.

Twenty-sixth Sunday of the Year

Ez 18:25-28; Ps 24 (in part); Phil 2:1-11; Mt 21:28-32.

At first sight, this gospel is disconcerting. It looks as if it is no more than a parable about two naughty boys, one who says that he will do what his father wants him to do and doesn't, and the other who says, 'I won't' and then goes and does what his father has asked him to do. Then towards the end of the gospel passage there is the daunting saying about prostitutes and other wrong doers making their way into the kingdom of heaven. How are we to reconcile the two sets of sayings?

We note that Jesus is addressing the chief priests and the elders of the people, as we read a little later on (verse 45), 'the chief priests and scribes realised he was speaking about them'. The parable then is about the people of Israel to whom God has addressed his word through the prophets, and of whom he had demanded obedience when he made the covenant with them in the desert after their escape from Egypt. It was then that God gave them the law. Had they not obeyed it? The scribes and Pharisees certainly thought not only that they had kept the law but that they had kept it more perfectly than anyone else.

What then was wanting? The scriptures of today are indeed about obedience, but about an obedience that goes much farther than the observance of the law merely by external actions. But the scriptures are also about repentance as is shown by the little parable. The second son 'thought better of' his refusal, and went and did his father's will. He changed his mind, he turned his mind and his will towards what he should do. And that is repentance.

It is to this that Ezekiel is referring in the first reading. Here too are two kinds of men. There is the upright man who lives a good life or seems to do so and then, in circumstances not explained, he turns away from God, disobeying him and perhaps finally rejecting him. Then there is the other kind. He repents, he turns away from sin and turns back to God. As the text says, 'He will certainly live, he shall not die', he will not die the eternal death of separation from God.

This provides the link with the second part of the gospel. Jesus is continuing his parable, though in a rather different way. Those who have listened to his word, those who have 'obeyed' by accepting it in their hearts and have repented, will go into the kingdom of heaven before those who have not listened, those who have not received the word and repented will not go into the kingdom.

So, like the first boy, we all have to listen to God and his word, we have to take it into our hearts and make it our own, we have to be obedient. We have to be obedient, as St Paul says, when he speaks of the obedience of faith when, as we should, we submit our minds to what God has revealed, the faith that is communicated to us by the church. This is not a tyranny because, as the scriptures themselves tell us, we are to 'search the scriptures', become familiar with them and find there answers to some of our questionings. The scriptures also tell us to have a 'reasonable faith' which means reflecting on what is revealed by God through his church and discovering reasons for believing. This is all part of the 'obedience of faith', all part of the normal Christian life which is very important in the age in which we live when the Christian faith is being rejected.

But as we all know, obedience is not easy. It means the submission of mind and will and that can be painful. But St Paul today shows us where the source of obedience is. Jesus, the Son of God, lowered himself to our human condition, he took on even the form of a slave and, always in obedience to his Father, he submitted to death on the cross, dying like a slave and a common criminal. Like those disreputable people mentioned in the gospel, and one with them, he died completely despised and rejected by all.

But the secret of that obedience is not yet revealed. Jesus came to do the will of his Father with an immense, an immeasurable love: 'God loved us with so much love that he was generous in his mercy: when we were dead through our sins, he bought us to life with Christ' (Eph 2:4, 5). It was with this love in his heart that he took on our human nature, that he suffered and that he offered himself for us and for our salvation, for the whole human race.

That is the power of obedience, an obedience transfused and sustained by love. That loving obedience is the source of our ability also to obey even when it is very difficult. And that love is communicated to us as we celebrate the eucharist today. We have turned to God, we have repented of our sins, we have listened to the word of God and now, in union with his Son, we are about to offer ourselves and our lives to God and to receive the body and blood of his Son Jesus Christ and, with him, the strength to love and serve him in our daily lives.

Twenty-seventh Sunday of the Year

Is 5:1-7; Ps 79 (in part); Phil 4:6-9; Mt 21:33-43.

Sometimes parables have two levels of meaning, the first to those to whom it was originally addressed, and the second as it has come to be understood and used in and by the church. As it stands in the gospel, it is a very terrible story. It seems to be speaking of the rejection of a whole people, the people of the Old Testament.

Yet they were the beloved people, chosen by God to be the means by which his word of salvation was to be made known to the world. It was for this purpose that he had liberated them from the slavery of Egypt and through the centuries had shaped and formed them, like a man making a vineyard. He had dug the soil, put a fence around it to keep out marauders, animal and human, and had planted choice vines in it. That is how Isaiah saw the matter and it is this that Matthew takes up in his gospel. But he adds something to it. Pondering on the long history of Israel, he remembers how God had sent one prophet after another to the people to convey God's message and his warnings to them. He had held them together as a people in spite of invasion and exile, he loved them, he lavished his gifts on them, and yet finally they had rejected him. In the words of Isaiah, 'What could I have done for my vineyard that I did not do? Why did it yield sour grapes instead?' Matthew, working in the Christian context for converts from Judaism, adds that after the prophets God had sent his own Son and the workers in the vineyard seized him and put him to death.

The reference is of course to the Jews and it seems a terrible con-demnation of them. Here is a matter of great delicacy which we must approach with great caution. Perhaps we need to be re-minded that the Second Vatican Council felt the imperative need to issue a document in which it condemned all forms of anti-Semitism and rejected the age-old accusation that the Jewish people were responsible for the death of Jesus. Some, not all, had a hand in bringing Jesus to his death, but not the Jewish peo-ple as a whole, and in any case the Jewish people since and for the last 2,000 years cannot be blamed for what happened then.

That is not all. If we are to understand this matter, we need to turn to St Paul's Letter to the Romans (9-11) where, with great force, he tells his readers, and so us, that the Jewish people were the chosen of God, endowed with the promises of salvation and God does not go back on his promises. Using a simile that is different from that of the gospel, he speaks of the Jews (who were his own people) as an olive tree. The original olive tree had been given all the gifts of God, it remains the object of his love and, as for us, we are like a wild branch which has been grafted on to the original tree.

One consequence of this is that we must not give ourselves airs, and another is that whatever rebukes and condemnations were addressed to them are addressed to us. Paul ends his statement on a note of optimism. One day, he does not know when, and somehow, but he does not know how, the people of Israel will be saved.

If we turn to the gospel according to John, we find there also a parable of the vine and the vine-stock on to which we were grafted by faith and baptism, for the vine-stock is Christ. There we hear that if we listen to his words and remain united to him we shall yield much fruit. But if we separate ourselves from the vine-stock we shall become useless branches and will be cut off and cast into a fire. So if we should reject Christ – and God forbid that we should – he can reject us.

That, it seems to me, is the second level of meaning of the parable and it is a message to us today, however uncomfortable it may be.

The vineyard is an image of the church, Christ is present is his church and he is present both in his word which is proclaimed and in his sacraments, especially the eucharist, which we celebrate. If, then, we give our minds and hearts to his word, and if we welcome him into our hearts and lives at holy communion, then far from being rejected by Jesus, he will be in us and we shall be in him, as he promised.

Twenty-eighth Sunday of the Year

Is 25:6-10; Ps 22; Phil 4:12-14, 19-20; Mt 22:1-14.

A banquet! We don't hear much about banquets nowadays.
There is the Lord Mayor of London's banquet in November to
which of course the likes of you and me are not invited, and anyway I suppose it must be pretty boring. We are more familiar
with wedding feasts which, as the years go by, seem to last
longer and longer. In the east they lasted a week and all and
sundry came, say a whole village. Wedding feasts are times of
rejoicing and hope, and it is this sort of image of the banquet we
find in the readings from Isaiah and the gospel.

It is in fact one of the great images of the Bible in both the Old
and the New Testaments and we may well ask what it is that it is
supposed to tell us and about what.

For Isaiah, who is writing a hymn of thanksgiving for what God
had done for the people of Israel in the past, the banquet, with its
rich food and fine wines and its rejoicing, was the image of a
time in the distant future when Israel will have been restored
and all peoples will be invited to sit down at the banquet: 'The
Lord will wipe away the tears from every cheek, he will take
away the people's shame everywhere on earth, for the Lord has
said so.' On that day it will be said, 'See, this is our God in whom
we hoped for salvation.'

He did not know when that would be, but the banquet of the
gospel is the fulfilment of what the prophet had written about.
The kingdom of heaven is coming with its banquet. It is the
kingdom or the reign of God that Jesus is bringing into existence
by his teaching, his life, his passion and resurrection. As we hear
today and in many other places, he called everyone to the feast.
He himself sat down to eat with sinners and the outcasts of society. In the parable all the 'bad and good alike' are invited. All are
called; the messengers are told: 'Go out to the cross roads and invite everyone you can find to the wedding'.

So the wedding feast becomes an image of the church which
continues the work of Christ. We remember that right at the end
of this gospel the Risen Christ tells his disciples to go and teach

all nations and to baptise them in the name of the Father, the Son and the Holy Spirit. This was the beginning of the new age foretold by Isaiah; this is the kingdom that Jesus brought into existence by his passion, death and resurrection; this is the time of the Messiah-Christ which will go on to the end of time.

And at the heart of the life of the kingdom is the banquet, the banquet that Jesus instituted before his death when, at the time of the Jewish feast of the Passover, he had a meal with his disciples and in the course of prayers of blessing and thanksgiving he gave himself to them in the form of bread and wine. It was the anticipation of his sacrificial death the next day and it was to be the memorial of his saving passion and death whereby we could share in the banquet and receive into ourselves the fruits of his redeeming death and resurrection.

Much of this is expressed in an antiphon for the Feast of Corpus Christi which we used to know very well: 'O sacred banquet in which Christ is received, his sufferings are recalled, our minds are filled with grace and the pledge of future glory is given to us.' We receive now, but the prayer looks on to the future as indeed does the church. With the scriptures we look on to the time of completion and glory when the church, the Bride of Christ, will be with the Bridegroom. As we read in the last book of the Bible: 'His Bride is ready; she is dressed in dazzling white linen and she hears the words, "Happy are those who are invited to the feast of the Lamb".'

As, then, we celebrate the eucharist, let us realise that through it we are beginning to enter into that joy which in heaven will be without end. We shall be with Christ and he will be with us as at a wedding feast. As we devoutly receive him in holy communion let the words of the same book, the Apocalypse, be in our minds: 'Look, I am standing at the door, knocking. If anyone of you hears me calling and opens the door, I will come to share his meal, side by side with him.'

Jesus is calling us all the time and, if we respond with love, then the future joy and glory will be ours.

(The last part of the gospel today may be omitted and it is better that it should be. It is part of another parable that has become attached, perhaps by accident.)

Twenty-ninth Sunday of the Year

Is 45:1, 4-6; Ps 95 (in part); Thess 1:1-3; Mat 22:15-21.

The appearance of the name 'Cyrus' at the beginning of the first reading may surprise you. It does not sound a very Jewish name, nor is it. It is the name of a pagan king of Persia which we now called Iran. It is even more surprising when we note that he is the 'anointed' of God. Why then is this passage chosen for today?

It would not be too much to say that almost the whole of the Old Testament puts before us God's plan for his people, Israel. He is with them in all the events of their history, even the painful ones, like captivity and exile. The Israelites were in exile and the prophet is saying that they will be set free through the agency of a pagan king, and from the Books of Nehemiah and Ezra we know that this was Cyrus and that he did in fact release the Israelites, that he facilitated their return to the Holy Land, and supported them as painfully they rebuilt their land and the Temple.

Cyrus then is portrayed as the servant of God, the servant of God's purposes for his people, and since he collaborates with God he is called his anointed: the Lord says to Cyrus, 'It is for the sake of my servant Jacob (the Israelites), my chosen one, that I have called you by your name, and conferred a title though you do not know me.'

This passage from Isaiah has an obvious reference to the gospel: 'Give back to Caesar what belongs to Caesar – and to God what belongs to God.' The way these words have been understood and lived through the centuries is a very long history. Up to the early years of the fourth century, the Roman Emperors, literally Caesars, persecuted the church from time to time, demanding that Christians should make a gesture of worship to the image of the Caesar. Refusal to do so led to death. As the martyrs said, following St Peter, 'we must obey God rather than man.' In the time that followed, the Emperor Constantine (born in Britain) gave the church its freedom and he himself died a Christian. But emperors became more and more demanding and wanted to rule the church as well as the Empire. Tension between monarch and church became very acute in the Middle Ages. Popes, struggling for the freedom of the church from the secular power, frequently quoted the words of the gospel: 'Render to Caesar what is Caesar's and to God what is God's': The authority and powers of government are limited by what the church is and by what it must be allowed to do, if it is not to become the lackey of the state.

This too we have experienced very painfully in our own time. There was the rise of atheistic communism in Russia after 1917 when for some seventy years every effort was made to obliterate every form of religion. There were many martyrs among the people of the Russian Orthodox Church. In the 1930s the Fascists took power in Italy and from 1929 until he died Pope Pius XI carried on a determined opposition to the dictator Mussolini and against his attempts to limit the freedom of the church. In the 1930s there rose up Hitler who did everything in his power to suppress the liberty of the churches, both Protestant and Catholic. But his greatest crime was the annihilation of at least six million Jews, just because they were Jews, and some Christians as well.

Things are easier now. Parliamentary democracy has become, in wide areas of the world, the normal way of conducting the affairs of state and this gives a certain freedom to citizens. They elect members of parliament (as they are called in this country) or deputies, as they are usually called in other countries. They can be got rid of at elections if people think fit and this is one of the safeguards the people still have. Relations between church and state have become easier also, though there are still black spots in the world. What then is our duty as citizens and Christians?

There is a positive and a negative side to this. Positively all of us, as far as circumstances allow, must play our part in the affairs of our country whether at local or at national level. It is a great pity that too few Catholics nowadays are found in public life in Britain. If there were more they, and we through them, could exercise a greater influence on public affairs, especially where they

concern moral matters. In acting in this way we should be giving
to Caesar what belongs to him.

But there is the negative side. We live in an increasingly pagan
society, the standards of moral conduct are no longer Christian
and legislators are all too prone to go along with the tide of what
they conceive to be public opinion. Thus the divorce laws have
been loosened to such a degree that it is said at least a third of all
marriages end in divorce. There are also the, what shall I call
them?, 'arrangements' about abortion and other horrific activities concerning insemination. There are also other matters that
go beyond personal morality, the fall in standards of honesty in
business, the seemingly insoluble problem of unemployment of
vast numbers of people, especially men. These are all moral matters and Christians must be concerned with them. In so far as
government or other public authorities are involved, they are at
least in danger of usurping the things that belong to God.
Politics are a moral matter, whatever the politicians may say. It
is then up to Christian citizens not only to exercise their rights
but to make a positive contribution to social life and thus play
their part in rendering to God what belongs to him.

Thirtieth Sunday of the Year

Ex 22:20-26; Ps 17 (in part); 1 Thess 1:5-10; Mt 22:34-40.

Year by year we hear this commandment of the Lord and we
may feel a little guilty, if only because our practice has fallen
short of what we know we should have done. As we have listened to the word of the Book of Exodus we may realise that we
have not lived up to the commandments of the Old Testament,
quite apart from the great law of Christ in the gospel. 'You must
not molest a stranger or oppress him.' We may not have done
that, but there are many strangers in this country, black or
coloured, who have not only been molested but murdered. 'You
must not be too harsh to the widow or the orphan'; yet one-par-
ent families often have a hard time trying to make ends meet.
'Do not take another's cloak as a pledge; but if you do you must
give it back before sunset because he has nothing else to cover

himself at night.' This reminds me of those rapacious men and institutions who by guile and dishonest practises deprive defenceless citizens of their just due. We like to think that the people of the Old Testament were not strong on love of neighbours, but our world does not seem to be living up to the standards set up for the Israelites some three thousand years ago.

'You must love the Lord your God … you must love your neighbour as yourself'. It is a very high ideal and we know that the world judges us Christians rather by the second half of the commandment than the first. For Jesus, the two parts of the commandment are one. As we read in the first Letter of St John, 'You cannot love God unless you love your neighbour.' So let us think about both parts of the commandment.

To love God with heart and soul and mind, that is with all we have and are, is, as we know, very difficult and we may wonder how we can do it. It helps, I think, if we remember that, in Matthew and Mark, these words were uttered close to the passion of our Lord. And in St John's gospel we find Jesus saying, 'Greater love no one has than to lay down his life for his friends', words that, according to that same gospel, were spoken during the Last Supper, the night before Jesus would give his life, his whole self, for the salvation of the world.

There is the source of our strength. From that stupendous event, the giving of the God-man for us, we learn that love is essentially self-giving and not self-getting (if I may use the phrase). 'You must love God …', that means that we must try to give ourselves to God, to offer our lives to God, and always through Jesus Christ. Though difficult, we, if we try, may realise that we are doing this by our daily living, by prayer at home, by our Sunday worship when we praise and thank God as we offer the Mass, and ourselves, through Jesus Christ who empowers us to do so by his presence.

That is the secret power of Christian love. It is a response to the love that God has shown us and shared with us. As St John says, 'This is how we know what love is, that he gave his life for us.'

To put the matter as clearly as possible, the love with which we love God and neighbour is implanted in our hearts. As St Paul puts it, 'The love of God is poured into our hearts by the Holy Spirit who is given to us.' It is because of this that we can love unselfishly; that is why we can, in the words of St John, overcome the sensual body, the lustful eye and pride in possessions.

We must love God first because he has loved us and still does and, as the scripture says, we must love others. There are problems here and may be there is a confusion about the meaning of love. Boy is attracted to girl and girl to boy. There is a strong emotional love between them. It may not last and often does not. Unwittingly there is also a self-seeking in the love, a desire for a certain sort of pleasure. It is natural enough and no doubt understandable, but if that love is to grow into true love they need to be aware that it is not love in the full sense of self-giving. That is something that has to be learnt and it takes time

At the other end of the life-cycle there is another expression of love. Husband and wife have grown old together. They hardly express their love in words. They express it by doing things for each other, by service, and, as we know, the bond between them is very close. That is the love of self-giving, the love that Jesus in the gospels speaks of so frequently, and it is the love that lasts.

Finally, there is the love of all others, of which Jesus also speaks, and to show us who the 'others' are he had to tell us the story of the Samaritan who helped one who in fact was an enemy, and he may have earned a good deal of unpopularity among his own people if his good deeds had become known. According to the gospel, everyone is our neighbour: 'Love your enemies, do good to those who hate you, and pray for those who treat you badly.' Yes, it is very difficult to love some people, very difficult to love some of the monsters of our time, and fortunately the gospel does not tell us to *like* them. But always, we must pray for them, pray that God's grace may penetrate their hearts and make them change their ways.

So then we can and must love God and serve him because he has first loved us, and we love him with the love he implants in our hearts. And we can and must love others because God loves them, whoever they are and whatever they have done. So we pray that through God's love they may turn to him, for God does not will that they should die in their sins but that they should repent and live.

Thirty-first Sunday of the Year

Mal 1:14, 2:2, 8-10; Ps 130; I Thess 2:7-9, 13; Mt 23:1-12.

There are two difficulties about the scripture texts today. The first is this terrific denunciation of the Jewish leaders, the sect of the Pharisees who exercised considerable influence in the time of Christ, and of the scribes who made more and more regulations which they imposed on the people and did not life a finger to help them. Even if the Pharisees and the scribes were in the wrong, we find it difficult to believe that Jesus spoke to them in these terms, and it is the opinion of scholars that these denunciations were a development of certain sayings of our Lord that we find in other gospels and were put together here. It is an accepted view that this passage is mostly the work of the evangelist.

The second difficulty is that if Malachi and the gospel are to be regarded as a message to the church today, we are faced with denunciations of the wrong-doings of the clergy, and that provides a problem for the preacher. Is he, am I, to go on about the short-comings of the clergy? No doubt we have our short-comings, no doubt there are priests who are unfaithful to their calling and to their ministry, and indeed one is conscious of one's own short-comings and wrong-doing. But it does not seem very helpful to talk about such things. It may even be depressing to you and, as for me, I would not like to set myself up as a Pharisee and suggest that I am better than the rest. I remember the word of the Lord, 'Physician, heal yourself'.

I think it is better to try and be positive, and this is suggested by one little phrase in the gospel that may pass unnoticed: 'The greatest among you must be your servant.' That is an echo of the great saying of Jesus, addressed to his disciples not long before he went to his death: 'I came not to be served but to serve and give my life as a ransom for many.'

The priest is, above all, the servant of the people. He is ordained for them, he is a man for others, and his supreme model is Jesus Christ himself who, as it is said in the Acts of the Apostles, 'went about doing good'. He went about caring for the sick and healing them, he went about consoling the troubled and distressed. He went about calling the sinner to repentance and forgiving their sins. He was God's love incarnate, present here on earth, as he is still present in the church, in his word and in his sacraments.

He was Teacher and the priest is a teacher, but the word he has to communicate is not his own but the word of Christ. He does his best to hold up the truth that God is love, a love that is revealed in Jesus Christ.

He is consoler when he tries to comfort people in distress or bereavement. Like Christ, and joining himself to him in prayer, he pleads for them and all others day by day.

Day by day also he tries to give himself to his people by his service of them and that may take him far down the road of suffering, as it did Archbishop Romero in El Salvador who was murdered at the altar, or the young Polish priest, Fr Popieluszko, who was brutally murdered by the Secret Police before Poland got its freedom.

No doubt not all of us are called to that and I, for one, wonder whether I should have had the courage to act like them. But to compare small things with great, let me say that the daily grind of the priest can, and often does, impose on him suffering of one sort or another. This is particularly so when there is only one priest to look after 2,000 people or more in a large urban parish.

However, one does not wish to indulge in heroics. The priest goes on doing his best day after day and some may think that the 'best' is not very good. If so, the first thing they should do is to pray for him and secondly, and not less important, to offer, not waiting to be asked, what service or help they can give. We are all members of the church and the total work of the church falls on us all. The word of Christ, 'The greatest among you must be your servant' is addressed to all. All of us in one way or another are servants of the Lord, servants of one another and servants of the church.

Thirty-second Sunday of the Year

Wis 6:12-16; Ps 62:2-8, 1 Thess 4:13-18, Mt 25:1-13.

There is a certain charm about this parable. Here are the twelve bridesmaids, no doubt all arrayed in garlands and beautiful gowns and eagerly awaiting the wedding. But there are also puzzles. There does not seem to be any bride whom one would expect them to accompany, the wedding was to take place at night, which was unusual, to say the least, even for Jewish weddings at the time. Nor are we told to whose house, whether the bride's or the bridegroom's, they were going. Then there is the harsh conclusion, 'Lord, Lord, open the door to us' and the reply, 'I do not know you'.

But we have to remember that it is a parable and in parables not all the details are important. Jesus may have been using a popular story to convey a very serious message.

If we put the gospel in the context of today's readings, we find that its message is about the end-time, sometimes called 'the end of the world'. In the second reading, St Paul is speaking about the resurrection of the dead when we shall be with our Lord Jesus Christ who, after his suffering and death, rose again to be the source of eternal life for us. The reading from the Book of Wisdom has the same message. If we look for wisdom, the wisdom that is Christ and his kingdom, we shall be received by him into it. This is made clear in a verse that is not included in our reading today: 'The desire for wisdom leads to a kingdom', that is, the kingdom of Christ that will never have an end.

We find the same if we remember that this parable comes in this gospel after a long chapter about the end-time. Then will come the sorting out. Those who have sought the Lord, those who have desired to be with him, those who have listened to his word and lived by it, will be welcomed into the kingdom. This meaning is suggested by a passage in St Luke's gospel. There Jesus says, 'Strive to enter by the narrow gate. Many will try to do so but will not be able.' They will stand outside and knock on the door, saying, 'Lord open to us. We ate and drank with you', but the Lord will say, 'I do not know where you come from'. They have not listened to his word, they have not tried to live by it, they have gone their own way and have done wrong.

What then are we to do? As in all the gospel discourses about the end-time, there is a sentence that comes right at the end of our passage today: 'Stay awake, for you do not know either the day or the hour.' Stay awake like the prudent maidens who were prepared with oil in their lamps and something over. Evidently that means we must be aware of God in our lives but it does not mean that we must always be thinking anxiously about the hour of our death or about the end of the world. If we turn to the message from the Book of Wisdom and from the psalm, we shall be re-assured: 'Watch for wisdom early and you will have no trouble ... Be on the alert for it, and anxiety will quickly leave you. Seek wisdom and you will find it.' And wisdom is the Word of God, Jesus Christ himself, who reveals the all-loving God. So we can pray with the psalmist, 'O God, you are my God ... for you I long: for you my soul is thirsting. My body pines for you like a dry weary land without water.'

Staying awake then, and being on the alert, seems to mean that we should have a desire for God, a desire that we express in prayer. As St Augustine taught, prayer is fundamentally a desire for we cannot be praying all the time. Prayer is a desire for God and this we express in prayer from time to time and so remain aware of God in our lives. As Augustine also said, prayer does not consist of many words: to use many words is one thing but a continuing desire is another, and that can be expressed in the actions of our daily life.

The desire for God; does that mean that we reject the things of this world? It means rather that we should see this world and all its business as transient. The world is destined to pass away, the world is imperfect and unfinished, and we are imperfect and unfinished. We are destined for something greater than this world can offer. We are destined for God, and in him we shall find complete fulfilment. So that we can move towards God, let us make another saying of St Augustine a prayer that will sustain our desire for God until the end of our days: 'You have made us for yourself, O Lord, and our hearts are restless until they find rest in you.' If we make that our prayer we shall always be aware of God, we shall always be awake to him, always on the alert for his coming.

Thirty-third Sunday of the Year

Prov 31:10-31; Ps 127:1-5; Thess 5:1-6; Mt 25:14-30.

There are two illusions that I think have to be dispelled if we are to come to some understanding of this difficult parable. The word 'talents' has nothing to do with what natural talents we may have and the point of the parable is not that we should use them to the best of our ability. A 'talent' was cash and the 'five talents' of the gospel was a very large sum of money. Nor is the parable about working industriously and making a lot of cash and then investing it to make more cash. If the parable did mean that it would be a contradiction of other passages of the sayings of Jesus elsewhere in the gospel: 'Do not hoard up wealth in this world where the moth consumes it or robbers break in and steal it'.

What then is the parable all about?

Matthew was addressing a largely Jewish convert community, perhaps based on Antioch, and he is using the parable to point out to his converts that they must not cling to their past with all its Old Testament laws and customs. These had indeed been a treasure for them in the past; the moral demands of the Law, the Torah, were higher than any other codes of the law of the time or for many centuries past. His audience and their forebears had received the revelation of God through Moses and the prophets. They and their ancestors had heard year by year at Passover time that God had made a covenant, a love pact, with his people. He would be their God and they would be his people if they were faithful to the covenant.

Now all that was over, good as it was, and something new had broken into the world and into their lives. That was Jesus Christ, the Son of God and all his saving word and work. His word was a precious treasure, because it showed them that God is love, that he cared for them, that he wished to raise them to a new level of existence; they were to be and were now in fact sons and daughters of the Father through his Son Jesus Christ. Jesus, through the days of his public ministry, had sown the seed 'which is the word of God'. Now they must make it their own and let it enter the depths of their hearts. There it must be fruit-ful in faith and works of mercy and if it is, then they will hear the words, 'Well done, good and faithful servant ... Come and join in your master's happiness.'

And the work of Christ? He not only proclaimed the word that invited all to salvation but he made a new covenant with them. At the Supper and on the Cross, Jesus offered himself as a 'ran-som for many' and to take away the sins of the world. At the Supper, Jesus instituted the meal through which all who accept Christ by faith can enter into union with him, a union that is a foreshadowing of the eternal banquet when we shall be with Jesus the Lord and we shall hear the words, 'Blessed are those who are invited to the wedding supper of the Lamb!' Of this eternal banquet the eucharist we celebrate here and now is an anticipation, a 'pledge of the future glory and joy that will be given us'.

The word of Jesus and the gift of Jesus himself to us are the trea-sure, the 'talents', the richness God has given to us and to those people whom Matthew was addressing. We do not know very much about them though there are indications in Matthew's gospel that they, or at least some of them, were clinging to the past. What Matthew was telling his converts is that though there were good things in the old law, Jesus had come not to abolish it but to bring it to fulfilment (5:17) and that, on the other hand, there were things they must give up, like circumcision (1 Cor 7:19 and the Letter to the Galatians), like the distinction of foods (Acts 10:9-15; all foods are 'clean'), and certain regulations con-cerning marriage (Mt 6:23 and Acts 16:29). As we know from the New Testament, there were many who wanted to hang on to these observances and this caused a great deal of trouble in the early church.

We too, in our own time, have experienced a similar tension between the old and the new. Many have thought and some still do that the 'old' church, that before the Second Vatican Council, should have been left unchanged. Everything that the Council did, and all that has followed, has been a disaster. They are rather like the man who buried his talent. It had to remain sterile. It could not produce anything. Such an attitude assumes that the church cannot grow and develop, but a church that cannot, or does not, develop is doomed to extinction.

What Vatican II urged upon us is that, like the church itself, we should be concerned for the world in which we live, that we should realise we have a word of life, the word of God, to communicate, and that the church and ourselves should be open to others and be able to present the word of God and the sacramental treasure of the church to others in a way they can welcome and receive.

Thirty-fourth Sunday of the Year

Feast of Christ the King

Ez 34:11-12, 15-17; Ps 22 (in part); 1 Cor 15:20-26; Mt 25:31-46.

When in 1925 Pope Pius XI added this feast to the calendar, he did so because he saw that society, especially western industrialised society, was becoming less and less Christian. Christian moral and social teaching was making ever less impact on the way people lived and on how they conducted their affairs. The pope wanted to show people that, if they were to be faithful to Christ and his teaching, it was not sufficient to be personally pious, but that they had a duty to others, a duty to society. According to their circumstances and ability, they must seek to permeate the structures of society with the Christian values of social justice. His teaching found expression in what was called Catholic Action, whose purpose was to instruct and train people to move out into their world and at least to attempt to restore the reign of Christ to human living. Various movements were set in motion, perhaps the best known being the Young Christian

Workers who made a considerable impact before, during and after the Second World War.

This outlook and this teaching reached its culmination in the Second Vatican Council with its great and important statements on the place and role of the laity in the worship and work of the church. Everyone is involved, all by baptism share in the royal priesthood of Christ, and all are committed to the mission of the church. All should seek to spread his reign of justice and peace in the world in which we live. Our model and our inspiration is Christ the King himself, who is Lord of the world, Lord of the whole human society.

But what sort of King is he and what sort of people should we be if we are to be his true followers?

Jesus Christ is indeed Lord of the world; as the scriptures of today tell us, all powers must be subjected to him and 'when everything is subjected to him, then the Son himself will hand over all things to his Father who will be all in all.' But that does not mean a sort of spiritual dictatorship, or that the whole world should become a sort of church. As we have heard in the first reading, the role of the king will be shepherd-like. In Israel the leaders have been unfaithful to God, they have neglected the sheep and now, through the prophet, God sends his message. He will shepherd the flock, he will search for the stray, he will bandage the wounded, he will make the weak strong and watch over all. In a later verse, unfortunately not included in our reading, we read: 'I shall raise up one shepherd, my servant David, and put him in charge of them to pasture them.' For us, this is Jesus Christ, the descendant of David, the familiar Good Shepherd of whom we sing in the psalm: 'The Lord is my shepherd; there is nothing I shall want ...'

In the gospel we are told what the work of the King-Shepherd-Judge is and how it is to be done, and we see that the burden falls on us, his followers. As St Paul says we are co-workers with Christ (2 Cor 5:20 and 6:1), his mission is our mission, the people to whom he came are the people to whom we must go, especially those in the greatest need: 'Feed the hungry, give drink to the thirsty, clothe the naked, welcome the stranger, visit the sick and the prisoner': by doing these things we shall be doing them to Christ in his members. At the same time we shall be showing who he is, the Shepherd-King who cares for everyone.

It is not difficult to translate this gospel into modern terms. There are thousands of deprived and homeless people even in this country, there are thousands of 'strangers', black, coloured and white who have come to this country, some refugees fleeing from oppressive regimes, some seeking a better standard of life or the very means of livelihood. There are tens of thousands in prison, who, guilty or not, need our care and attention, and there are the sick, the old and the housebound all around us. Towards them all we have an obligation and if, according to our ability and opportunity, we fulfil that obligation, we shall be doing something to bring justice as well as love. For, as the present pope has said, justice and love go together. We must not only try to help the casualties of our society, we must also try and change the conditions that have caused their plight. An enormous task lies before us and the Christian communities in this country, to mention no other, but that is our vocation. In fulfilling it we shall be helping to bring about the reign of Christ:

The kingdom of truth and life,
the kingdom of holiness and grace,
the kingdom of justice, love and peace.
(Preface of the Feast)

Year B

Second Sunday of the Year

1 Sam 3:3-10, 19; Ps 39 (in part); 1 Cor 6:13-20; Jn 1:35-42.

Christians by their very name are followers of Christ, attached to him and committed to him like his first followers who were called 'disciples' in the gospel, a word that we might translate as 'learners', for they had to listen to Christ, to take in his teaching, first about the man they called 'Messiah' and then to learn who he was: the One promised throughout the ages, the chosen and anointed one of the Father, and finally the one who was the Son of God, sent by his Father into the world because he loved us.

If we in our turn are to be followers of Christ we too must be called – and perhaps we have not thought of that, or have taken it for granted. Jesus said to his first followers 'Come', as he did to Andrew and Peter and the rest. They came, they responded to the call and 'Leaving all things they followed him'.

What in various ways the scriptures are saying is that the call, our vocation, comes from God. It came to the boy Samuel in the sanctuary and he replied, 'Speak, Lord, your servant is listening.' And what that involved is suggested by the psalm that follows the reading: 'You do not ask for sacrifice and offerings, for holocausts or victims but an open ear. So here I am Lord, I come to do your will.' Samuel's response was not just 'I am listening' but 'I am ready to do what you want of me'. He did not know what lay ahead, any more than Mary did when, at the end of the Annunciation, she said, 'Let it be to me according to your word.'

But those words, 'Here I am. I come to do your will', link up with Jesus himself, for in the Letter to the Hebrews the words of the psalm are quoted and applied to him. Although we may not often think of it, Jesus was also called. He was called in his baptism when his Father's voice, said, 'This is my Son, the beloved; my favour rests on him.' That marked the beginning of his mission, and throughout John's gospel he is constantly referring to

125

his Father who has sent him. He is the first and supreme apostle of God to bring us salvation, grace and love.

Through Christ, God's call was, as it were, extended to the disciples who in their turn became apostles, men sent. God's call is extended to us also and it is for us to respond to it and to follow the Son of God.

How then do we do this? We respond first by faith which is given us in baptism, a faith that should grow throughout our lives as day by day we commit ourselves ever more deeply to Christ. We are called to the eucharist and in the eucharist which strengthens our faith, and we are called in our sacraments too, notably in marriage and ordination. And always in prayer we must continue to listen to God so that we may know his will and be ready to do it.

But here is a difficulty that many people feel in the course of their lives. 'How do I know what God's will is for me in these circumstances?', they ask. It is not always as difficult as we may think. If people enter into marriage with due seriousness and preparation, then marriage is God's will for them – as is all that follows, the bringing up of children and indeed even the difficulties people encounter in the course of their marriage. Ordination is a response to God's call made know to a man through the church, and more immediately by the bishop who represents the church. He too will be doing God's will though he, like everyone else, will not know what difficulties and sufferings he will encounter in trying to live according to the will of God.

Or again, there are people struck down in the full vigour of their life by a serious and lasting illness and understandably they ask, 'Where is God's will in this? I am useless, I am a burden on those I ought to be supporting.' It is indeed difficult, perhaps impossible to see God's will in this and it may take time before the sick person, through counselling and prayer, can come to see that, however mysterious and painful God's will is, it is to be found there. It is not easy, I admit, to accept that this is God's will, but if we can accept the suffering and the distress we shall be doing

God's will for us, at this time, even if there is little else we can do about it. It is perhaps in these circumstances that we can make the prayer of Jesus on the cross our own: 'Into your hands, Lord, I commend my spirit.'

These examples do not of course solve all problems, but the word of God today gives us some indications of the way we should go. Like Samuel we can say, 'Speak, Lord, your servant is listening', with Mary we can pray, 'Let it be me according to your word', and with Jesus Christ our Lord, as he lay on his cross of pain, we can pray, 'Into your hands, Lord, I commend my spirit.

Third Sunday of the Year

Jon 3:1-5, 10; Ps 24 (in part); 1 Cor 7:29-31; Mk 1:14-20.

Yesterday I was reading in *The Tablet* that there are nearly as many members of the National Trust as there are Catholics in this country. It does not seem a very eloquent statistic but it serves to remind us that we are still very much a minority. It has also been said that when you put together all the church-going Christians of this country they come to something like ten million. This is in a population of about fifty-five millions.

Today the message is about apostleship or mission, and the figures I have quoted, even if not exact, show the size of the task that lies before us. It seems to me that the scriptures we have heard offer us two things that I hope will encourage you.

First, there is the extract from the strange Book of Jonah. We do not know who he was or even if he existed; he is only remembered because of the fictitious story of his being swallowed up by a whale, which wasn't a whale but, as the Hebrew says, 'a big fish'. Not that that helps much. The scene is set again in a fictitious Nineveh which once had been a big city, the capital of the Assyrian empire. Its ruined site is now in Iraq. What is important is that the Assyrians in the time of Isaiah had been the great enemy of the people of Israel, they had invaded their country more than once and swept off into exile a part of their people.

What then is the point of the story? It is this: At a time when the Jews were becoming more and more exclusive and thought they had no mission to anyone outside their own territory, the word of God, the word of repentance comes to the people of Nineveh through this bizarre story. It is telling the Jews that they have a duty to proclaim the one true God even to their enemies and to urge them to repentance. Like all good stories it had a happy ending. One man converted a whole city.

The second piece of encouragement comes from the gospel.

Jesus is beginning to proclaim the good news of salvation and the gospel of repentance, a turning to God with the whole of one's mind and heart which is an essential part of the good news. If we turn to God then we can receive God's saving word into our hearts and live by it.

Then there is the call of the disciples, Simon (Peter), Andrew, James and John. Let us look at them for a moment. They were humble, ordinary men, fishermen and as such they earned their living. In the Acts of the Apostles some supercilious persons called them 'illiterates and (merely) private persons'. They had not attended the Rabbinic schools. As we should say they had not taken a course in holy scripture, much less in theology. They were not rabbis, they were not teachers, they were not prophets, they were not priests, they had no public status or function. And yet Jesus was committing them to the enormous and seemingly impossible task of proclaiming the gospel to their world and to draw the vast pagan world of the time to repentance. As we know, in spite of hostility, persecution and martyrdom, by the end of the first century the good news had been proclaimed to almost all parts of the Roman Empire and numberless people had been drawn to Christ, to faith in him, to repentance, and to incorporation into the church by baptism and the eucharist.

It may be that our world is not so much hostile as indifferent to the gospel, though in some parts of the world people are still being oppressed or even persecuted for their Christian faith. In our own country the gospel has been proclaimed for some fifteen hundred years and we may suppose there is still in many people a residual faith that needs only the word of God to spark it into life.

As I have said, we can take encouragement from today's message. Although Jesus, the Son of God, was resisted, and his work seemed to be a failure and he died as a common criminal, yet his word proved to be irresistible and overcame. His apostles seemed poor and ineffectual men, but after they had received the Holy Spirit they went on boldly and in the end died for the faith they preached.

They were ordinary people like us and, like them, we are all called to spread the good news, to make it known and to draw others to Christ. It may not be given to all to do so by word, but our lives should be a living witness to our faith and that is possible to all of us. Alarming as it may seem, it is through us that the saving word of God will be brought to others and that our Lord Jesus Christ will be made known to a world that is so badly in need of him, of his forgiveness, of his healing and of his truth.

Fourth Sunday of the Year

Deut 18:15-20; Ps 94 (in part); 1 Cor 7:32-35; Mk 1:21-28.

People sometimes wonder why we have readings at Mass from the Old Testament. Its concerns seem so remote from ours and it is often difficult to understand. The Old Testament never seems to have been popular with Catholic people, though I remember priests, who were old when I was young, who knew their Bible very well and used the Old Testament in their sermons – which were much longer than they are now!

Why then should we read the Old Testament? Several answers might be given, and one is that it is a record of God's dealing with the human race as represented by the people of Israel. But the reading of today suggests another reason.

From the beginning, and guided by the Holy Spirit, the church has seen in the Old Testament what I would call a massive movement towards the fulfilment of God's purpose which, in the gospel today, is made known in the word and work of Jesus, the Messiah. He was promised throughout the ages, even at the moment of the fall of our first parents (Gen 3:16), a promise repeated again and again in the pages of the Hebrew Bible. This Messiah, Jesus, as we hear in the gospel, 'taught them with authority', and after the exorcism we hear the comment of the people, 'Here is teaching that is new' and (in another translation), 'With authority he commands even the unclean spirits, and they obey him'. Authority to teach is combined with power. All this seems to be a strange and uncanny echo of the words in the Book of Deuteronomy: 'I will put words into his mouth and he shall tell them all I command him.' It is God who is speaking.

The writer of Deuteronomy sees a long line of prophets, the successors of Moses who in the gospel is called the Prophet, even though we may think of him primarily as the lawgiver. But for the writer, 'law' and 'word' were very closely related. The law, the Torah, was the utterance of God, the 'Ten Words', so to say, by which the Israelites were required to live. This law, first given in the desert, was repeated and re-promulgated in this book, hence its name, Deuteronomy or the second promulgation of the law.

What this reading is doing, then, in the context of today's Mass is to throw light on Jesus himself as prophet, but also as the promised Messiah who was the Son of God. We have heard 'I will put my words into his mouth …', but Jesus utters words out of his own mouth, out of his own heart. He is the Word of God and his words are divine words and that is why they have power. Now the past is being fulfilled, now is the final and decisive intervention of God in the world, which is being brought about by the word and work of his Son, Jesus Christ.

So now we hear not only the words of a man inspired by God, we hear the very word of God himself and that is why that word has authority. If we realise that, it makes it easier for us to understand the exorcism. This was an exercise of authority and power, the casting out of the evil spirit was a sign that the new age had begun, that the reign of God was beginning and that it was being effected by the power present in the word of the Messiah, the Christ, the Saviour of the World.

From the lips of Jesus, then, we hear the very word of God and that is why we take up the psalm today and make it our own prayer, 'Oh that you would listen to his voice. Harden not your hearts.'

As an encouragement to do so, I give you some words written by St John Fisher, Bishop of Rochester, who was martyred for the faith in 1535: '(God) did not spare his own Son but gave him to redeem us all, disregarding the fact that we, naturally thankless, pay no attention, nor consider how much God's love is shown to us, but forget and neglect to follow the example of our merciful Lord in his great compassion for sinners.'

'Paying attention' to the word of God, remembering, remembering that Jesus is not only the Word of God but that he is also the Love of God that is made known to us and made present to us in the word of God that is proclaimed to us every Sunday. He is present to us as love in this our eucharist if we take his word into our hearts and take him to ourselves in holy communion to live by him.

Fifth Sunday of the Year

Job 7:1-4, 6, 7; Ps 146:1-6; 1 Cor 9:16-23; Mk 1:29-39.

The message of today's Mass is straightforward and should be very consoling to those who suffer – and that is most of us at one time or another.

Job, whoever he was and whether he existed or not, is presented to us as a picture of a human being in all its wretchedness. In an earlier chapter he is pictured as a man stricken with sores and ulcers from head to foot and sitting on a dunghill, lamenting his lot. He is a figure of the human race seemingly bereft of God and without any earthly help. We may think the picture somewhat overdrawn but we have only to recall the many and distressing pictures of diseased and starving people we have seen on TV and still see in different parts of the world.

We see something similar in the gospel we have just heard: 'All who were sick and those who were possessed by devils', those suffering from various kinds of diseases, were brought before Jesus and he healed them. Jesus cared for and still cares for both body and soul, for he came to 'save', heal physically and spiritually, those who were suffering in any way. It may seem shocking to say so, but Jesus was not just a 'religious' man or a 'holy' man, concerned only with 'souls'. He was fully human and he wanted to relieve physical suffering as well as diseases of the soul.

As we read constantly in the gospel, he had compassion on the people, that is, he suffered with them in their suffering as he did when the five thousand followed him. They were not only a people without shepherds, leaderless and spiritually starved, they were hungry and he fed them. Or we remember the widow's son of Nain. Jesus sees a funeral procession coming out of Nain and on the bier is a dead young man, 'the only son of his mother'. She is weeping and Jesus' whole being is moved with pity for her. He halts the procession and says to the young man, 'Rise up' and he sat up and began to talk. That is all. Jesus saw the weeping mother, his heart was moved, he must do something for her and he raises her son to life.

I have used the word 'compassion' and that is the third part of today's message. Understandably we are puzzled and distressed by the prevalence of disease and illnesses of all kinds. We are particularly distressed when babies and young children are afflicted with heart malfunctions or leukaemia, and we ask ourselves, 'Does God care?' Is he someone remote, up there, who indeed rules all things but for his own inscrutable purposes? We know one thing at least. Here in Jesus Christ is the compassion of God, here is God in Christ showing his compassion for all who are suffering, for all who are oppressed, for all who are sinners, and that movement of the divine heart towards suffering humanity did not cease when Jesus left this earth. It is as real now as it was then, even if God's ways with us are hidden or mostly hidden.

The compassion of God, the pity of God and the healing that God offers are continued into the present time to all who suffer.

It is continued in the constant prayer of the church, but most notably in the sacraments of penance and the Anointing of the Sick. Just as Jesus in his lifetime did not repel the notorious sinner we call the Magdalen, just as he forgave the murderer-thief on the cross, so now he is ready to accept any and every sinner who approaches him with a repentant heart.

And just as Jesus healed the sick, so does he now through the anointing of the sick, which used unhappily to be called 'Extreme Unction' or the Last Sacrament. It can be stated emphatically that it is not the sacrament of the dying but the sacrament of those who are seriously ill. Furthermore, as the church teaches us, it is the sacrament for the healing of the whole person, body and soul. And it is principally through this sacrament that the healing of Christ is brought to people now.

For all this we can thank God, even if all our problems and our questionings are not solved or answered. But with the psalmist we can pray, 'Praise the Lord for he is good. He heals the broken-hearted and binds up all their wounds'.

There is also, I think, one practical conclusion. All can have some part in the healing that comes from Christ. In the splendid and official book, *The Pastoral Care of the Sick*, the church urges you, the people, to care for the sick, to visit them, and above all to pray for them. The priest is instructed to lay hands on them, as Christ himself did, and after prayer with the sick, I do not see why you should not do likewise. It is in this way that the compassion and the healing of Christ is brought to the sick and suffering now. Think then of your ministry to the sick, perhaps in your own homes, and then to others who would welcome your care. You will be a co-worker with Christ.

Sixth Sunday of the Year

Lev 13:1, 2, 44-46; Ps 31 (in part); 1 Cor 10:31, 11:1; Mk 1:40-45.

If we are to understand the gospel of today more deeply, it will be best to put it in the context of this first chapter of Mark which we have been hearing for two or three Sundays. It has been described as a picture of a day in the life of our Lord, and what is clear is that Mark has grouped together a number of healing incidents in one place. They will in fact have happened at different times. But he has another purpose too. In the Roman world of the time, there were a number of bogus healers about, wonder-workers, and Mark was very concerned to show that the Christ he was writing about was not one of them. He was something else and something much more but what he was, the Messiah and the Son of God, would only be fully revealed through the cross and the resurrection. That is really the explanation of the saying, so many times repeated in Mark's gospel, 'Do not say anything about it', the cure, but go and tell the priests who will pronounce you clean of the leprosy or skin-disease.

We need also to realise that there is something of a parable about this story of healing. First, leprosy, or whatever the skin-disease was (and we hardly know), made a person unclean; a leper had to be separated from the rest of the community not for hygienic reasons but because he was ritually unclean. Lepers were excluded from worship. We remember how in the Old Testament Miriam, the sister of Moses, criticised him and as a punishment she was stricken with what was called leprosy which was healed only through the prayer of Moses and Aaron and then she was restored to the community. Here, in this gospel incident, Mark is showing that Jesus had pity on the sick man, that he ignored the rules about ritual impurity and healed him. That is one reason why, as in Luke's account, the man came back to thank him.

Secondly, in the Old Testament and to a certain extent in the New, physical illness was closely associated with spiritual illness or sin. This was not just a crude judgement: 'Your sins have found you out, you have got only what you deserve'; it was based on an understanding of the wholeness of the human person and of the interaction of mind on body and body on mind. Only in our own time have we come round to seeing that this is true.

On account, then, of the ritual uncleanness, for ages in the church, leprosy, the leprosy of this miracle story, has been seen as a symbol of sin, and the Fathers of the Church and other writers after them have so seen it. This is also suggested by the psalm chosen for today: 'Happy the man whose offence is forgiven, whose sin is remitted.' But this view of things leads us on to a more profound understanding of this story. Mark wishes to turn our minds to the supreme event, the great healing, the remedy for all sin, namely the passion, death and resurrection of Jesus. As we read in the First Letter of St Peter: '(Jesus) was bearing our faults in his own body on the cross, so that we might die to our faults and live for holiness; through his wounds you have been healed. You had gone astray like sheep but now you have come back to the shepherd and guardian of your souls' (2:24). Like silly sheep we have gone astray and sinned, but we are healed by the wounds of the One who is the guardian of our souls.

If you ask, 'How is this healing brought to us?', I would draw your attention to the sacrament of penance and the services of penitence that are celebrated during the course of the year. On these occasions we can pray with the psalmist, 'I have acknowledged my sins … I will confess my offence to the Lord' and he will forgive us. In the sacrament of penance, when the priest pronounces the words of absolution, we are brought close to the Lord Jesus who reconciles us to his Father, to the church and to those we have offended or to those who have offended us. Reconciliation means healing, the healing of the hurts and rifts that can occur between ourselves and others, but also the healing, the restoration of our relationship with God after serious sin.

I venture to remind you of the words of absolution the priest pronouces after you have confessed your sins:

God, the Father of mercies,
through the death and resurrection of his Son
has reconciled the world to himself
and sent the Holy Spirit among us
for the forgiveness of sins;
through the ministry of the Church
may God give you pardon and peace,
and I absolve you from your sins
in the name of the Father, and of the Son and of the Holy Spirit.

Seventh Sunday of the Year

Is 43:18-25; Ps 40 (in part); 2 Cor 1:18-22; Mk 2:1-12.

The account of the healing of the paralysed man occurs in all three synoptic gospels. Evidently it was part of the early preaching of the apostles and it is apparent in their action. When Peter was at a place called Lydda he found another paralysed man and he said to him, 'Aeneas, Jesus Christ heals you; get up and fold up your sleeping mat' and the man did so. There is however no mention here of the forgiveness of sins. The first reading and the psalm strongly suggest that today we should consider God's forgiveness both in the Old Testament and in the New.

The prophet is speaking of the sins of the people. He, like all his contemporaries, saw their exile and wretchedness as punishment for their earlier sins, most notably their lack of faith in God and their failure to keep the holy law. Now they were on the point of regaining their liberty and returning to the Holy Land, no need to think about what was done before … 'I it is, I it is, who must blot out everything and not remember your sins'.

Then there enters the paralytic and it is not too far-fetched to think of him praying the psalm, 'Lord, have mercy on me. Heal my soul for I have sinned against you.' So his friends bring him in, going up the outside staircase, because of the crowd, and let him down at the feet of Jesus. The first words Jesus addressed to him perhaps surprise us, as they may very well have surprised his friends, and as they did in fact those who were hostile to Jesus: 'My child, your sins are forgiven'. The word 'child' suggests that the paralytic was a young man, perhaps not much more than a boy and if so, his sins cannot have been very great. May we speculate? Did this sick young man represent the human race? We remember the saying of John the Baptist, 'Look, there is the Lamb of God who takes away the sin of the world.' Here, as in other incidents of a like kind, Jesus is beginning his work of salvation.

Another feature of the story cannot but impress us. The paralytic's friends show a great charity towards him – they were determined that he should be brought close to Jesus – but also a touching faith: 'Seeing their faith ...' Jesus was immediately moved. And as we know from many other stories in the gospels, faith in Jesus was necessary both for forgiveness and healing. It is as if the faithlessness of the people of the Old Testament was being reversed by the faith of the young man and his friends.

The heart of the account however is to be found in the words, 'Your sins are forgiven ... Get up, pick up your stretcher and walk.' This Jesus says and this is what happens. Whether or not the account was touched up by the disciples in their early preaching, as some think, there is no doubting the majesty and the assurance of Jesus that he has the authority to forgive sins, the prerogative of God – but he was the Son of God.

As in the previous miracle stories, Jesus is here beginning his mission of salvation which he would effect by his passion, death and resurrection when he gave himself for the ransom of the world. So it was that immediately after the resurrection Jesus first reconciles his weak and faulty disciples: 'Peace be with you', and then they hear the words, 'Receive the Holy Spirit. For those whose sins you forgive, they are forgiven; for those whose sins you retain, they are retained.' The ministry Jesus had received from his Father is now passed on to those who would be called apostles, men sent by him to continue his work. This, in the Acts of the Apostles, we find them doing. On Pentecost Sunday Peter goes out to the people, he proclaims Jesus as the Messiah and the Son of God, he proclaims his death and resurrection, and when the people ask, 'What shall we do, Peter replies, 'Repent and be baptised' for thereby their sins will be forgiven and they will be reconciled to God through Jesus Christ.

This ministry is continued in the world today by the church when, in the name of Father, Son and Holy Spirit, she initiates people into the family of God and the life of Christ, but also in the sacrament of penance when we too can hear the words of Christ, 'Child, your sins are forgiven.'

Eighth Sunday of the Year

Hos 2:16-22; Ps 102 (in part); 2 Cor 3:1-6; Mk 2:18-22.

How do we see the church? Do we see it as just a great organisation present in every part of the world? Do we see it as pope, bishops, priests and other officials who are sometimes prominent in society, the sort of people the newspapers write about? Or do we think of it largely as an institution with laws and regulations we must all keep? If we do, we are seeing only the external part of the church, a part that is ultimately not the most important. The scriptures of today suggest another view of the church that takes us much deeper, takes us into the inner nature of the church. They are talking about a relationship between ourselves and the church, a relationship that we may not have known existed.

Today it is first sketched out in this somewhat strange passage from Hosea. The Lord, speaking through his prophet, is saying that the whole people of Israel are wedded to him. The people have gone astray, they have been unfaithful to him, they have gone after false gods, the *Baalim*, whose worship involved ritual prostitution. They have, as it were, committed adultery and cut themselves off from God. They have to repent, and God leads them out into the wilderness. As the text (not given today) says, God will block the way to their false lovers and if she looks for them she will not find them. Through this rigorous penance the people 'will respond to me (God), as she did when she came out of the land of Egypt'. When the day of repentance is over she will be able once again to call God her husband. Or, as we hear today, 'I will betroth you to myself for ever ... I shall betroth you in uprightness and justice and faithful love and tenderness.' As we read in the later chapters of Isaiah, the people are the bride of the Lord and he is their bridegroom.

If this was true of the people of the Old Testament, we should expect it to be true of the people of the New Testament, and if Jesus' reply surprises us, it did not surprise the disciples of John the Baptist. They had heard him speaking of the bride and the bridegroom and that second term refers to Christ; his voice is heard and this gives joy to both John and his followers (John 3:29). In our gospel today the followers of Jesus also rejoice: 'Surely the bridegroom's attendants would never think of fasting while the Bridegroom is still with them.' Only after he is taken away (by death) will the time of fasting come because that will be a time of conflict and suffering, even if mixed with joy that the word of Jesus and his saving death and resurrection are bringing men and women into the church.

The saying looks on to the future and we have to look ahead to the last book of the Bible, the Apocalypse, where the full teaching about the bridegroom and the bride is given: 'I saw a new heaven and a new earth ... I saw the holy city, the new Jerusalem, coming down from God out of heaven, as beautiful as a bride all dressed for her husband.' There is the church complete and in glory as it will one day be. But, though as yet imperfect, it is already here. As the text goes on to say, 'Here God lives among us all' and it repeats the Old Testament saying, 'They shall be his people and he will be their God'. And in this city, in this church, there is a well, a well that gives life to all who will drink from it (Apocalypse 21:2, 6). From the heart of Christ, dwelling in his church, will flow fountains of living water that will enter the hearts and lives of all who will come to it and drink from it.

If we reflect on those words, 'They shall be his people ...' we shall see that the church is not a mere institution, however impressive, but that it is a network of relationships that are both vertical and horizontal. They are vertical to our pastors but beyond them to Christ who is the head of the church, and they are horizontal because, through the grace of Christ we all share, we are related to all our fellow Christians, our brothers and sisters in Christ. In this sense the church is *ours*, not some remote institution of officials, and we make the church *real*, by our worship surely when we are drawn into unity with Christ, but also by understanding that we have obligations to each other, obligations of service and support. But we also have the joy of what for once is rightly called fellowship, a sharing together of the gifts God gives through the liturgy and sacraments of the church and a sense of closeness to Jesus Christ who is God-with-us.

Ninth Sunday of the Year

Deut 5:12-15; Ps 80 (in part); 2 Cor 4:6-11; Mk 2:23-36.

When I was young – which is a very long time ago – there were many laws of the church that had to be kept. You had to be fasting from midnight if you wished to receive holy communion. You were not allowed to eat meat on Fridays and there were various prohibitions about what was called 'servile' work on Sundays. What bulked large in the minds of most people was the obligation to go to Mass every Sunday. Although dispensations could be asked for and given for various matters, and people could be excused in others, the impression was that Catholics lived very much under a system of law. It was not always possible to see that the law was trying to save something very precious.

Here in the scriptures today, in both the first reading and the gospel, we have teaching about the Sabbath, which for Christians is Sunday, to show not so much that its observance was a matter of law but that it was holy. By the time of Christ the laws concerning the Sabbath were very burdensome and demanding; no one was allowed to walk more than a mile, and this legalism obscured the very purpose of keeping the Sabbath. The passage from Deuteronomy gives the reason for keeping it: 'Your servant, man or woman, shall rest as you do ('sabbath' in Hebrew means 'rest'). Remember that you were a servant in the land of Egypt, and that the Lord your God brought you out from there with a mighty hand and outstretched arm.' The deliverance of the Israelites from Egypt was regarded by the authors of the Old Testament as a salvation, a great act of God that saved them from slavery and extinction in Egypt, and enabled them to go out into the freedom of the desert where they could become the people of God.

If this was true of the Jewish Sabbath, it is all the more true of the Christian Sunday. Within New Testament times the church had transferred the observance and celebration of the Sabbath to the Sunday, the Day of the Lord. Every Sunday we recall and celebrate our salvation brought about by the passion, death and resurrection of our Lord Jesus Christ. As the Constitution on the Liturgy teaches (106), 'Following the apostolic tradition that originated on the very day of Christ's resurrection, the church celebrates the paschal mystery every seventh day, or Sunday ... rightly called the Lord's Day or Sunday. Christians must gather together to hear the word of God, to partake of the eucharist and, in this way, to call to mind the passion, death, resurrection and glory of the Lord Jesus, giving thanks to God.' This is the fundamental reason for keeping the Sunday holy and if we understand this, it is obvious that all should make every effort to come and celebrate the eucharist on the Day of the Lord. If we understand that this is the truth of the matter, then we shall not willingly let a Sunday pass by without coming to church. In this sense, obligation and a sense of obligation is a good thing and not just a piece of legalism.

When we come to consider the gospel, we find a different emphasis. Jesus is going about his work of liberating the Jewish people from the burdens of the legal system. Things must be seen in the right proportion. David with a few followers was fleeing from King Saul and, coming to the Tabernacle or Tent of Meeting, he asks if he and his company may eat of the sacred bread that was displayed before the Mercy-seat week by week. They were hungry, they had had nothing to eat, their need overrode the rules, and the high priest allowed them to eat of the loaves. Later, we hear the question of Jesus, 'Is it against the law on the sabbath day to do good or to do evil?' The answer was obvious and the whole teaching of Jesus on the matter is summed up in his words: 'The sabbath was made for man, not man for sabbath.' The law of love of neighbour comes before observance of the sabbath or, for that matter, the Sunday. What is of primary importance is to understand what the law, even the law of God, is trying to protect and then act accordingly. We are sons and daughters of the Father, not slaves under oppression in a permanent Egypt.

In the light of the teaching of the gospel, we should be able to order our Sunday. It is a holy day, 'a day sacred to the Lord' but in our own time it has been horribly secularised and even desacralised. Are we willing to go along with this trend? Is it not our business as Christians to show a rather different example? Sunday is a day for worship but it is also a day of joy, and families can and do find ways of enjoyment that are completely within the spirit of the Christian Sunday. But on the other hand, let us not treat it as any other day of the week. 'Sabbath' means rest; let the family, and especially the mother, rest and relax on the Day of the Lord after resting in the Lord in the celebration of the eucharist.

Tenth Sunday of the Year

Gen 3:9-15; Ps 129; 2 Cor 4:13-5:1; Mk 3:20-35.

I remember that I have said to you more than once that the word of God challenges us, challenges us to act rightly but also to think rightly, and we have such a challenge today.

In the first chapter of Genesis we have an account of the creation of the world and the first human beings, and we read that God saw all he had made and they were very good. How then did sin and evil enter the world? The authors of the Book of Genesis recalled the age-old myth of the temptation of the first man and woman who represented the whole human race. They rebelled against God who had made them, and let in, so to say, the forces of evil which the writers personified as the Satan, the Adversary of God. He, by his temptation of Adam and Eve, led them and the whole human race into sin, alienation from God. That this may well have been the way the writers thought can be gathered from the Book of Wisdom, which was written almost at the end of Jewish history. There we read: 'God did not make death and he does not delight in the death of the living … But ungodly men by their words and deeds summoned death, considering him a friend …' (2, 13, 14). We do not take Genesis as a factual, historical account of what happened millions of years ago, but we find that it contains a profound truth that resistance to God, rebellion against God, is the source of all sin and all evil.

It is this reading of the passage from Genesis that connects with the gospel.

By his proclamation of the good news of salvation, by his urgent call to repentance, by his miracle of healing, and by his casting out of evil spirits, Jesus is reversing what happened in the beginning and all its consequences. He was bringing in the kingdom, the reign of God, when sin would be done away with and the empire of the Evil One would be eventually destroyed. In doing so, he was fulfilling the promise made long before when the word of God came to fallen man and woman: 'I will put enmity between you and the woman, between your seed and her seed, he shall bruise your head and you shall bruise his heal.' The power of Satan would be broken and Jesus was doing that by his exorcisms, precisely the casting out of evil. The victory would come with the cross and the resurrection when all who came to Christ by faith, baptism and the eucharist would be made free with the freedom of the children of God.

Unhappily, some Jewish leaders, called scribes, ranged themselves on the side of the Evil One. As we have heard, they accused Jesus of casting out devils through the prince of devils and Jesus, by a parable, easily refutes their argument. But his whole life and work was the decisive answer. Recalling the ancient messianic title, the Strong One – a title the scribes must have known very well – he proclaims that he is the Strong Man who now comes to deprive Satan of his ill-gotten spoils. What is more, Mark in his gospel shows that the Strong One was prompted and supported by the Holy Spirit. He had received the Spirit in baptism, in the strength of the Spirit he had wrestled with the Evil One in the wilderness, and now Mark is indicating that if the scribes and others refuse to recognise the power of the Spirit in the words and works of Jesus, they are self-blinded. That is the meaning of the saying about the unforgivable sin against the Holy Spirit. As Mark comments, this was 'because they were saying "An unclean spirit is in him".'

In this event we are brought very close to Jesus in his life and work. We may be inclined to think that for him it was all very easy. It wasn't. He had to contest foot by foot the evil that is in the human heart and in the world and he won the victory only at the cost of immense suffering and his own life. We too in our world are confronted with evil, with many evils; we too have to make the same pilgrimage as Jesus made. The only difference – and it is an enormous difference – is that he is with us and his grace and his strength are within us so that, with him and through him, we can overcome evil, overcome the unregenerate world, the world that would draw us to sin. Like Jesus, we must resist and if we remain close to him the outcome will never be in doubt.

Eleventh Sunday of the Year

Ez 17:22-24; Ps 91 (in part); 2 Cor 5:6-10, Mk 4:26-34.

The message today is about the kingdom, the kingdom of God. Once it was regularly interpreted as meaning the church here in this world and there was a strong tendency to see it as the institutional, visible church to which all the sayings in the gospels could be applied. We can now see that this term 'the kingdom' has wider and deeper implications.

It can be said to be foreshadowed in the Old Testament where the people are called by God and made his people. Writing of the restoration of Israel after it had been in grave danger of annihilation on account of captivity, Ezekiel sees a new era opening up for the Israelites: 'I will take a shoot and plant it myself … It will sprout branches and bear fruit, and become a noble cedar. Every kind of bird will live beneath it …' This comes very near the parables of the gospel but the restoration was not destined to last. Greeks came, then Romans, and by the time Jesus appeared Israel was under Roman occupation. More disturbingly the spiritual life of the people seems to have been running low.

It was into this atmosphere that Jesus the Messiah came and began his preaching of the kingdom, the reign of God. By his miracles, by his contests with the spirits of evil, he was bringing into existence the kingdom foretold by the prophet and by his word. As we learn from the parable of the sower, his word is a word of life. It is planted in the heart and there by the action of God but it does not lie inert. It 'produces first the shoot (the sign of life), and then the ear and then the full grain in the ear'. The reign of God is working within us even when we are unaware of it, *provided* we are willing to receive it. Among other things, it is a parable about the power of God's word within us.

But the parable has not simply a personal sense. The shoots come, the ear and then the full grain appear, they become visible, in the lives of those who receive it but also in the whole land which becomes productive. Then, as the second parable shows, it becomes a large shrub 'so that all the birds of the air can shelter in it'. This is the church as it appeared after the resurrection when the apostles inspired by the Holy Spirit go out and proclaim the living word of Christ. The church begins to appear as an organised institution doing the work of Christ in a very hostile world.

What we are being told then is that the kingdom begins first in the interior life of those who receive it and only then in the great visible church that gradually spreads throughout the world.

Of course there were set–backs, people refused to listen, the apostles and their immediate followers met with opposition and sometimes martyrdom, and the church has had its ups and downs ever since. Nonetheless it will go on to the end of time: 'When the crop is ready, he (the farmer) loses no time: he starts to reap because the harvest has come.'

We may get discouraged from time to time. We may say to ourselves or openly, 'The Church ought to be doing this or that' but we need to realise two things. The progress of the kingdom is primarily God's work and growth will not come from merely human effort. Even so, and secondly, it will not come without human effort, our effort. St Paul, the great apostle of the word of God who spread the good news throughout the Roman Empire, was keenly aware of both considerations. Speaking of himself and Apollos, the preacher, he said: 'I planted, Apollos watered but God gave growth. So neither he who plants not he who waters is anything but only God who gives the growth.' But elsewhere Paul has another phrase we might like to ponder on: 'We are God's fellow workers.' God has chosen that his saving work should be done by human beings and it is being carried on by innumerable priests, religious sisters and lay people whether at home or abroad but, within our own capacity and according to our circumstances, it is our work too. And if they or we should become discouraged, let us be like the farmer who was both patient and hopeful.

As I have said, God's work begins within, invisibly, and then and only then do its effects become visible. So it seems to me that these parables can be applied to our own personal life. To use another metaphor of St Paul's, 'you are God's field'. We too have to receive the seed, we too have to grow and most of us are aware that the growing in Christ is a very slow business. We are aware of our imperfections, our weaknesses and our backslidings. We pray and strive and the results are meagre or visibly none at all. But God is at work in us all the time and if we will let him into our lives, then God will give the growth although we shall probably not be aware of it until we come to meet him at the end of our lives. Patience, patience with ourselves, hope in the love and power of God, and a calm submission to his working within us will bring us into the presence of God.

Twelfth Sunday of the Year

Job 38:1, 8-11; Ps 106 (in part); 2 Cor 5:14-17; Mk 4:35-41.

The gospel sometimes raises questions in our minds that it does not answer. Some 'modern' people will say that the nature miracles of the Bible could never have happened. For them the world is a finished mechanism, they know all its laws which can't be broken; there is nothing outside it. Although they pride themselves on being free-thinking and undogmatic, they are making a very dogmatic statement. Scientists nowadays are ready to declare that the universe is mysterious or fades off into mystery.

Job, for his part, was confronted with another and a greater mystery. He thought he had been afflicted by God and he almost quarrelled with him. Towards the end of his suffering God asks him questions: 'Who pent up the sea behind closed doors when it leapt tumultuous out of the womb?' God, revealed in truth in Jesus Christ, remains the supreme mystery. We cannot define him, we cannot comprehend him in the sense of grasping the whole truth about him. If we could, we should have reduced him to our limited, very finite minds and such a being would no longer be God. As there is mystery in God, so there is mystery in the world around and it is not for us to set limits.

We turn then to the miracle of the calming of the sea and the saving of the disciples, and again we ask: what did Mark want to convey by it? In the earlier part of the gospel we have seen people being drawn to Jesus by his healing of the sick, by his compassion for sinners and by his teaching, and the crowds cry out, 'Here is one who teaches with authority and not as the scribes and Pharisees.' But what the source of that authority was they did not know and the disciples themselves were only beginning to understand. It is only later that through Peter they will make their first profession of faith, 'You are the Christ', i.e. the Messiah. Here and now they were still learning. They had been drawn to Jesus so strongly that they had left their trades and followed him. Now, with him in the boat, with the storm raging, they spontaneously turn to him, 'Master, save us, we are sinking.' Then comes the calming of the sea and the winds and the saying of Jesus, 'How is it that you have no faith?' And the gospel account goes on, 'They were filled with awe. Who can this be? Even the winds and the sea obey him.'

They were beginning to grow in faith and confidence and, because they were God-centred men, they felt they had caught a glimpse of the power and majesty of the transcendent God whom they had worshipped since childhood, no doubt in the words of the psalm:

He stilled the storm to a whisper;
all the waves of the sea were hushed.

It was because of experiences like this that the disciples felt they could go on following Jesus and sharing with him the unpopularity and growing hostility that pursued him until his death. Even later, after the resurrection, when they were confirmed in their faith, when they were put in prison and condemned to death, the words 'Why are you frightened?' may have echoed in their minds.

In the early centuries of the church, the boat in a storm was often regarded as a symbol of the church. At the end of the sixth century, when Rome was dangerously threatened by the Lombards, Gregory the Great wrote of the barque of Peter as being almost overwhelmed and seemed to be in danger of going down before the forces of evil. Even so, and thanks to him, the church was expanding into a far-off and hardly known land, England, to which he sent St Augustine to convert the English.

So it has been all through the history of the church. It has rarely been a success story. If Jesus said, 'I will be with you until the end of time' he never promised that the church would always be flourishing. The faith of the church, its confidence in its Lord and the love that is at the heart of its life, are the only guarantees that it will endure to the end of time.

But we too are in a position similar to that of the disciples. Our lives also have their ups and downs; there are times of trouble, times of pain, times of heartbreak. Like Job we may question God, we may feel we must argue with him, we may even come somewhere near despair. Then is the time to remember the power and love of God that is revealed and made present to us through Jesus Christ. He suffered the agony and humiliation of the passion and the cross, and after his resurrection the disciples recognised him with joy and a new faith. In our infinitely smaller troubles and whatever our anguish, let us keep before us the Christ who suffered and died for us and for our salvation. He is with us, as he will be until the end of our lives. In times of trouble and suffering we might like to make our own the prayer of St Paul, 'I know in whom I have believed and I am sure he is able to guard the treasure entrusted to me until he appears on the Day', the Last Day, but also the last day of my life.

Thirteenth Sunday of the Year

Wis 1:13-24; Ps 29 (in part); 2 Cor 7:9, 13-15; Mk 5:21-43.

There are two ways of reading the stories we have just heard. The first way is to see them as revealing Jesus in all his human attractiveness. Here he is among the people, being jostled by the crowd. A leading man of the synagogue comes up to him and asks him to heal his daughter. A woman pushes her way through the crowd just to touch his garment. These two and dozens of others saw in Jesus something they could hardly describe. The woman may have thought he was some sort of wonder-worker and the synagogue leader evidently thought he was a holy man with special powers. But whatever they thought, Jesus deals with them gently. The woman thought he might be angry, but no, he turns to her and kindly says, 'Be well again'. He took her willingness to come to him for faith: 'Your faith has saved you.' As for the man, Jesus immediately gave way to his request; he went to his home, he laid hands on the little girl, he raised her up by the hand and he and he alone remembered that she would be hungry, 'Give her something to eat'.

That is how people were drawn to him, that is why his disciples became so deeply attached to him, ready eventually to die for him. What Jesus was then he is now, even if we cannot see him. And for all this we give thanks. We too can be drawn to him.

The second way to read the stories is to look deeper. First, we find certain words that recur. Thus the leader of the synagogue says to Jesus, 'Come and lay your hands on her and she will be saved.' To the woman Jesus said, 'Your faith has saved you.' To both he uses the word 'faith': 'Do not be afraid; only believe.' But to the little girl he says 'rise up', using the same verb used in the New Testament for his own resurrection. Finally, he took with him into the room Peter, James and John who would be witnesses to his resurrection and would proclaim it to the world.

Taking all this into account, I think we can see these healings as pointing on beyond themselves. The 'saving' of the little girl and, in a different sense, the 'saving' of the woman, suggested to Mark another and comprehensive saving: the salvation of the human race by the suffering, death and resurrection of the Jesus he was writing about.

This understanding of the text has a certain likelihood when we remember that to the Hebrew mind sin, disease and even death were not so sharply separated as they are for us. St Paul could write, 'By one man sin came into the world and by sin death', and he did not mean only spiritual death. Again we have heard in the first reading, 'Death was not God's doing, he takes no pleasure in the extinction of the living.' He created them to live, he made them imperishable because they were made in his own image. The death that Jesus came into the world to destroy was first spiritual death, the death caused by sin. This he achieved by his own death and resurrection. As we pray after the consecration, 'Dying you destroyed our death, rising you restored our life, Lord Jesus, come in glory.' The saving and the raising of the little girl was a foreshadowing of his resurrection as it was of the final victory over physical death when we shall say with Christ, 'Death, where is your victory?' Death has been swallowed up in victory.

Jesus also came to heal our bodily ills. As we read in the prophetic passage of Isaiah (53,4), he took upon himself 'our sicknesses and pains'. During his lifetime Jesus was beginning his work of healing though now, even now, sickness and suffering are only gradually and partially being overcome but in the end we shall be made whole, receiving the health such as Jesus gave to the woman who had been troubled for so many years.

Finally, there is the word 'faith', in some ways the most important in the whole account. The woman believed, or perhaps we should say that Jesus turned her desire into faith. The leader of the synagogue was told to believe and his daughter was raised to life. And this faith was not some sort of belief in Jesus as a wonder-worker, a role that Jesus rejected. The faith of which the gospel speaks is belief in Jesus himself, a trust in him leading to a total commitment to him of self and one's whole life. Such a faith takes time to grow; even the disciples did not fully believe until after the resurrection. As for ourselves, if we pray and read the scriptures, if we ponder on Jesus and all he did for us, our faith will grow, and if sickness and pains afflict us, if physical death is the destiny of us all, one day we shall be transformed by the same power that raised Jesus to life and we shall enter into the joy of the kingdom.

Fourteenth Sunday of the Year

Ez 2:2-5; Ps 122; 2 Cor 12:7-10; Mk 6:1-6.

The gospels rarely strike a note of personal emotion, but here today we can discern a certain sadness.

Jesus had gone out on his first mission. He had gone among the people, they had listened to his word, they had seen his compassion for the sick and the sinner and he had gathered his first disciples. By and large the people had welcomed him and indeed at times thronged around him to hear his word and receive his loving care. Now he goes back home and begins teaching in the local synagogue. Luke expands this incident and tells us that he read from the book of Isaiah: 'The spirit of the Lord is upon me, because he has anointed me to preach the good news to the poor ...'. Then he began preaching on the text. The people were astonished. Here was the local boy who had come back. They had known him as the village carpenter and not unnaturally they asked themselves where he had got all his wisdom and how was it that he had worked miracles, of which they had evidently heard.

Then comes the note of sadness: 'They would not accept him.' They rejected him and Jesus sadly comments, 'A prophet is only despised in his own country, among his own relations and in his own house.' And he went away, 'amazed at their lack of faith'.

As we know from the rest of the gospel, he was rejected by most of the people, even by some of his disciples. After his teaching on the eucharist, the bread of life, many of his disciples said, 'This is a hard saying; who can listen to it?' and they walked no more with him. Then there was the final rejection on Calvary when, as he lay on the cross, some jeered at him. Mark of course knew all this and, as he wrote his gospel, he may have in mind the words of Isaiah: 'He was despised and rejected by men; a man of sorrows and acquainted with grief; as one from whom men hide their faces he was despised and we esteemed him not' (53:3; RSV).

Is this, however, all that is to be said? Was the rejection final? Let us remember that many of his disciples did follow him. After the ascension we read in the Acts of the Apostles that 120 were gathered in the upper room in Jerusalem with Mary the mother of Jesus. There was Joseph of Arimathea, a would-be disciple, and Nicodemus who had come to Jesus by night, both of whom saw to the burial of Jesus. Some Pharisees were converted and there was the wise Gamaliel who stood up in the synagogue after the resurrection of Jesus and, speaking of the new Christian movement, said, 'If this undertaking is of men, it will fail; but if it is of God, you will not be able to overthrow them. You might even be found opposing God.'

I recall these facts as they help us to understand the style of the Bible, and the passage from Ezekiel in particular, as well as in a measure the gospel. The biblical style is to state things in black and white. There is either acceptance or rejection, someone is entirely good or entirely bad and that is the end of the matter. But as we know the human mind moves slowly, we take in new ideas only gradually and it is only at the end of a whole process of reflection that we make up our minds to accept a new idea or reject it. That, I think, was true of the people of the New Testament we have been considering. That men like Joseph of Arimathea and Nicodemus, as well as some Pharisees, came into the church later on shows that for them there was a slow process of conversion.

So it is with us. Although we may not think much about it, we were first converted by baptism, by confirmation and, when we listen to the word of God, we re-affirm our faith and receive Our Lord Jesus Christ in communion. It is this that supports and strengthens our faith throughout our lives. But if we neglect word and sacrament, then there is grave danger of rejecting

Christ instead of receiving him into our hearts and lives.
Acceptance or rejection is as much part of the life of Christians as
it was for the people of the Bible.

Fifteenth Sunday of the Year

Amos 7:12-15; Ps 84 (in part); Eph 1:3-14; Mk 6:7-13.

The question may have arisen in your minds before now: What
is the link between the church now and Jesus Christ, his teaching
and his work of salvation? It is to be found here in this gospel
passage which is among the more important of the gospels of
Mark, Matthew and Luke, and in a different way and in different words we find it in the gospel according to John: Jesus says
to his disciples: 'You did not choose me, but I chose you and I
commissioned you to go out and to bear fruit, fruit that will last.'
Like Amos, who was taken from his flocks and sent to prophesy
to the people of Israel, so the disciples were 'taken'. This miscel-
laneous collection of men were taken from their fishing boats,
the counting desk, from their village tasks, and who knows
what else. Like Amos they were called, like him they were sent,
and like him they were sent to proclaim repentance, but unlike
him they were also sent to heal the sick and cast out evil spirits.
Under the guidance of Jesus they were bringing in the kingdom.

This was but a beginning. For two or perhaps three years they
followed Jesus, they listened to his word, they came to know him
and became deeply attached to him. From him they received
special instruction, as we read, 'To you it is given to know the
mystery of the kingdom of God', but those outside (those not of
the Twelve) were to learn only through parables (4:11, 12). Later
on, at the Last Supper, Jesus told his disciples that they would be
given the Holy Spirit who would teach them all things and bring
to their remembrance all that he had said to them. After he had
gone, he would send the Holy Spirit who would lead them into
all truth.

But we know that, alas, at the supreme test when their Master
was taken from them and tortured and crucified, they all aban-

doned him. But their faith was revived by their sight of the Risen
Lord. From him they received their final commission: 'Go out
into the whole world and proclaim the gospel to every creature'.
They were to instruct, to baptise, and Jesus promised to be with
them to the end of the ages. Then at Pentecost there came their
final confirmation. As Jesus had told them, they were to be his
witnesses to the ends of the earth and, after ten days, the Holy
Spirit came upon them as it were in tongues of fire.

This had an immediate effect. Peter went out and preached to
the crowd, proclaiming that Jesus was Christ and Lord, that he
had suffered, died and rose again for them and for their salvation. He called to the people to repent and, as we read in the Acts
of the Apostles, large numbers did so and were incorporated
into the church by baptism and the eucharist. In the same place
we read that the new converts came together, that is, they joined
the assembly and, with the other Christians, listened to the teaching of the apostles and prayed and took part in the 'breaking of
bread', that is the eucharist. Thus was the church born.

What was begun then has continued ever since. The word of
God has been proclaimed, people all over the world have believed and been converted, they have received the baptism of
the Lord, and as the Christian community they have celebrated
the eucharist.

There we have the vital links between Jesus Christ, his apostles
and the church today. The living word of God has been handed
on to us throughout the ages and that is why we can believe. The
very life of Christ has been conveyed to us through the eucharist
and the other sacraments and that is how we can live as
Christians here and now.

All this is the truth we hold and the treasure that has been committed to us. Relying on this foundation, we can be confident in
our faith and secure in mind that we have the basis for Christian
living. The world has taken other ways, it poses strains and
temptations on us, but let us not be like the apostles when they
ran away but like them when they proclaimed Christ and in the
end died rather than deny the Christ who had saved them, the
Christ who is the Saviour of the world.

Sixteenth Sunday of the Year

Jer 23:1-6; Ps 22; Eph 2:13-18; Mk 6:30-34.

In some parts of the church, the priest in charge of a parish is called a pastor, which is really a Latin word meaning 'shepherd'. The texts of today are very much about shepherding, the care of the people committed to the parish priest (the pastor) and his assistants, if any.

This is true of the passage from Jeremiah where he is taking a very dim view of the shepherds he is talking about: 'Doom for the shepherds who allow the flock of my pasture to be destroyed and scattered.' He was in fact speaking of the kings of Israel and their many wrong-doings and neglect they had been guilty of for centuries. The rulers of Israel were both kings and shepherds, as the psalm reminds us: 'The Lord is my shepherd' and what is more, as we see from the lives of David and Solomon, they were priest-kings who led worship in the tabernacle and the Temple. The moral well-being of the people was to some extent regarded as dependent on the conduct of their king. They were ministers of God for the people.

As in so many human arrangements, it did not work out like that and now on the eve of the exile and captivity of the king and his people, Jeremiah utters his rebuke but also looks on to the day when God will raise up a king who will be wise, honest and just. He will indeed be a descendant of David for Jesus is of the line and house of David whose throne and kingdom he will inherit but transform.

It is however Jesus the pastor, the shepherd, we meet in the gospel story today. For some months now he has been teaching the people, healing their sick and calling disciples. These he has sent out on their first mission to do very much the work he had been doing, and now that they have returned he invites them to come to a place apart to rest and pray. But they are interrupted. The people clamour round Jesus and his disciples and Jesus 'took pity on them because they were like sheep without a shepherd'. They wanted to hear him, so he taught them but it was this same crowd, it seems, whom in the next chapter he fed with the five loaves and two fish. That was his shepherding: food for the spirit and food for the body.

The work of the pastor or parish priest is the same today, although he can never hope to perform as Jesus did or even as his disciples would do after the resurrection. For we can discern in the gospel account what is already suggested in the passage from Jeremiah, the pastor must be with the people. Through them says God, 'I will gather them … I will bring them back to their pastures.' This Jesus would do through his life, his teaching and by his death and resurrection; he would 'gather together in unity the scattered children of God' (Jn 11:25) and when he was 'lifted up' on the cross and in the resurrection he would draw everyone to himself (12:32).

This indicates something of the depth and breadth of the shepherding of Jesus, of whom the pastor in his parish is but a faint and imperfect image. He must be with his people, understanding and sharing to the best of his ability their joys, their sorrows and their hopes.

To them too he must deliver the word, the word of God, mindful always that it is God's word and not his own that he was to communicate. For them Christ, through ordination, has put in his hands the celebration of the eucharist and the other sacraments through which Jesus Christ our Saviour communicates his life to us. Through the sacrament of reconciliation and his reconciling work in the community, the priest seeks to bring together those who are divided in opinion or at enmity with one another. He is with the sick, offering them the holy anointing, and he is with the dying absolving them and giving them the viaticum that will accompany them into the next world. With the local community he offers the eucharist for them and, when they die, he prays with the bereaved at the grave that the deceased will enter into the everlasting light and peace of heaven.

There are many other activities, very mundane activities, that are forced on the priest by the demands of modern life and he may not be very good at handling them, but if he is with his people, if he is always ready to offer them what Christ has put into his hands, then he will be a true minister of his Lord, reflecting his compassion and his love.

Seventeenth Sunday of the Year

2 Kings 4:42-44; Ps 144 (in part); Eph 4:1-6; Jn 6:1-15.

For the next five Sundays the gospel readings are taken from St John, partly because Mark's gospel, the shortest of the four, does not provide enough material for all the Sundays of this year. There is another reason too. This series of readings from the long chapter 6 gives us almost the whole of Jesus' teaching on the eucharist, which lies at the very heart of the church's life.

You will remember that last week's gospel (from Mark) ended with the saying that Jesus had pity on the people and taught them at great length. Today's gospel in a way takes up from there. After feeding the people's minds, he feeds their bodies.

This feeding of the five thousand at first sight seems to be an ordinary meal. The people sat down and ate, probably not wondering where the bread and fish came from. But, as recorded in the gospel, and apart from the miraculous element, it has certain special features. First, Jesus takes the loaves and the fishes, and as the other gospels record, he looked up to heaven. Secondly, he tells his disciples to distribute the food to the people. From the rest of this chapter of St John we shall see that Jesus wanted to lead the people's minds from earthly bread to heavenly bread and this he did through both words and actions. This will be unfolded in the coming Sundays.

In the gospel accounts, we can see a certain pattern of words and actions and that is what I want to talk about today.

In Mark's gospel Jesus first taught the people at length and only then multiplied the loaves and fishes. If we think about this for a moment, this is a pattern of the Mass we celebrate every Sunday. We first hear the word of God and then celebrate the sacrament of the eucharist. These two parts, said Vatican II, make up one whole and both are necessary in the celebration of the Mass. Why?

The word of God – that is a very important term, one of great depth. As we read in the Letter to the Hebrews, the word of God is a living word. It is like a sharp sword penetrating into our inmost being, if we will let it. Jesus Christ makes himself present to us by his word. As the Constitution on the Liturgy states, 'He is present in his word since it is he himself who speaks when the holy scriptures are read in church', and again, 'In the liturgy God speaks to his people and Christ is still proclaiming his gospel.' This is the word by which, as Christians, we are meant to live and, whatever the difficulties of understanding that sometimes occur, we should listen, take the word, the message, to heart and make it our own. We can help ourselves by reading over the texts of the day at home before Mass and better still become familiar with the Bible by reading it. Then we shall find that in some ways the Old Testament foreshadows the New as is suggested by the readings of today.

First there is the story of Elisha and the feeding of some people with twenty barley loaves. This is seen as foreshadowing the multiplication of the loaves and fishes in the gospel. It may seem a bit far-fetched, but it is meant to lead us to the thought that in the Old Testament God cared for his people too. This is the message of the psalm which links the reading from the Old Testament with that of the New. We rejoice in the generosity of God: 'All your creatures thank you, Lord ... You give them their food in due time,' and we acknowledge God's goodness as we pray, 'You open wide your hand, O Lord, and grant us our desires.'

But the generosity of God far outstrips anything either Elisha or the psalmist could ever have imagined. In the accounts of the Last Supper, we find Jesus giving *himself* to us: 'Take and eat, This is my body; Take and drink, This is my blood,' the blood of the covenant, the covenant made by God with the people of Israel so long ago and that is now being brought to completion by the self-giving of Jesus in the supper and on the cross.

These considerations suggest the second reason for the proclamation of God's word in the Mass. It prepares us for and leads us into the celebration of the sacrament, into our self-offering through Christ, our High Priest, who is ever living to make intercession for us with his Father. It leads us on further to holy communion when we receive, in deed and in truth, the body and blood of our Saviour: 'Anyone who eats my flesh and drinks my blood has eternal life ...'

The proclamation of God's word and the offering of Christ's sacrament-sacrifice when we receive him into ourselves – that is the Mass and through it we are able to give thanks, eucharist, to God our Father through Jesus Christ for the immeasurable riches of this sacrament.

Eighteenth Sunday of the Year

Ex 16:2-4, 12-15; Ps 77 (in part); Eph 4:17, 20-24; Jn 6:24-35.

There is an old saying, a respectable saying, that we are saved by faith and the sacraments of the faith. And sometimes in the past the faith element of salvation has been underplayed or forgotten.

Yet, as we look at the four gospels and St Paul's account of the eucharist in his First Letter to the Corinthians, we become aware that in these writings, as in their preaching, they were expressing the faith of the church of the Apostles. As we examine the writings of the Fathers of the Church who came after them, we find the same unwavering faith in the presence of Christ in the eucharist. Later on, in the Middle Ages, there were indeed disputes about the eucharist, but the faith and teaching of the church remained what it had been from the beginning.

Here, in this part of chapter 6 of the gospel according to John, Jesus is emphasising the importance of faith, of faith in himself and of faith in what he did, or was going to do.

But first let us recall what had gone before this passage of the gospel. Jesus had fed the five thousand and then escaped from them because he was afraid they wanted to make him a king. They follow him and now Jesus speaks at length to them. He tries to raise their minds from earthly bread to heavenly bread, from the sign to the reality: 'Do not work for food that cannot last but for the kind of food the Son of Man is offering you.' When the people ask what this work is, Jesus replies that the first work is faith: 'You must believe in the one God has sent.'

What does this imply? What does it mean? If they were to accept anything he said or did, they must accept him for what he is. They must acknowledge that he came forth from the Father: 'I came forth from the Father', and elsewhere 'I came to do the will of my Father', and the doing of the divine will has been his very life, the very 'food' of his whole life. The people ask for a sign that they may believe in him and Jesus replies that he himself is the sign of God, that he himself and his whole redeeming work is the sign that his Father loves the people: 'God so loved the world as to give his only Son that all who believe in him might be saved.' So secondly, Jesus is asking them to accept him and all he said and did, as also his sufferings, his death and resurrection that would take place later on. If they can believe in him, accept him in faith as the Son of God, as the redeemer of the human race, they will be able to accept him as the bread of life that far transcends the manna in the desert, or anything they could imagine. 'I am the bread of life. He who comes to me will never be hungry; he who *believes* in me will never thirst'.

As Jesus, all through this passage, was leading the people on to faith in himself, so is he leading us on today to a deeper faith in himself. He is inviting us to give ourselves and our lives as he gave himself to us and for us. It is not surprising then that Sunday by Sunday we are asked to profess and renew our faith, which we do by listening to the gospel, to the homily that expounds it, and in the Creed. What we have heard, what we have listened to and tried to make our own, we now proclaim by word, publicly. We believe, we say, in God the Father who made all things seen and unseen, we believe in Jesus Christ his Son whom he sent, Jesus Christ who became one of us and who suffered, died and rose again for us and for our salvation. And so that we might not be orphaned, so that his presence could remain with us, he sent the Holy Spirit, the giver of life and the divine remembrancer of the church.

From our profession of faith we move to the celebration of the eucharist, to the offering of ourselves with and through Jesus and the reception of him into our hearts and lives.

That is the Mass. Let us listen, let us give ourselves and let us receive the body and blood of Christ with faith and reverence.

Nineteenth Sunday of the Year

1 Kings 19:4-8; Ps 33:2-9; Eph 4:30, 5:2; Jn 6:41-51.

It may surprise some of you if I tell you that there was a time when people went to holy communion very rarely, two or three times a year, or at most eight times, on the greater feasts. There were those, some of them theologians, who ought to have known better, who taught that holy communion was the reward of virtuous living rather than the means for the ordinary Christian of living in Christ. This sort of thinking has now disappeared, largely thanks to the strong recommendations of Pope Pius X in the first decade of this century to frequent communion. Now it is taken for granted that when we go to Mass we receive holy communion. It is now clearly seen that communion is the food of the spiritual life, and that is what is emphasised by the scriptures today.

As an introduction to the subject, we have the story of Elijah who was in great distress, his life was threatened, he escaped into the wilderness and there, as we have heard, he was mysteriously fed, and in the strength of that food he walked for forty days and forty nights to Mount Horeb where God had revealed himself to Moses long centuries before. Elijah would be another Moses and would continue his work long after the forty days and forty nights.

Then we note that the last sentence of the gospel is about the holy eucharist as food: 'Anyone who eats this bread will live for ever; and the bread that I shall give is my flesh for the life of the world'.

We have followed the narrative of St John's gospel from the feeding of the five thousand to Jesus' insistence that faith in him-

self was an indispensable condition for accepting him for what
he was, the One sent by his Father, and now we are approaching
the point where he offers himself as food. This the people could
not understand and they complained and questioned and became disgruntled. They thought they knew who Jesus was very
well. Was he not the son of Joseph, the village carpenter of
Nazareth, didn't they know his mother and their siblings who
lived round about? Who was he to make the extraordinary statement that he had come down from heaven? Was he a greater
man than Moses who had given their ancestors manna in the
desert?

Once again Jesus tries to raise their minds to a higher level of understanding, an understanding that would in fact be faith. This
can only come from the Father; no one can come to him 'unless
he is drawn by the Father'. If they are willing to be drawn, they
will be taught by God and hear the teaching of the Father. And
what will that teaching be? They will learn that Jesus is the bread
of life, the bread that gives life, a bread that so far transcends the
manna that it will give them an everlasting life: 'Anyone who
eats this bread will live for ever.' To this we can add the saying
in the next part of the gospel: 'If you do not eat the flesh of the
Son of Man and drink his blood you will not have life in you'.

When all this is put so starkly and strongly, it almost shocks us,
familiar as the teaching may be. But perhaps we can understand
now all the better how important it is to have faith in Jesus
Christ, in his word and all that he was and did. Theologians
may, and rightly so, discuss the manner of Christ's presence
under the appearance of bread and wine, but both they and we
are finally dependent on the word of Jesus which has been faith-
fully handed down to us through the centuries.

Bread and life, these words recur through the gospel passage,
and we can, I think, discern why Jesus at the Last Supper chose
bread and wine to be in the holy eucharist. Bread and wine were,
and to a great extent still are, the staples of life in the Medi-
terranean region, and Jesus clearly wanted us to understand that
he himself is the food that gives us life, his life, a life which sustains our Christian living until we die: 'Anyone who does eat my

flesh and drink my blood' under the appearance of bread and wine, 'has eternal life'. It is a life-in-Christ that continues until Jesus raises us up 'at the last day'.

But at the Last Supper the bread that was given was broken bread and the wine that was given was a symbol of the outpouring of the life of Jesus as he lay on the cross. Jesus was giving his whole self on the cross, and what we receive in holy communion is the whole Christ, the sacrificed Christ who bore the marks of his wounds of the crucifixion and, if he is the High Priest with and through whom we offer ourselves, he is also the victim who gave up his life for us. To receive communion is to be united with the Christ who suffered, died and rose again for us and who is ever-living to make intercession for us before the throne of his Father.

Through the eucharist, then, Mass and communion, we are in Christ and Christ is in us, but it is the living, crucified and risen Christ whom we receive and who lives in us. For this and all that it implies we can make our own the psalm of today: 'Bless the Lord at all times, his praise always on my lips … Taste and see that the Lord is good, He is happy who seeks refuge in him.'

Twentieth Sunday of the Year

Proverbs 9:1-6; Ps 33 (in part); Eph 5:15-20; Jn 6:51-58.

We come to Jesus by faith, he offers himself to us as the food of life, he makes himself present to us, he is always with us and this he began to do when he offered himself *for* us.

To put the matter in more familiar terms, Jesus is present under the appearance of bread and wine, we receive him in holy communion and are made one with him, but, as we say, we offer the eucharist. Or as the catechism said, it is a sacrifice. It is this last that is suggested in the gospel passage of today.

For long it has been noted that, in the gospel according to John, there is no account of the institution of the Last Supper. There is indeed the moving account of Jesus washing the feet of his disciples and here he is acting as their servant, and as the servant of

God and his people he offered himself on the cross. He had come, as he said, not to be served but to serve and give his life as a ransom for the multitude (Mk 10:45). His action was a fore-shadowing of his death. If we look into today's gospel we shall find that Jesus is speaking of his self-offering and his death.

It is true that his meaning is partly obscured in the text, but when Jesus was using the words 'give', 'flesh' and even 'for', he was speaking of giving himself for the salvation, the 'life', of the world: 'I am the living bread … the bread that I shall give is my flesh' for 'the life of the world'. As we read in Luke's gospel, 'This is my body which will be given up for you.' This my body, my living flesh, will be handed over to death, as it was on the cross. All here is active, as according to John, Jesus was through-out his passion, and Jesus is active in the Mass. He is not primar-ily the object of adoration, and even in communion it is he who gives himself to us through the hands of the priest. As he was of-fering himself to his Father and for us on the cross, so he is active now in the eucharist, drawing us into his eternal self-offering which endures for ever.

Like the first Christians who had celebrated the eucharist from the beginning (Acts 2:42), we too remember the words of the other gospels: 'This is my body', my whole person that is given over to death for you; 'This is my blood', my life that is poured out in sacrifice for you for the taking away of sins. We remember too that these words occurred in the blessing prayer over the bread and the thanksgiving prayer over the cup, and in this very gospel of St John we have heard how Jesus 'gave thanks' over the loaves before they were distributed to the waiting people.

In more formal manner, we do the same in the celebration of the Mass. After the liturgy of the word we come to its climax, the Eucharistic Prayer, The Thanksgiving: 'Let us give thanks to the Lord our God', a thanksgiving in which you join, 'We lift them up to the Lord'. There follows the first part of the Eucharistic Prayer (the Preface) when we praise and thank God for the sav-ing works of his Son, Jesus Christ. To this we all respond with the hymn of praise, 'Holy, holy, holy Lord …'. The thanksgiving continues as the Holy Spirit is invoked so that the bread and wine may become the body and blood of Christ. The words of institution, 'This is my body ... This is the cup of my blood', are said and thus we make the memory of what Jesus did at the Last Supper, repeating his injunction, 'Do this in memory of me'. This is continues as the church calls to mind the passion, death, resurrection of Jesus Christ, and, looking on to his second coming, offers to the Father through Jesus Christ 'in thanksgiving this holy and living sacrifice'. The prayer then looks on to holy communion when we pray that we 'may be filled with the Holy Spirit, and become one body, one spirit in Christ'. The whole prayer comes to an end with an ascription of glory and honour, through Jesus Christ in union with the Holy Spirit, to the Father.

And so we come to the moment of communion, having in our minds the words of the gospel, 'He who eats my flesh and drinks my blood lives in me and I live in him.' Union with Christ, that is the end-purpose of our celebration of the eucharist. It is thus that the church is built up, it is thus that all are drawn into union with one another, for though we are many we are all one body 'because we all have a share in this one loaf' (1 Cor 10:17).

Twenty-first Sunday of the Year

Jos 24:1, 3-15, 18; Ps 33 (in part); Eph 5:21-32; Jn 6:60-69.

It comes as something of a shock to hear that there were disciples of Jesus who had listened to his words, who had known him, perhaps for some time, and yet turned away from him and left him. Evidently something more than listening or liking was necessary and this is what the passage from St John is about today.

The reading from Joshua suggests that as then, so long ago when the people of Israel had captured much of the Holy Land, when even more important than that, God had bound them to himself by covenant and led them from slavery into freedom, there were those who wished to abandon the God who had saved them. As we know from their later history, some did, but today we hear the reply of those who were determined to remain faithful: 'We too will serve the Lord for he is our God.' Peter in the gospel, the leader of the Twelve who represented the twelve tribes of Israel, makes a similar reply, 'Lord, who shall we go to? You have the message of eternal life, and we believe ...'

In a way, this passage brings us back to the earliest part of this long discourse of the sixth chapter of St John: the one 'who believed in me will never thirst' for Jesus is 'the bread of life' and everyone who believes in him 'has eternal life'. Only those who believe in Jesus, only those who accept in faith his saving work that was being accomplished before their eyes, only those who accept him as the One sent by the Father, would be able to believe that he was 'the living bread come down from heaven' and that the bread was 'his flesh for the life of the world'. What was required was a total commitment to Jesus the Christ as Word of God, as Son of God, as Saviour, if his followers or anyone else were to be 'in him' drawing their life from him: 'As I who am sent by the Father myself draw life from the Father, so whoever eats me will draw life from me.'

But as the reception of the Holy Spirit was necessary for this complete adherence to Jesus and all he was and stood for ('It is the Spirit who gives life'), so is the Spirit necessary if we are to believe that Jesus, the bread of life, is present and active in the eucharist that we celebrate today. In relation to our understanding of the eucharist, these words of Jesus have another relevance for us. The eucharist is a 'mystery of faith', we can never fully understand it but it is of crucial importance that we should not *mis*-understand it. 'It is the spirit that gives life, the flesh has nothing to offer.' A materialistic way of thinking of the eucharist would lead us into the gravest error. If by the eucharist we are made one with Christ, we are united with him through the symbols of bread and wine, and these symbols are not empty symbols as if they were some sort of images of the body and blood of Jesus. It is his power that makes them efficacious symbols, actually making present Christ and his redeeming love and communicating to us his whole self really and truly in holy communion. If you like, through the symbol of bread we, as St John says, eat the flesh of Christ and through the symbol of wine we drink his blood. As I have said before, we receive the whole living Christ who was sacrificed for our salvation and who now gives himself to us in and through the holy eucharist.

The eucharist is a great mystery and it is no wonder in the end that some of Jesus' followers could walk no more with him. Let us put ourselves with Peter, who said, 'You have the message of eternal life.' Jesus has the message that gives a life that begins here and endures into eternity; because of this 'we believe; we know that you are the holy one of God'. Because of a faith like that, we can believe that Jesus in the eucharist is eternally drawing us into his sacrifice, his self-offering, and that we receive as the food and drink of our Christian, spiritual life, the sacrament that is the pledge and promise of life with God to all eternity, for Jesus will 'raise us up on the last day'.

Twenty-second Sunday of the Year

Deut 4:1, 2, 6-8; Ps 14:2-5; Jas 1:17-27; Mk 7:1-8, 14, 15, 21-23.

I wonder if this gospel has anything to say to us? It seems to be addressed to the scribes, the religious lawyers, and to the strict sect of the Pharisees. It would be easy to bash the scribes and Pharisees and indeed the gospels have harsh things to say about them. But we have more fruitful things to do.

In any case, they were trying to protect and uphold the holy law, the Torah, which they and all Jews believed had been delivered to them by God through Moses, as we can see from the first reading. Their fault was that they imposed on the people what Jesus in the gospel of today calls man-made additions. As we read in the gospel of Matthew, they imposed heavy burdens on the people, they took tenths of the smallest growing things like mint and cumin (a little seed-bearing plant), and they did not lift so much as a finger to help them in their needs. It was a system that made life very uncomfortable for ordinary Jews. If they did not wash their hands before eating, or sprinkle themselves with water when coming home from market, they were considered unclean, unable to take part in worship, among other things.

There was something worse. As we read in the next part of this chapter (not given in the Missal), there were those who perverted the law. This said, 'Honour your father and your mother', but instead of supporting them in their old age, these people said all their goods were *Corban* that is, dedicated to God, with the consequences that they could not give any of it away to anyone. This, Jesus says, was a striking example of their hypocrisy. Their radical error was that they concentrated on mere words, on externals, on washings and sprinklings, on not touching unclean people, sinners or the dead. That is why Jesus reminded them of the saying of the prophets:

These people honour me only with lip-service,
while their hearts are far from me.

The service of God, the worship of God, was not for them a movement of mind and heart towards God, but the keeping of certain human customs.

What then had this gospel to say to us? Are we likely to fall into the same error?

Years ago, as many of you will remember, there were a lot of church laws, a law about abstaining from meat on Fridays, a law about fasting in Lent and some other days. There was, and still is, an obligation to go to Mass on Sundays and certain other days unless we have a reasonable excuse. There were other laws of a similar sort and there was some misunderstanding of what they involved and what was their purpose. They were in fact intended to hold up to us an ideal: the Christian life requires some discipline, some self-denial, if we are to be true followers of Christ. Some did not understand this and, unhappily, if they had eaten by mistake the smallest bit of meat on a Friday they would rush off to confession thinking they had committed a sin.

Some years ago the Church abolished the laws on abstinence and left only two days of fasting and abstinence in the year, Ash Wednesday and Good Friday. The church wants us to practice self-discipline for that is the only kind of discipline worth having. Deeper still, she has recalled us to one of the basic teaching of Christ: 'If anyone would come after me, let him take up his cross daily and deny himself and follow me.' And St Paul was constantly calling us to be Christ-like in the depths of our being. He himself prayed that he would know Christ and the power of his resurrection and share his sufferings so that he might become like him in death (Phil 3:10, 11). If religious practice does not come from the heart, it is empty, a fake. That is why Jesus could exclaim, 'Nothing that goes into a man from outside can make him unclean; it is the things that come our of men's hearts that make him unclean.'

Interior religion, the religion of mind and heart, that is what is important and it is important for our worship too. The obligation to celebrate the Mass week by week is still an obligation, but it is not just an obligation. As the church has made very clear, if the Mass is to be a genuine act of worship, it must involve our minds, our hearts, our whole selves and we are urged to express our interior worship of God in prayer, in action, by taking part and by offering ourselves and our lives to the Father through his Son, Jesus Christ, by the power of the Holy Spirit. Let us beware. External actions, rites and gestures are not enough but if we give *ourselves*, in and through the Mass, then our worship is genuine and through it we shall receive the great gifts of God.

Twenty-third Sunday of the Year

Is 35:4-7; Ps 145:7-10; Jas 2:1-5; Mk 7:31-37.

'The Day of the Lord' is one of the great phrases of the prophets of the Old Testament and it has several aspects. Sometimes the prophets foretell a day of wrath and calamity, a day of terror and judgement of those who have not been faithful to God. But sometimes there is a gleam of light shining through the dark clouds and a Messiah, the Anointed of the Lord, is promised, as in today's passage from Isaiah: 'Vengeance is coming, retribution is coming': that is the gloomy part. But the prophet also has a message of comfort: 'God is coming to save you.' Here the Day of the Lord is the day when the Anointed One (Messiah) will come. It is a day that lies in the far distant future, a future that goes beyond the reckoning of the prophet. Only in the New Testament with the coming of Christ-Messiah will that day dawn when he ushers in the reign of God, the messianic age, the age of the church which will last until the end of time. Then the saving work of Christ will be completed, then will all have been accomplished and he will hand over the earthly kingdom of the church to his Father. At that time – or out of time – it will be united with the heavenly city when there will be no more sickness or death or weeping or mourning, but all who have been faithful will see God as he is and seeing him will become like him and be filled with joy.

At the same time, and while proclaiming the Day of the Lord, the prophet describes what the Messiah is to do and sketches out his portrait: 'Then the eyes of the blind will be opened, the ears of the deaf unsealed and the tongues of the dumb will sing for joy.' Elsewhere, a later prophet completes the picture: 'The spirit of the Lord is upon me, the Lord has anointed me. He has sent me to bring good news to the afflicted, to soothe the broken-hearted, to proclaim liberty to captives, release to those who are in prison (and) to proclaim a year of favour from the Lord', words that Luke will put on the lips of Jesus at the beginning of his mission (4:16-19 and cf Is 61:1,2). With Jesus, the Day of the Lord has come and we see the prophecy being fulfilled in the gospel. Jesus is bringing in the reign of God, he is gradually rolling back the forces of evil, he is beginning to break the power of sin, suffering and illness and this, his redeeming work, will continue to the end of time.

We may be prompted to ask: how is this work continued? Let us return to the gospel narrative, not only here but in other places too. When Jesus is healing he sometimes says just a word, some-times he lays his hand on the sick person and sometimes, as here and in the healing of the man born blind in the gospel of St John, he goes through an elaborate process. He puts his fingers into the deaf man's ears, he touches his tongue with spittle, he prays, looking up to heaven, and then he speaks the word of power, 'Be opened.'

Why did he do all this? We cannot be sure but I think he wanted us to understand that his work of healing and redeeming could take quite concrete forms. With such forms we are in fact quite familiar. By water and the word we are made sons and daughters of God, by anointing with chrism in confirmation we are inserted more deeply into the church, and Jesus gave us bread and wine, symbols of himself and his self-offering, so that we could continue to do what he told us to do at the Last Supper. These we call sacraments. They are something that we can see, something we can handle, something that impinges on our senses, showing us that the healing, forgiving and loving Christ is still among us. In a way, the sacraments are extensions of Christ who united human flesh, human nature, with his divine nature, who in that flesh suffered, died and rose again, and so brought into existence the great sacrament, the church, which is the radical sacrament, for through it Christ communicates himself and his grace to us now. For our part, this way of sanctifying us also shows that both body and soul are being redeemed, that we can be and are united wholly as human beings to Christ and that we in turn can give our whole selves to God through him.

Today, then, we give thanks to an understanding and gentle Christ who has shown us this way to salvation. Through the material we can be raised to the spiritual, through the human Christ we can be made sharers in his divinity, through the visible, the church and its sacraments, we can be raised up to God here and now, and at the end in our very bodies we shall see his glory and be filled with unending joy.

Twenty-fourth Sunday of the Year

Is 50:5-9; Ps 114 (in part); Jas 2:14-18; Mk 8:27-35.

If, when we hear this gospel, we recall the commission to Peter in Matthew's gospel, we may find Mark's account of the same incident puzzling or disconcerting. But Mark, even though, as it is thought, a disciple of Peter, was not here concerned with the promise that Peter would be the foundation stone of the church. He was concerned with the passion and death of Jesus which of course he knew about and, with all the early Christians, he had been pondering on for years. It is about the passion and death that the church would have us think today, as is indicated by the choice of the first reading from Isaiah. It is the third of the Songs of the Suffering Servant, that mysterious character of the Old Testament, whom the first Christians identified as Jesus. As in the gospel, we read that the servant suffered insult and violence: 'I offered my back to those who struck me, my cheeks to those who tore at my beard. I did not cover my face from insult and spittle.'

With this as a guide, we can see how carefully Mark composed his narrative. Jesus has now for some time been preaching and teaching and moving among many people. His words and his actions have raised questions: Who was he? Where did he get authority to teach? Was he a new prophet? Jesus summarises these questions and then, turning to his disciples, he asks them what they think. Peter, answering for the rest, makes the great confession of faith, 'You are the Messiah.' That seemed and indeed was the right answer, but 'Messiah', what did that word mean? What sort of man would the Messiah be? Several ideas were current but one, that seems to have dominated the thought of those who considered the matter at all, was that he would be an earthly king with great power, who would conquer the occupying Roman power and set up a new Israel where God would reign. It was because of these notions that Jesus was always reluctant to acknowledge directly that he was the Messiah and here, significantly, we hear him speak of the 'Son of Man' in reply to Peter's 'Messiah'.

What sort of man then would the true Messiah be? The answer comes in words that are no doubt coloured by Mark's experience. The Messiah was the 'Son of Man' who would suffer, be put to death and after a short time be raised again. The destiny, the vocation of the Son of Man, was to suffer and to die; as we read in this same gospel, 'to give his life as a ransom for many', that is, for all. But in the tradition about the Messiah there was nothing about a suffering Messiah and Peter was deeply shocked. Speaking, it seems again for the rest, he rebukes Jesus for having such thoughts. Alas, alas, he was totally wrong. Neither he nor the other disciples had yet come to understand that the Messiah's 'kingdom was not of this world' and worse, that they were trying to deflect Jesus from the mission he had from his Father. The whole purpose of Jesus' life was to do the will of his Father who had sent him into the world to die for sinners and to re-unite them to God. Hence comes in turn Jesus' rebuke to Peter. He is a Satan, an adversary of the will and purpose of God. The way Peter was thinking was not God's way of thinking. It was so very different from his thinking when Jesus commended him for his confession of faith, 'Blessed are you, Simon son of Jonah ... It was not flesh and blood that revealed this to you but my Father in heaven.'

The theme of suffering or, better perhaps, of self-giving is continued in the last part of the gospel. Discipleship involves suffering of whatever sort and self-giving, for we give up (self-denial) so that we may give more effectively. This is the fundamental 'imitation of Christ', a giving of self to others and for others, as Jesus did. This comes from the heart and then issues into action. We are of course infinitely less than Christ and anything we can do is done through him and by his enabling grace. If we want to 'save' our life, hoard it up so to say, and shut ourselves away from others, our life will become sterile and without fruit. But if we are willing to 'lose' our life for Jesus Christ and his people, then indeed riches, unknown to us, will be ours.

Twenty-fifth Sunday of the Year

Wis 2:12, 17-20; Ps 53 (in part); Jas 3:16, 4:3; Mk 9:30-37.

There are times when God seems far away, even absent from our world, times when Jesus seems to us not much more than a remote historic figure. We may feel that in the world in which we live God is conspicuously absent. There are those jockeying for power, lobbying the powerful, thrusting down rivals or suspected rivals so that one or other can get his foot on a higher rung of the ladder to what is regarded as 'success'.

One of the ugliest features of our society, not only in this country but elsewhere, is the desire and the effort to exclude Asians, blacks and Jews, as well as others who do not fit in with certain preconceived notions. The whole phenomenon is called Racism and, though we would like to think our country is free of it, we know that it is not and that there are certain groups who would like to kick out all they consider 'aliens', even if they have been born here and lived here all their lives.

Thirdly, in recent years we have heard of appalling brutality to children, even to babies, and other kinds of abuse that are hard to listen to, stories that make us wonder what the human race is coming to. No doubt it is not helpful to be alarmist or to condemn our own times as the worst that have ever been, but I do not think it is an exaggeration to say that we are witnessing a breakdown of morality over a very wide extent of human behaviour.

In direct contrast to these ugly features are the words of Christ we have heard in today's gospel: 'Anyone who welcomes one of these little children in my name welcomes me.' A little later in the gospel we hear Jesus' condemnation of those who would lead astray 'the little ones', including the unprotected: 'Anyone who is the downfall of one of these little ones who have faith, would be better thrown into the sea with a great millstone round his neck.' It is thus that Jesus expresses his abhorrence of the abuse of children or the defenceless and of violence done to them.

Let us however look into the first saying of Jesus: 'Anyone who welcomes one of these little children in my name welcomes me.' 'Welcome' means much more than saying 'Good day' to someone; it means receiving, accepting, a willingness to accept them into one's own life if necessary. When we do this, as the saying of Jesus tells us, we are welcoming him in them, we are finding him in them, we are becoming aware that Jesus Christ is in others, as is emphasised in another saying of Jesus: 'Where two or three are gathered together in my name, I am there among them'.

There is no doubt that seeing and finding Jesus in others is very difficult. There are all those characteristics and habits in others that we find off-putting, there are those people we find it almost impossible to like, there are the monsters and murderers of our time who fill us with detestation. We may suppose that they have driven out Christ by sin, though it is not for us to judge. On the other hand, there are those people we meet whom we sense are holy. We know that association with them does one good. We are glad to have been in their presence. Through them we have been encouraged to pray better and to try and come closer to God. In all this we can be sure that Christ is present, present in them and through them in us.

If we cannot aspire to all this, if we cannot recognise Christ in others, if we feel like condemning certain people, let us remember that Jesus 'received' the sinner-woman Magdalen, that on the cross he welcomed the robber who asked for forgiveness, and that he was accused of welcoming sinners and sitting down at table with them. If Jesus welcomed such people and so many others, we can pray that through his welcomings we can do likewise. Or, to put the matter in more conventional language, we can pray that he will give us the grace to see him and welcome him in others, whoever they may be.

Meanwhile it would be as well to realise that every Sunday at Mass we are welcoming, accepting others. Before communion, as a sign of reconciliation and unity we exchange the Peace which in Latin is called *osculum pacis*, the Kiss of peace, by which we welcome and accept those near us and then together we go to receive the bread and the wine that makes us one body in Christ. Therein is the source of our ability to see Christ in all others and to receive and welcome them into our lives and hearts.

Twenty-sixth Sunday of the Year

Num 11:25-29; Ps 18 (in part); Jas 5:1-6; Mk 9:38-43, 45, 47, 48.

At first sight, this gospel seems to be made up of three different groups of sayings, as indeed it is. But if we remember the prediction of the passion in last week's gospel, I think we can see how these sayings are connected. The reading from the Book of Numbers gives us the first hint. Unauthorised men are proclaiming the word of God and Moses sees no reason for stopping them: 'If only', he says, 'the whole people of the Lord were prophets and the Lord gave his spirit to them all.'

The predictions of the passion of Jesus I have mentioned included, of course, a reference to the resurrection, and the resurrection of our Lord Jesus Christ marked the beginning of a new age when the good news of salvation would be preached throughout the world. As we know from St Paul, there were others than the apostles who were preaching the gospel but Paul said that it was not so much a question of who was preaching as that what they were preaching was in fact the teaching of Jesus Christ which had been handed down from the beginning. Writing to the Phillipians, he said, I know that some are preaching the gospel as rivals but what did that matter? What mattered was that in every way, though without false pretences or untruth, the gospel of Christ should be proclaimed (1:15-19). His words seem to echo those of Jesus in the gospel of today: 'If anyone is casting out evil spirits (and perhaps preaching) in my name, do not stop him.' He is unlikely to speak evil of Christ, for 'those who are not against us are for us.' Although the preaching of the gospel can be and has been abused throughout the ages, the saying of Jesus seems relevant to our time when there are many varieties of Christians preaching Christ, even if they are oversimplifying badly. Their message may well be incomplete, but they may be reaching out to people who would not otherwise ever hear the gospel. I have long thought that if people expose themselves to the word of God, things may happen to them.

But the gospel, the good news, is concerned not only with preaching but with doing and so, 'If anyone gives you a cup of water because you belong to Christ he will not lose his reward', for as we read in Matthew's gospel, in so far as we do this we do it to Christ who loves everyone. These words are also encouraging to us when we see in our world so many helping others, when we become aware of the vast amount of giving to people in distress that is a mark of our otherwise not very Christian society. It is indeed very strange and suggests, as a great theologian of our time has said, that there are great numbers of 'anonymous Christians' about. We can only hope and pray that they will get their reward at the end, union with the unknown Christ they have served.

The next set of sayings are about what we must not do. If anyone causes the 'little ones', the poor, the defenceless, the weak, children, to fall into sin, if anyone preaches a false doctrine to lead them astray, if anyone teaches them immoral ways, then they deserve the severest punishment. This too had a melancholy relevance when we think of the child-abusers who have been revealed in our time, of the drug-pushers who are destroying the morals and the very lives of young people.

Finally, the message of the gospel applies to ourselves. It challenges us to ask, 'What are our priorities?' Do we think that Christ's teaching must give way to the values of modern life? We might usefully recall some other words of Jesus: 'What does it profit a man if he gains the whole world and loses his life', his life in Christ and his eternal salvation? Do we think that self-indulgence, including sexual indulgence, is compatible with the teachings of Christ? What Jesus is saying to us today is that if we should think and act in that way, we are in danger of cutting ourselves off from God, and that is what 'hell' means. God does not condemn us to hell; as the scripture says, 'God does not desire the death of a sinner.' No, we condemn ourselves. If we spent a life of sin and died impenitent, the vision of God would be unbearable, we would turn away from it and be separated from him for ever.

I am well aware that this is a sombre message, but often enough the gospel summons us to serious thoughts about ourselves and our life. It is meant to turn us to God, to help us to review our daily living under the eye of God, and if we let it do that and if we repent, then we have nothing to fear: 'God does not desire the death of a sinner, but rather that he should repent and live.' He is 'full of compassion and rich in mercy', and today we can pray the psalm: 'From hidden faults acquit me, from presumption restrain your servant and let it not rule me. Then shall I be blameless and clean of all sin'.

Twenty-seventh Sunday of the Year

Gen 2:18-24; Ps 127; Heb 2:9-11; Mk 10:2-16.

As I am sure you know, the institution of marriage has run into serious trouble in recent times. It is credibly reckoned that some 50% of all marriages in this country end in divorce and that about one third of Catholic marriages end in the same way. Indeed it seems there are few outside the Catholic Church who believe in the indissolubility of marriage, that it is for ever. This means that very heavy pressures are put on Catholics and many are involved in unhappy situations which sometimes are not their fault. All of us must bring to them compassion and understanding and we must not do anything so unChristian as to judge others. Judgement belongs to God alone. The gospel today should help us to see where we stand.

First, let us realise that the words about marriage are the words of Christ and not the words of ecclesiastics or canon lawyers. What the church teaches stems from Christ's words which are found in this gospel of Mark, in that of Luke, in Matthew with one variation, and in St Paul's First Letter to the Corinthians. Even then, however, marriage is not seen just as a law, much less a law that might be changed. There is something deeper here, something that concerns the very nature of marriage.

Let us then turn to the words of Jesus: 'From the beginning of creation, God made them male and female' and when they are married, husband and wife become one body. *Therefore*, as Jesus says, what God has joined, let no one divide. You will have noticed that he is quoting from the Old Testament. He sees marriage as instituted by God at the very beginning of the human race.

We can see the whole matter from a different point of view if we consider the teaching of the Letter to the Ephesians. There marriage is put in the context of Christ and his church. The author of that Letter quotes the words of Genesis as Jesus had, but he carries the matter further and deeper. Christian marriage is a sign or symbol of the union between Christ and his church. This union is so close that, as he says, it is a 'great mystery' whose depths we can never wholly plumb. The union between Christ and his church is so intimate that it is unbreakable, for if it were broken the church would cease to exist. Of this union marriage is the sign, symbol or sacrament, sharing in the qualities of intimacy and unbreakableness. In a word, marriage is a sacrament because it shows forth that intimate, unbreakable union between Christ and his church, that is his people. That is why marriage is indissoluble, that is why it is for ever.

To make this matter of marriage clearer, the author begins his chapter with these words: 'Try to imitate Christ and follow him by loving as he loved and gave himself up for us as an offering and a sacrifice to God.' The union of Christ with his church was made in the suffering of the cross and with love, with all the love he has for us. That is the very meaning of his sacrifice. Therefore, the Letter can conclude, 'Husbands should love their wives as Christ loved the church and sacrificed himself for her.'

As love is the meaning of the cross, as love is bond that binds the church to Christ, so it is love that binds husband and wife together. But like Christ's love, it is a love of self-giving, and like Christ's love it is an enduring love to which the partners on their wedding day commit themselves: 'I take thee ... for better or for worse ... until death do us part'; and these words are simply the echo of gospel teaching.

All this I think helps us to understand where we are in this matter. But of course married people know better than I that marriage is fraught with many dangers and difficulties. There are many temptations to infidelity. And the demands of self-giving and self-sacrifice are very high. But I believe that if married people have a firm belief in the teaching of Christ, if they have a firm conviction that he is with them in their marriage, enabling them day by day to give themselves to each other and then to their children, their marriage will endure. Like Christ, they may be called upon to suffer in various ways but that very suffering is part of the self-giving and the self-sacrifice, and Christ is with them in that also.

Twenty-eighth Sunday of the Year

Wis 7:7-11; Ps 89 (in part); Heb 4:12, 13; Mk 10:17-30.

In our own time we have seen a great number of people getting rich, some of them getting rich very quickly, and some by dubious methods. It might then be possible to read this gospel as a denunciation of riches or of the people who get rich and sometimes very rich. That is not the purpose of this gospel passage, so let us find out what is.

A man, called young in Matthew's gospel, sees Jesus, comes up to him and asks him a rather extraordinary question, 'What must I do to inherit eternal life?' He is asking about a life that goes far beyond anything in this world. He is asking for a life that begins here and yet endures so that it can be called an everlasting life. Jesus replies by referring to six of the Ten Commandments which were the summary of moral living in the Old Testament. This is how an Israelite was required to live and this, as the young man replied, he had tried to do.

What comes next is also surprising. Jesus tells him that he lacks one thing; he must go and sell everything he has and give the proceeds to the poor and if he does he will lay up treasure in heaven. But there is something else: 'Come, follow me.' That is really what the gospel is about. Jesus is calling the young man to total commitment, he is asking him to follow without preconditions or any entanglements with worldly affairs. In a word, he was calling him to be a disciple. That the young man did not feel he could do and he went away sadly.

That this gospel is about following Jesus can be gathered from Peter's question, which seems rather an ungracious question, 'What about us?' Jesus gives the same answer in different terms. Those who give up everything to follow him will receive the eternal life that the young man had sought and wanted. The following of Christ, then, demanded renunciation, renunciation of worldly advantages and power, and would involve persecution and rejection, as Jesus himself endured persecution and suffering. To put the whole matter as briefly as possible, Jesus was telling the young man and his disciples that the giving up of possessions, whether great or small, was the necessary way of giving oneself to Christ, to God, and indeed to others. We give up so that we may give.

Does this mean that every Christian has to give up everything? As the passage from the Book of Wisdom and the psalm make clear, it is a matter of a clear understanding of respective values: 'I prayed and understanding was given me, I entreated and the spirit of wisdom came to me. I esteemed her more than sceptres and thrones; compared with her, I held riches as nothing. I reckoned no priceless stone to be her peer, for compared with her, all gold is a pinch of salt'. It is a matter of proportion. Wealth is not bad and if there were not wealth-making whole peoples would be destitute, as we know some are, in what we call the Third World. But where wealth is pursued regardless of the consequences, or with indifference to those who may be impoverished or deprived of what is their just due, then wealth can be described, in the terms of the gospel, as the Mammon of Iniquity, money, wealth, possessions that breed wickedness.

But it is not only in the upper reaches of the economy or commercial and business life that there is an ugly lust for wealth. We can all be affected with a desire for 'things' and more and more things about which we can be possessive and perhaps nearly obsessive. Of course it is not wrong that we should have the necessities of life as it is also true that the definition of 'necessities' has grown very considerably in our own time. What is required of us is that we should see these things not as ultimate goods that we should be striving for, and that we should always be aware of those, whether in our own country of elsewhere, who are in need.

In the first reading we have heard the word 'wisdom' and in the Old Testament this can mean prudence or a right judgement about the things of this world. At its highest, it means seeing things from God's point of view rather than from the world's. All these things that so much concern us, and often understandably concern us, will one day pass away and, since we are children of light, born of the Risen Christ in baptism, we would do well to make our own the words of St Paul: 'Since you have been brought back to life with Christ look for the things that are in heaven where Christ is ... Let you thoughts be on heavenly things, not on the things that are on earth', for 'when Christ is revealed – and he is your true life – you too will be revealed in all your glory in him' (Col 3:1-4).

Twenty-ninth Sunday of the Year

Is 53:10-11; Ps 32 (in part); Heb 4:14-16; Mk 10:35-45.

The message of the scriptures today is both sombre and very important. It is about authority, it is about service and it is about suffering. The message also poses serious questions to us.

Authority, whether in church or state, nowadays is not highly regarded. Civil laws are flagrantly broken day after day. Government, politicians of all kinds, church people and journalists all deplore the rise in the crime rate and great numbers of people ask, Why, why should it be that people are becoming lawless? In the church, many just disregard the laws of the church and even the laws of God. It is of course not possible to attribute to a single cause this deplorable situation, but if we reflect on what the scriptures have to say about authority, service and suffering, we may get some light on the matter.

From the gospel we learn that even towards the end of Jesus' life – for the passion was imminent – the disciples had not learnt what Jesus had meant when he spoke to them about the 'kingdom'. They still thought of it as an earthly kingdom and they wanted to have the highest places in it. The reply Jesus gave to them must have shocked them: 'Can you drink the cup that I must drink?', the cup of suffering, and the baptism he speaks of would be a baptism of blood. What Jesus is saying is that in his kingdom authority involves suffering, and that is not something that even we think of readily. One reason for this is that those bearing authority in the church are the representatives of Christ, receiving whatever authority they have from him, and, since they represent him, they must in some way or another be like

him. In our own time, Archbishop Romero in El Salvador was a
striking representative of Christ when he was shot down at the
altar for upholding justice and doing what he could to defend
the oppressed. The conventional term used of saints, 'Servants
of the Lord' was fully verified in Archbishop Romero.

That something of the sort was in the mind of Jesus can be gathered from the words of the gospel I have referred to already, but
also from the lesson he has to give them about service: 'If anyone
among you wants to become great he must be the servant of all.'
And perhaps with his eye on the high priest and the Roman occupying power, he teaches them what authority is not: 'You
know that among the pagans their so-called rulers lord it over
them, and their great men make their authority felt.' If what
Jesus castigates is a travesty of authority even in the secular
sphere, it would be equally true if it were found in the church,
and Jesus points up the sharp contrast between that sort of authority and the authority of the church. Authority is essentially
service: 'Anyone who wants to become great among you must
be your servant' and indeed if anyone would be first he must be
the 'slave of all'. Office holders in the church, popes, bishops,
priests and deacons, are the servants of the community and that
must inspire and control all their work.

But even that is not the whole message and here we come to the
climax of this gospel passage, as is suggested by the first reading
from Isaiah who puts before us the picture of the Suffering
Servant, in which the church from the beginning has seen the
Servant Christ. Whether echoing these words or not in the
gospel, we find Jesus, as it were, identifying himself with the
Servant: 'The Son of Man did not come to be served but to serve
and give his life as a ransom for many.' Here in Jesus, service
and suffering are joined, and the gospel text seems to be saying,
'This is the foundation of all authority in the church.' By this and
through the preaching of it through the centuries, countless men
and women have been drawn to Christ, have been incorporated
into his church and in turn have gone out to serve the world.

The teaching of this gospel was enshrined in the documents of
the Second Vatican Council which proclaimed that the church is

a servant church, a church that seeks no domination anywhere, a church that shares the sufferings and the joys and the hopes of the human race whom she wishes to serve in any way open to her. In the end, authority means growth, growth in Christ, growth in well-being and social justice for all, growth in the kingdom of which this world is the theatre until it becomes the new heaven and the new earth at the end of time.

All of us then who are followers of Christ the Servant are called to offer our service to the church and service to the society in which we live so that Christ, through us, can reach out to others and so that the world in which we live can be a society of justice, love and peace.

Thirtieth Sunday of the Year

Jer 31:7-9; Ps 125; Heb 5:1-6; Mk 10:46-52.

Coming after the solemn sayings of Jesus in this same chapter of Mark, this little miracle story may seem surprising. In fact the evangelist seems to have included it quite deliberately here. What might be called the great central part of the gospel runs from 8:22, beginning with the cure of another blind man and includes three predictions of the passion of Jesus, and ends with the healing of another blind man called Bartimaeus.

There are two reasons for this. The first is that all the events and sayings of these central chapters are about the breaking in of the kingdom which Jesus will bring into existence by his passion, death and resurrection. The reading from Jeremiah seems to suggest this point of view. He is foretelling the return of the exiles in Babylon. They will be brought back from the land of the North, they will come, all of them, including the blind and the lame, women with child and in labour, perhaps they will come singing the psalm 'When the Lord delivered Zion from bondage, it seemed like a dream'. Their mouths were filled with laughter and on their lips there were songs.

Now in the gospel a new Israel is coming into existence and it too was accompanied by marvels. The blind man receives his sight. In the Jeremiah passage the prophet calls God 'a Father to Israel'; it is he who has liberated them. In the gospel Bartimaeus, with a certain touch of affection, calls Jesus 'Rabbuni', my Master; it is he who has given him back his sight. Like the pilgrims of old he was filled with joy. They had gone out full of tears but had come back 'full of song'.

The second reason for the inclusion of this story here at the end of chapter ten is, I think, that it suggests that the bringing in of the kingdom and its establishment as the early Christian community would be wrought in pain and suffering. As we read in Luke's gospel, the Christ had to suffer if he was to enter into his glory; it was the Risen though crucified Christ who confirmed the disciples by the giving of the Holy Spirit and sending them out as apostles to be witnesses of him and his passion, death and resurrection to the ends of the earth. But the witnessing and the preaching brought suffering too. Peter and John and other apostles were put in prison. James was put to death by Herod not more than ten years after the resurrection. Then Saul, later called Paul, come on the scene 'breathing out threats to slaughter' and seeking to 'arrest and take to Jerusalem any followers of the Way, men or women, that he could find' (Acts 9:1, 2). But on the way to bring death to the followers of the Way, Saul/Paul saw the light on the way to Damascus. There came a blinding light and the voice asked him, 'Why are you persecuting me?', and to his question came the reply, 'I am Jesus whom you are persecuting.' Afterwards he saw the light through baptism and he began to teach the Way he had sought to exterminate.

'The Way' was a well known term for Christians who followed the way of light, who followed Jesus who said he was the way, the truth and the life. Bartimaeus too saw the light of day again and, as Mark says, he followed Jesus 'on the way' (RSV). The evangelist seems to be delicately hinting that Bartimaeus followed the Way.

Those healed in the gospel are not usually named. The man born blind in St John's gospel has no name, and it may be that Bartimaeus later became a Christian and his name was remembered by the community. In baptism, called enlightenment in the early church, he received another light that united him to Jesus and with him he walked on the way.

All of us have been enlightened in baptism when we received the gift of faith in Christ, and all of us are called to walk on the way, the way of Jesus Christ who told us that if we follow him we shall not walk in darkness but will have the light that gives life.

Thirty-first Sunday of the Year

Deut 6:2-6; Ps 17 (in part); Heb 7:23-28; Mk 12:28-34.

In the second half of the first century AD, when the gospels were being written, there was often considerable hostility between Christians and Jews and I fear these early Christians, whom we must not romanticise, paid the Jews back in their own coin. They did not always practise what they preached. So it may come as something of a surprise that a Jew also could repeat in the gospel the great law of love which was promulgated in the Old Testament, namely in the Book of Deuteronomy, as we have heard. It is sometimes thought that the Old Testament had not much to do with love. There was a great deal about fighting and even hatred. God himself is thought by some Christians even now to have been a sort of tribal God, remote and terrible, more concerned to punish than to save.

Such views are a travesty of the truth. Frequently in the Old Testament God is shown as a Father who 'loved Israel'. He is like a shepherd who seeks those who have gone astray; he binds up the wounds of the injured and carries them home and feeds them. He calls the people his child and holds him to his cheek. His people are told to do justice, to act kindly and to walk humbly before God. If a poor man pledges his cloak it must be returned to him before nightfall because he has nothing else with which to cover himself. Strangers must be welcomed and slaves must be treated humanely. Then, in this very legalistic book, Deuteronomy, comes the great law of love of God and neighbour which was turned into a prayer and recited daily, as it still is by practising Jews. Finally, it was so important that Jesus took it over into his teaching and we find the doctrine of love everywhere in the gospels and the rest of the New Testament.

What then is the difference between the law of love in the Old Testament and the love spoken of in the New? The difference is not to be found in the fact that Christians are more charitable than the Jews. We have seen too many wars, too many horrors, too much brutality in this century alone to be able to maintain that proposition. The first difference is that whatever Christians have done, love dominates the whole life of Christ and, as I have said, dominates the whole of the New Testament. At a time when Judaism was emphasising law rather than love, when the scribes were piling regulation on regulation, Jesus re-promulgated the law of love and showed that it was the very meaning of his whole life and mission. As his life was drawing to its end, as he knew that the 'hour' had come for him to pass from this world to his Father, he wished to give his disciples proof that he loved them to the uttermost. So he gave himself first in the eucharist at the Last Supper which was the sacramental sign of his self-giving on the cross. He is the supreme model and example of love: 'God so loved the world as to give his only Son ...'

The second and radical difference between love in the Old Testament and the New is that it is not just a law that we must keep but a life that we must live. In all the discourses of the Last Supper, as handed on by St John, when Jesus speaks of love he also speaks of our being, dwelling, living in him and in his Father through him: 'If you love me you will keep my commandments ... and anyone who loves me will be loved by my Father and I shall love him ... and my Father will love him and we shall come to him and make our home with him' (14:15, 21-23). Jesus gave himself on the cross, he gives himself to us now, his love is within us, it is the source whereby we can keep the commandments and live as Christ would have us live. Love is a gift, love is implanted within us, and St Paul puts this truth very simply: 'The love of God has been poured into our hearts by the Holy Spirit who has been given us' (Rom 5:5).

It is then because love is within us that we can love, love God and love all others. It is a source, a power that supports and transfuses all our actions, that is, all our actions that are in accordance with the will of God. It is a love that makes our love a love of self-giving after the model of Jesus Christ himself. It is a love that purifies our love that is so often fraught with self-seeking. It is a love that makes it possible for us to go on loving even when it is unpleasant and seems impossible to do so.

In the early church, Christians celebrated the eucharist in conjunction with a love-feast which was called an *agapē*. We celebrate the same eucharist which is the sacrament of God's love for us and before we receive the body and blood of the Risen Christ we offer each other a sign of peace, the *osculum pacis* as it is called in Latin. By it we express our love and union with each other, a love and union that brings peace and reconciliation.

Thirty-second Sunday of the Year

1 Kings 17:10-16; Ps 145 (in part); Heb 9:24-28; Mk 12:38-44.

The widow in the ancient world, even in the Jewish world, had a very low status. She had no rights, no share in her deceased husband's property and unless she married again she had to return to her family and there live more or less as a servant. It is a little surprising then that, in both the Old Testament reading and the gospel, widows are set up as models of generosity, all the more so as we remember that Jesus recalled that God had sent the prophet to the widow of Zarepta of Sidon, a foreigner, rather than to a widow of Israel, and that God had compassion for her. She unknowingly was doing God's work in feeding the prophet in a time of famine.

In the gospel there is a very sharp contrast between the wealthy scribes who devour the property of widows, and the poor widow with her two small coins, her whole livelihood, which she put into the Temple treasury. The implication is that God would look after her for, as the psalm says, 'The Lord upholds the widow and the orphan.' The widows gave their all and God rewarded them. The 'jar of meal was not spent' and 'the jug of oil was not emptied'. Later Elijah would raise the widow's son to life.

But what about the widow of the gospel. It is often said that the Christian church has not had a very high regard for women. There may be some truth in that but it is sometimes forgotten that during his ministry women accompanied him, providing for his material needs. There was Joanna, a well-to-do lady, there was Mary the Magdalen and Susanna and many others. There were the Marys who, with the Magdalen, stood at the foot of the cross, among them Mary the Mother of Jesus whom Jesus committed to the care of his beloved disciple. Later, after the resurrection, women played an important part in the life of the church. There was Prisca who with her husband Aquila had a house church; there was Phoebe described as a deaconess; there was yet another Mary and Olympias and others unnamed who accompanied the apostles and their disciples. In the Letter to Timothy we hear of Lois, his grandmother, and Eunice, his mother, women of faith who had brought him up.

In a later age, it is not difficult to find great abbesses like Hilda of Whitby who ruled over a double monastery of women and men. She and many others had real jurisdiction within their communities and on them lay the task of the spiritual formation of the members of their communities. We can think of Hildergarde of Bingen in Germany, a learned nun, a poet and a musician, of Mechtilde and Gertrude, also of Germany, who were saints and mystics. There was St Catherine of Siena, also a mystic, who did not hesitate to rebuke popes, and in the sixteenth century the great St Teresa of Avila in Spain who reformed the Carmelite Order and was the 'mother' of the many houses she founded. Later still, there have been those many foundresses of almost innumerable congregations of women who have nursed and taught and done every kind of work for others throughout three centuries.

But let us return to our widow of the gospel. Was she rewarded in any way? We do not know. Perhaps she was remembered and the evangelist wrote her story. What we do not know is that the early Christian communities were urged to look after the widows among them. Those who have brought up their children well, those who have practised hospitality, those who have relieved the afflicted and have spent or are spending their days in doing good, must be looked after by the community in which they are to have an honoured place. In fact this continued and in all the early centuries of the church we find that virgins, widows and what were called ascetics, were supported by the local communities, so much so that it could be said there were large numbers of people on the pay-roll of the church.

In our parish communities to this day there are many widows and other single ladies who unobtrusively do work for the church. Let us remember them and their work with gratitude and when they in turn need help, let us give them our company and all the care they need.

Thirty-third Sunday of the Year

Dan 12:1-3; Ps 15 (in part); Heb 10:11, 14-18; Mk 13:24-32.

As the year draws to its end, the church reminds us that our life on this earth will end and that this world is not everything. One day it too will come to an end. Even scientists and others are warning us that if we do not respect and use this physical planet with the care it deserves then we, the human race, will bring about its destruction. There is then nothing bizarre in thinking about the end, whether of our own lives or of the world as a whole. The heavens and the earth, the whole of creation, will pass away, said Jesus, but my word will not pass away, and it is to that word we now turn our attention.

We notice that, both in Daniel and the gospel, the word 'distress' appears. There will be a time of distress when there will be turmoil of various kinds. And when there are such times people's minds turned to the end, as they still do. I daresay that as the year 2000 approaches, there will be various unbalanced people who will be proclaiming that the end is nigh. If so, we should remember the words of Jesus, which are the most important words of the gospel, that no one knows the day or the hour when the end will come.

Out of this sense of the time of distress or tribulation there came a certain kind of literature called *apocalyptic*, both biblical and non-biblical, and we have two examples of it today, in Daniel and the gospel. There were vivid descriptions of the world falling apart, of wars and rumours of wars, of destruction and of conflict between nations and even families. In the midst of all this turmoil, one called the Son of Man will appear 'with great power and glory' who, as we know from the great parable of the sheep and the goats in Matthew's gospel, will judge the whole of the human race. We must understand, however, that all is this picture language. We are not required to believe that the various horrors spoken of are factual descriptions of what will happen or even that Christ, the Son of Man, will gather the whole human race before him, because that would be an impossibility – millions upon millions of human beings from the beginning of the world until its end!

Can we then discern the underlying purpose and meaning of the biblical text? It can be summed up in one word, Judgement, the Last Judgement, as we learned to say long ago. But even that word needs understanding. We have to think of it in this way. Throughout the centuries, as we learn from the Old Testament, God was working out his plans of salvation for the human race. It seemed to fail and then, in the fullness of time, God sent his Son to save the human race from their sins. As time has gone on we see that some have rejected him, that others have flouted God's purpose in the world, that vast injustices have been perpetrated on countless millions of people, that the poor have been oppressed and that justice has been withheld from them and many other innocent people. Is all this to go unnoticed and unpunished? Are we never to see that God's purpose has been worked out and that justice will replace injustice? At the end, God's purpose will be revealed and vindicated. Those who have persevered to the end, those who have done God's will, 'the wise will (then) shine as brightly as the vault of heaven and those who have instructed many in virtue (will be) as stars for all eternity'. Those who knowingly have resisted God to the end will receive their just deserts. The last book of the Bible, the Apocalypse, was written to give comfort to the first Christians in their time of tribulation and to assure them that their faithfulness and perseverance would not go unrewarded.

Even so, all this may seem remote from us. How are we affected by all the Bible says? Does it indeed concern us at all? There is an old saying, *Respice finem*, 'Look to the end', and in a world that seems to be determined not to look to the end but to want everything immediately and never to look beyond this world and their instant needs, it is incumbent upon us as Christians to remember that we and this world are destined to pass away. And then what? It is the traditional teaching of the church that when we die there will be a private judgement. But this too needs understanding. We shall meet God and in the presence of his holiness and love we shall recognise our sinfulness but if we have repented and persevered in the way of the Lord then we shall hear the words, 'Come, blessed by my Father and possess the kingdom prepared for you since the foundation of the world.'

The Feast of Christ the King

Dan 7:13, 14; Ps 92 (in part); Apoc 1:5-8; Jn 18:33-37.

As once again we come to celebrate the Feast of Christ the King, we may well feel the need to ask: What sort of kingdom are the scriptures speaking about? What sort of kingdom was Jesus talking about?

Long ago, in the past, there were those who wanted to set up a the theocracy, the rule and empire of God of which the pope would be the earthly representative, and all through the Middle Ages there was the conflict between the church and the secular power. At times it looked as if the pope was indeed trying to set himself up as a sort of super-emperor. To be just, one must say that popes and bishops were fighting for the freedom of the church, freedom to do what God had committed it to do for the people. Nonetheless a wrong impression was given and the popes did become temporal rulers over the papal state in Italy.

Whatever is to be said about all that, one thing is clear from today's scriptures: that is not the kingdom that Jesus was speaking of.

Let us turn to that mysterious passage in the prophecy of Daniel. 'A son of Man', evidently a more than human being, approaches the 'Ancient of Days' who is God. On the 'Son of Man' is conferred a kingdom, sovereignty over all peoples and nations but it seems clear that it is not to be an earthly sovereignty for it will never pass away or be destroyed. Nor does the text say how this kingdom is to come about.

For this we turn to the gospel. Here is Jesus before the Roman official, the representative of the Roman empire that extended from the river Euphrates to the Atlantic, a man of power but weak and well-intentioned. 'Are you a king?' he asks, and Jesus, with calm and dignity, questions the man who is his judge with the power of life and death. Jesus had already been condemned by the Sanhedrin for claiming to be the Messiah and the Son of the Blessed One (God his Father) and now he confesses that he is indeed a king but not the sort of king that either the chief priest or Pilate thought he was. His kingdom is not of this world, it is no earthly kingdom that he is seeking. He is a king only in the sense that he came into the world to bear witness to the truth.

This seems a strange answer but, all through the fourth gospel, Jesus is constantly saying that he has come to bear witness to the One who sent him and to communicate the message, the truth, he has received from his Father, the truth he has been commissioned by his Father to make known to the world. Jesus reveals his Father, he reveals the love his Father has for the whole human race and he proclaims that he has come to do the 'work' of his Father. This he had done by his teaching, by his very life and by the miracles which were the signs showing who he was and what he had come for. Now this witnessing to his Father and indeed to the world was coming to an end. His death and his resurrection would be the supreme sign, the very sacrament of the divine love that would redeem the world. That was (and is) the 'truth', the truth of his mission, the truth that he *was*. All this is summarised in the reading from the Apocalypse: 'Jesus Christ is the faithful witness, the first-born from the dead, the ruler of the kings of the earth. He loves us and has washed away our sins with his blood.'

But how is the reign of Christ to be made present in the world? The rest of the verse continues, '(He has) made us a line of kings, priests to serve his God and Father.' By baptism we all share in the kingship and priesthood of Christ and like the disciples, for whom Christ prayed at the Last Supper, we too are sent: 'as you sent me into the world, I have sent them into the world'. Like the disciples we are 'consecrated in truth', consecrated to proclaim the Christ who is truth. Like Christ, who came not to be served but to serve, we are called to serve in the world. In the language of the New Testament, 'kingship' means service, not rank or honour and we by our word must try and make Christ known to a world that seems largely ignorant of him. By our service of whatever community we live in, we can bring to bear the moral principles of social living and, by our daily lives, we can show that Christ is present and active in this world, in families, in individual people, in husbands, wives and children.

All this seems very humdrum and uncreative, but this is where we must start if, by the power of Christ our King, we are to bring into existence his reign of 'justice, love and peace'.

Year C

Second Sunday of the Year

Is 62:1-5; Ps 95 (in part); 1 Cor 12:4-11; Jn 2:1-11.

When we find the word 'sign' in the fourth gospel – and there are seven of them – it is an indication that what seems a simple narrative has more than one meaning. Here the first meaning is that the changing of the water into wine is a manifestation, a revelation that Jesus is Lord, the Messiah, sent by the Father for the salvation of the human race. The disciples had already sought out the Messiah and identified him in Jesus and now, at this first sign of his power, they come to believe in him, though in the years that followed their faith would have to grow stronger and deeper.

The second meaning of the miracle takes us very far, seemingly far away from the simple scene of the marriage feast of Cana.

The gospel story is set in the context of Isaiah 62. The prophet is speaking of the people in the Old Testament. He is recalling what had happened through the centuries. At Sinai he had made them his own people; he had led them through the desert into the land of freedom; he had protected them and promised them an even more glorious future. But they had been unfaithful to him. In the words of Jeremiah, 'they have abandoned the living waters and dug for themselves leaky cisterns'. They have worshipped false Gods in whom there is no life. For their sins they have been swept off into captivity but they have repented and now they have been brought back to their own country. They are no longer an 'abandoned' people or a 'forsaken' people. They are now to be 'God's delight' and the 'wedded'. The people of Israel are to be the bride of God: 'as the bridegroom rejoices in his bride, so will God rejoice in you.'

It is an astonishing teaching which is deepened and carried over

into the New Testament. In the Book of Revelation (or Apocalypse) the church, the new people of God, is spoken of as the
Bride, all adorned with jewels, prepared to meet the Bridegroom,
The Lamb of God, and to sit down with him at the eternal banquet of which the eucharist here and now is the foreshadowing.

But how was this brought about? In the gospel we hear those apparently mysterious words of Jesus, 'My hour has not yet come'.
What was that hour? As so much in the rest of John's gospel
shows, the 'hour' was the time of his passion, death and resurrection: 'It was before the festival of the passover, and Jesus
knew that the hour had come for him to pass from this world to
the Father' (Jn 13:1). By his self-offering in his passion and death
he brought to its climax that long history of salvation of which
we read in the Old Testament. It was through his passion and
death that Jesus reconciled us and re-united us, the whole human
race, with God. As an ancient writer of the church said, 'It was
from the side of Christ as he slept the sleep of death on the cross
that there came forth the wondrous sacrament of the whole
church.' This, as other writers said, was symbolised by the blood
and water that flowed from Jesus' pierced side. This is the bridal
church, born of self-sacrifice and love, to which we have the
privilege to belong, as we do by the water of baptism and by the
body and blood of the eucharist which sustains and nourishes
us throughout our life.

From this simple story of the gospel we have been led to a deeper
understanding of what the church is. Through it, through the
church's sacraments, through the whole liturgy of the church,
we are established in an intimate and personal union with
Christ which is comparable to the union of husband with wife
and wife with husband. It is not surprising then that the chapter
of the Letter to the Ephesians that speaks of Christian marriage
begins with these words: 'Try then, to imitate God, as children of
his that he loves, and follow Christ by loving as he loved you,
giving himself up in our place as a fragrant offering and sacrifice
to God' (Eph 5:1, 2). This does not apply only to married people.
It applies to all of us. All of us share that deep and intimate
union with Christ and all of us are called to respond to his love
with self-giving and love.

Third Sunday of the Year

Neh 8:2-10; Ps 18 (in part); 1 Cor 12:12-30; Lk 1:1-4, 14-21.

The relationship of the passage from Nehemiah to the gospel is not immediately clear. However let us see if we can find one.

The scene is set in Jerusalem. Jews have returned from exile. They are restoring their desolate city and its Temple. What is more important is that their leaders are seeking to bring about a spiritual renewal. The heart of the Old Testament religion was the law, the Torah, and the priest-scribe Ezra reads out to the assembled people parts of the Books of the Law, perhaps passages from Exodus and Deuteronomy. It is a solemn moment marked by the response of the people, 'Amen, Amen', by which they endorse the law and promise to abide by it.

All this seems very far from the gospel. Ezra proclaims the law; Jesus proclaims salvation, 'the Lord's year of favour'. Although the law was more a way of life than a code, it did of course contain many rules and regulations. Jesus proclaims God's mercy. He was sent to bring the good news (of salvation) to the poor, the humble, the underprivileged but also to the spiritually starved whatever their status in society. He is sent to bring freedom to captives, sight to the blind and liberty to the oppressed.

The contrast seems complete but there is a link between the first reading and the gospel. Ezra can be seen to be repeating what Moses had done hundreds of years before when, as the servant of God, he made the covenant between God and his people. As then, so now the law was proclaimed to the people: as then, so now the people give their assent, they will obey the law of God and live by it. Then Moses took the blood of the sacrificed animal, sprinkled the people with it and poured the rest round the altar saying, 'This is the blood of the covenant', of the sacred union between God and his people. On this occasion there was no sacrifice, perhaps because the Temple had not yet been restored. The people had a feast instead!

If we turn back to the gospel we shall find other and deeper things.

Jesus is the Messiah, the Anointed One of God. On him the Holy Spirit has descended at his baptism, he was led by the Spirit into the wilderness where he was put to the test, and now 'with the power of the Spirit in him' he returns to his native place and proclaims the good news of salvation to his own people. Taking up the prophecy of Isaiah and reading from it he says, 'This text is being fulfilled today, even as you listen.' He was showing the link between the long history of salvation, God's dealings with the people of Israel, and saying equivalently that he was continuing his Father's work. This was the acceptable time, now was the God-given moment to receive the good news of salvation, a time for which the world had waited for so long. It would indeed bring sight to the blind and freedom, but above all it was a freeing from sin, that act of God which we call redemption or ransom. As we read in St Mark's gospel, Jesus came not to be served but to serve and give his life as a ransom for many, that is for all who would accept his word, for all who would accept him as Lord and Saviour, for all who would commit themselves in faith to him.

Of all this, the sermon at Nazareth was but the beginning and as we turn the pages of the gospel we see Jesus healing the sick and going on his preaching tour to Capernaum and beyond. And in contrast to Ezra, what he preached was not a code of law but a proclamation of God's saving mercy and love: 'Come to me all you who labour and are heavily burdened and I will give you rest.' Though Jesus spoke with authority he did not command: he invited, he urged people to come to him, to be with him and to follow him, and as we know many did. But not all. The people of Nazareth were at first astonished that a local boy, a carpenter and the son of a carpenter, should stand before them and claim to be moved by the Spirit of God. Then their astonishment turned to hostility when he said, 'No prophet is ever accepted in his own country' and reminded them that God had sent Elijah to a non-Jewish town for help, and that Naaman from Syria had been cured at the instance of the prophet Elisha rather than any of the lepers of Israel. At this the people jostled him and tried to throw him down a cliff but he slipped through their hands and escaped.

We sometimes think that if we had heard Jesus we would have been instantly converted and have followed him. We find it difficult to understand how the people of the time could have rejected this Jesus who is so appealing to us, this Jesus who was so full of kindness, love and mercy to all. All we can say by way of explanation is that the people could not see through the man, the village boy, to the Saviour. In a word, they had no faith in him, as the gospel says.

It can be the same with us. We can listen to the word of God Sunday by Sunday but it does not bring us closer to him because we do not let it. It does not convert us and go on converting us because we fail to understand that the power of the Spirit by which Jesus spoke is present as the scriptures are read to us Sunday by Sunday. If we listen with the full attention of the mind and with an open heart, then the power of the Spirit will enter our lives and transform them.

Fourth Sunday of the Year

Jer 1:4-5:17, 19; Ps 70 (in part); 1 Cor 12:31-13:13; Lk 4:21-30

It is a strange thing that throughout history, and particularly as it is recorded in the Bible, human beings have struggled against God and even denounced him. Men and women have fought against God who only wants to offer them his love and to save them (and us) from their worst selves, their sinful selves. Yet all he wanted, and wants now, is that we should be whole and happy and he offers us his gifts of grace and love. Yet we, and it must be said, large parts of the human race, have shown a strange perversity to go our own way and to reject or ignore the God who loves us.

That, broadly, is the background of the scriptures today.

Jeremiah is sent to a people who refuse to listen to the prophet's word, even when the threat of invasion, destruction and captivity hang over them. He must resist them, he must be 'like a pillar of iron, like a wall of bronze'; he must proclaim the word of God

that is entrusted to him and for his pains he was abused, persecuted, thrust down a well where he nearly died. As another
prophet said on another occasion, these people look but they do
not see, they hear but they do not listen because their hearts are
far from God, words that Jesus himself uses elsewhere in the
gospel. Like Jeremiah, Jesus too was rejected by most of his own
people, beginning with his own relatives and the people of his
town.

But his references to the widow woman of Zarephath, and to
Naaman the wealthy man from Syria in the far north, raises a
curious question. Both the widow of Sidon and Naaman were
non-Jews, that is they were officially outside the divine plan of
salvation which, in the Bible, is apparently restricted to the Jews
although in the later prophets we read that the promises made
to Israel are for everyone. Jesus seems to be gently approving of
the widow and Naaman. Is he suggesting that through their
faith, no doubt an imperfect faith, they were entering God's plan
of salvation? If so, this raises a further question that concerns us.
Can those outside the church, those who do not know Jesus
Christ and his teaching be saved?

In the sixteenth century, after the Reformation, Catholics thought
Protestants could not be saved and Protestants thought Catholics
could not be saved either. But the world was opening up, the
Americas had already been discovered and St Francis Xavier
was the first to preach to the countless millions of India and the
Far East. He was in anguish that so many should be lost. Since
then we have come to realise the enormous antiquity of the
human race, which has existed for hundreds of thousands of
years before the revelation of God's existence and saving purpose
in the Hebrew scriptures. Were these primitive human beings
beyond salvation?

These facts have brought a new realisation of the complexity of
the problem and they have stimulated much theological thinking. Inspired by the passion of Christ, whose will it is that all
should be saved and come to the knowledge of the truth, the
Second Vatican Council declared those who, through no fault of
their own, do not know the gospel of Christ or his church can be

saved if they seek God, however dim their notion of God may be, and try to live upright lives according to the dictates of their conscience. Even those who do not come to an explicit knowledge of God but try to live a good life are also in the way of salvation. For whatever goodness is to be found anywhere is the work of the grace of God.

Clearly this is not an easy way of salvation, and it is all the more difficult nowadays when we witness whole peoples and cultures torn apart by wars and hatreds. On the other hand it does throw some light and give encouragement in the situation in which we live. In our own time there has been a remarkable response of the first and more opulent world to the needs of the Third World. There has been a vast outpouring of generosity, both public and private, in recent years and if we are inclined to be a little cynical about it let us remember the words of Jesus, 'If anyone gives you a cup of water to drink because you belong to Christ … he will certainly not lose his reward.' Or we might like to recall the Maundy Thursday hymn: 'Where is love and loving kindness there is God.' Wherever and whenever there is a good deed there is the grace of God.

It may be that our world is not as wicked as we think it is, but it is our task as Christians to live as Christ would have us live and by our lives bear witness to Christ's love that is in our hearts. St Peter, in his First Letter, exhorts us to do just this: 'No one can hurt you if you are determined to do only what is right … Reverence the Lord Christ in your hearts, and always have a ready answer for people who ask you the reason for the hope you have in you' (1 Pet 3:13-15). Then let what is in our hearts be expressed in deeds. The cup of water and the ready word are bearers of God's love.

Fifth Sunday of the Year

Is 6:1-8; Ps 137 (in part); 1 Cor 15:1-11; Lk 5:1-11.

At first sight, the connection of the first reading with the gospel seems tenuous. In the passage from Isaiah we have one of the great manifestations of God in the Old Testament and, as the psalm suggests, we seem to be invited to give glory and thanks to God who reveals himself to us. But let us note that the revelation is given in the Temple.

But when we turn to the gospel, we see that the connection between the two readings is the call, vocation, the voice of God calling prophet and apostle to the proclamation of God and the message he has for the human race. We notice too other parallels between the two readings. At the vision of the all-holy God, the prophet becomes aware of his unworthiness even to appear before God. 'I am a wretch, a man of unclean lips.' He, as it were, shrinks before the majesty and glory of God. When we turn to the gospel we find differences and likenesses. Here is no great manifestation of God, the Master is among familiar friends, they have been with him for some little time but they are also witnesses of an act of power, the great catch of fish against all expectations. They began to understand that they were in the presence of one who was more than a man and this is all the more understandable, if, as some think, this incident took place after the resurrection. Though the feelings of awe and reverence are less, Simon Peter goes down on his knees and like Isaiah he confesses his unworthiness to be in the presence of holiness and divine power: 'Leave me, Lord, I am a sinful man'. Isaiah's lips were touched and his sins taken away. It would take longer to 'cleanse' Simon Peter. He would have to experience the suffering and death of his Master, and his cleansing would only come after the resurrection when he would be forgiven his sin of denial: 'Simon, do you love me ...?'

After the cleansing, Isaiah is sent on his mission: 'Whom shall I send? Who will be our messenger?' and he replies, 'Here I am. Send me.' After the forgiveness, Jesus sends his disciples: 'As the Father sent me, so I am sending you.' With the Spirit of the Lord upon them and with the peace of Christ and his reconciliation in their hearts, they would go out after Pentecost and proclaim the saving death and resurrection of Jesus as the Saviour of the people. Peter, surrounded by the other apostles, would preach repentance and forgiveness of sins and would incorporate into the church all those who came to be baptised and to celebrate, 'the breaking of bread', in the first Christian community. The commission of Jesus, that the disciples would be 'fishers of men', was now in operation.

What was begun then has continued throughout the ages. The church has reached out to every part of the earth and countless men and women have proclaimed the gospel throughout the centuries. If we ask what they have said and done, the scriptures of today underline two things. If we turn to the reading from St Paul we find it contains one of his two sayings about 'tradition', what is handed on from the beginning: 'I want to remind you of the gospel I preached to you, the gospel you received and in which you are firmly established.' Or, as he puts it more clearly when speaking of the eucharist, what I have received I have handed on to you. But 'tradition' does not mean merely repeating in the same words that we learnt as children. Nor does the church merely repeat what she received in the beginning. Over the centuries the church, guided by the Holy Spirit, has penetrated ever more deeply into what was delivered to her by Christ so that people of succeeding generations could receive it, take it in and make it part of their own thinking, faith and action. 'Tradition' is the living word of God that we hear every Sunday and that is proclaimed in a great variety of ways by the church to all kinds of people in every part of the world.

The second message the scriptures give today is that of reverence. Isaiah is overwhelmed by the glory and majesty of God who is revealed to him in a vision. He seemed to see God enthroned in the Temple and the heavenly beings singing, 'Holy, holy, holy is the Lord of hosts. His glory fills the whole earth'. It is from this all-holy God that the word of the Lord proceeds and because it does, it must be treated with reverence. In church, the new temple, the book of the scriptures is enthroned on the lectern and, when the gospel is proclaimed, the book is accompanied by song. At the end of the readings we hear the words, 'This is the word of the Lord, This is the Gospel of the Lord' and we make the appropriate responses. In an age which is notably lacking in reverence or even respect for holy things, we celebrate the word of God with reverence, listening to it and responding to its proclamation. As Peter said, 'Here are the words of life,'

words which we can find nowhere else. And after the word of
God we sing the praises of God as we join with the angels and
other heavenly beings in singing, 'Holy, holy, holy Lord, heaven
and earth are full of your glory, Hosanna in the highest.' At once
we are reverencing the all-holy God and the word that comes
from him.

Sixth Sunday of the Year

Jer 17:5-8; Ps 1 (in part); 1 Cor 15:12, 16-20; Lk 6:17, 20-26.

We hear much these days of the rich getting richer and the poor
poorer, and as far as I can tell these allegations are true. Likewise
we hear of the wealthy North, meaning the industrialised nations, and the poor South, namely the developing countries who
are trying to move from a primitive economy to a more ad-
vanced one. Again, from my reading, this allegation also seems
to be born out by the facts. I read for instance that the international bank, the IMF, does indeed lend money to poor countries
but also demands such high interest that the poor countries cannot pay the money back and sometimes not even the interest.
Added to this is the practice of excluding the products of the
poor countries from importation into the rich countries. All this
is plainly unjust and reminds one of the gospel term, as the older
translations had it, 'the mammon of iniquity' which literally
meant unjust money, money unjustly gained.

Poverty and riches, Luke tackles the problem head-on: 'Blessed
are you poor ... Alas for you who are rich'. Using the style of the
language of his day, Aramaic, he does not use qualifiers, such as
'this rather than that'. Everything is black and white, there is
good and evil and nothing in between: justice and injustice
stand in stark contrast to each other. If we turn to Matthew's
statement of the first beatitude, we may think that he is softening
the contrast between poverty and riches: 'Blessed are the poor in
spirit ...' That does not mean 'those who have chosen a spiritual
poverty', those who have given up things like monks and nuns.
Matthew was thinking of the poor, the lowly, the unimportant
and the humble devout of the Old Testament and the devout

Jews in the New Testament like Zachary and his wife Elizabeth, like holy Simeon and the prophetess Phanuel who lived and prayed in the Temple. Such people, called the *anawim* in the Old Testament, were blessed, and by God, because they were open to his word, always ready to receive it and live by it. To this in the New Testament there was added the expectation of a Messiah. Simeon 'looked for the comfort of Israel' and Phaneul 'spoke of the child (Jesus) to all who looked forward to the deliverment of Israel.'

The beatitudes then concerned the kingdom, the reign of God that Jesus was bringing into existence by his life and teaching. He was setting out a programme for the kingdom and the first thing we learn is that the poor, the hungry and the sad will have a special place in it: 'yours is the kingdom of God': the hungry will be fed and the sad will be made happy.

But alas, this has not yet come about. The rich are doing well, they are filled and they are laughing all the way to the bank. Although Luke only hints that it won't always be so, 'you are having your consolation now', he leaves us with the question, 'What are we to do about it?', namely the whole problem of the rich and the poor. For us, it is very difficult to do anything, most of us have no wealth, none of us is in the seat of power, none of us has any desire to be a revolutionary. We know from experience that revolutions only manage to shift wealth from one section of the people to another. The communist bosses in the Soviet Union, in Czechoslovakia, in Hungary, in Romania and elsewhere feathered their own nests and lived in luxury just like the worst of Western tycoons.

Well then, what can we do about it? The first thing is that we should not be afraid to use the words 'the rich' and 'the poor'. They exist and the disparity between the rich and the poor is to be condemned and put right. It is not just a question of pointing to rich individuals. We can leave them to God. It is a question of pointing to those vast financial corporations which in recent years have made so much money that they have not known what to do with it. There are all those secret bank accounts abroad, there are all those monstrous office blocks which now ironically are empty. There are all those dubious characters who can operate stock exchanges to their own advantage and the ruin of others. In recent years there has been a disgusting lust for wealth regardless of the social evils that will be caused by it. There has been a thirst for profits, sometimes to the tune of 100%. We need to inform ourselves of these matters and, whether corporately or individually, we should have the courage to say that it is all wrong. That it is *unjust*. This is not my view. It is the view of the Second Vatican Council and of the popes for the last hundred years.

Since that council there has been a vast outpouring of giving through the national and international aid agencies, Caritas and our own Cafod, alongside all the other agencies which are doing the same kind of work. These call for our moral and financial support. And let it not be said that they are mere charitable agencies. They are not just pouring money into a bottomless pit. They are carrying out projects to enable poor nations to become economically viable, able to support their own people and to contribute to the wealth of the world. In other words, these agencies are promoting social justice and the church has pointed out, time and again, that you cannot have peace without justice. We then, even if only in a small way, can contribute to that justice that will bring the peace so long desired.

(*Note:* I have used 'blessed' as in the New Jerusalem Bible instead of 'Happy', as in the former edition. 'Happy' seems to me to indicate a subjective feeling. 'Blessed' is objective, a blessing from God, whatever may be our feelings!)

Seventh Sunday of the Year

1 Sam 26:22-23; Ps 102 (in part); 1 Cor 15:45-49; Lk 6:27-38.

It may seem rather odd that an Old Testament story should have been chosen to illustrate a New Testament commandment. Yet all told, it seems to be appropriate.

Saul, King of the Israelites, had pretty well adopted David as his successor. He became jealous of him for his popularity, he tried to kill him, David fled and became more or less a rebel. Here

Saul is at his mercy, unguarded, with his men lying asleep around him. David could easily have murdered him. He did not. He did good to the man who hated him.

When we turn to the gospel, which is Luke's version of the Sermon on the Mount, we find that we are in a world that seems very strange to us: Turn the other cheek, part with your overcoat as well as your jacket, give to all who ask and lend regardless. All this seems most impractical. If we lived like that there would be social chaos, and those who did these things would be ripped off right and left. How then are we to come to terms with this series of injunctions?

As last week, we are confronted with a way of speaking that is foreign to us. It uses sharp contrasts: 'Not this but that'; no 'rather this than that'. There are no grey areas. We are faced with a series of absolute statements: 'To the one who slaps you on one cheek, turn the other cheek too.' What, you may ask, about self-defence? 'Lend to all who ask.' You would be ruined. We can see that some of the injunctions concerned one's personal life and others that have a social dimension.

So first let us consider three things mentioned in the gospel: being hit by someone; giving your coat to someone who asks for it; and lending. The first question we have to ask, and it is a very important one, is, what do these sayings *mean*? As throughout the Sermon on the Mount, whether in Matthew or here in Luke, what Jesus is concerned about is our inner religion, or fundamental attitudes. If he says 'turn the other cheek' he means that we should not be unduly aggressive, that even if someone offends us we should not want immediately to retaliate. The model is Jesus himself who was slapped on the face during his trial. As St Peter wrote, Jesus 'was insulted and did not retaliate with insults; when tortured he made no threats' (1 Pet 2:23). What Jesus is saying (to put it crudely) is, 'Don't want to get your own back.'

What about giving away your coat or rather letting it go? I think here Jesus is telling us not to cling to our possessions too strongly and at the same time to be willing to help those in need. Perhaps you have two overcoats and could give one to a person in need. This is closely connected with the other saying, 'Give to those who ask'; what, to everyone? In the nineteenth century people divided the poor into the deserving and the undeserving. Only the deserving got help and then not much of it. The undeserving were left in their wretchedness. This was to sit in judgement on our neighbour and Jesus in the gospel tells us that that is precisely what we must not do: 'Do not judge and you will not be judged yourselves.' Of course there are problems here. If we know that a gift will be abused we must find some other way of helping the person. Discernment is different from judgement.

When we move to the social aspects of Jesus' teaching, the difficulties do not disappear: 'Love your enemies, do good to those who hate you ...' Have I any enemies? I don't know. What I do know is that I have lived through two great wars and have seen and known things that should not have been done. Is one allowed to hate those who are attacking one's country? No. We are not allowed to hate anyone. We can and must repel the enemy though nowadays war is so horrible and total, involving the killing of innocent people, the old and infants, that we can embark on it only with the gravest misgivings and after exhausting every possibility of peace. Any other sort of war is nowadays morally unjustifiable and, if you reflect on the matter, inconceivable. If we wonder if there is anything to be done about 'enemies', the answer is in the gospel: 'Love your enemies, do good to those who hate you ... and pray for those who treat you badly.' Prayer first and last can take hatred out of our hearts and prayer in the end will circumvent the enemy, as I believe it has done in our own time. The Berlin Wall fell in 1989.

In this Sermon on the Mount then, we have a whole programme of Christian living. It sets standards that are very difficult to live up to, but standards are becoming more and more important in our world. It is too slick to say that people must be taught the difference between right and wrong. It is one thing to know the difference between right and wrong and it is altogether another thing to do what is right, to love our enemies, to help the poor and to be generous to those in need. We all know that it is difficult and all of us fail at times and in one way or another. But we also know that without the grace of God, without the power of his love working within us, we could not do what is right and go on doing it. And grace comes from prayer and above all from the eucharist we celebrate week by week and that is why we should pray regularly, why we should come to church week by week to receive the life and love and power of Jesus Christ.

Eighth Sunday of the Year

Ecclus 27:4-7; Ps 91 (in part); 1 Cor 15:54-58; Lk 6:39-45.

I wonder if we remember that there is such a thing as a specifically Christian way of life that should mark us out as being Christians? I wonder if we realise that being a Christian lays on us certain obligations and duties and indicates to us how we should behave day by day? Some of those obligations and duties are suggested by the gospel today.

But first, it may be useful to remind you that today's gospel is the second part of Luke's version of the Sermon on the Mount and that it is a continuation of last Sunday's. As you will remember, it ended with some very radical and searching sayings: 'Be compassionate as your heavenly Father is compassionate. Do not judge and you will not be judged yourselves; grant pardon and you will be pardoned.' Those are fundamental attitudes we should all live up to. Today's gospel is a little more specific. There are what might be called three little parables showing us how we must behave in certain circumstances.

The first is about being superior, or rather about not being superior: 'The disciple is not superior to his teacher.' Sometimes we think we can hand out advice to others, but Jesus says you can't do that unless you have first learned from your teacher, as the student learnt (and still learns) from his rabbi, a word that means teacher. We need to know, we need to know in such a way that the knowledge becomes part of our way of living, something we have taken to heart and made our own. Only then are we fit to tell anyone else how to live. But knowledge, in the sense of mere information, is not enough. We have heard rather a lot recently about teaching the young the difference between right and wrong. Well and good, perhaps it is necessary, but unless the teaching is backed up by the example of good living it may well have little effect. I would add, it is one thing to know the difference between right and wrong and it is another to do what is right. As we all know, and as the scriptures remind us again and again, we know what is right but do not always do it, and if we are to do it we need the grace of God which comes from prayer and worship.

Luke's saying, 'The disciple is not superior to his teacher ...' appears in a slightly different form in the gospel of St John: 'No servant is greater than his master, no messenger is greater than one who sent him' (13:16). This gives Luke's saying a new dimension. Jesus himself is the great Teacher, the one who revealed the mystery of God and taught his disciples the meaning of his life, passion, death and resurrection. As we find elsewhere in the gospels, the voice from heaven tells us, 'Listen to him.' We need to listen to his word, we need to make it our own and live by it. We hear his word from the scriptures today, we receive his word as it is handed down to us by the church, and it is when we have listened and lived by the word that we can teach others.

The second parable of the splinter and the plank is about judging and carping criticism of others. We are all pretty good at picking holes in other people's characters and conduct and forgetting our own shortcomings. Alarmingly, Jesus is saying that it is easy to be a hypocrite. Correct yourself first, says Jesus, and remember that you too are going to be judged, and by God.

The third parable is the most important of the three and takes us deeper. Bad trees cannot produce fruit. Good words and good actions can come only from one who has a good heart. As the gospel says, our words flow out of what fills our hearts. That goes down to the root of the matter (if I may use that metaphor in this context). We speak what we are. If the human heart is full of bitterness and uncharitable thoughts, it will show in our words and our deeds, even when we do not realise it.

What then is the remedy, how can we come to have a good heart? What is certain is that we cannot produce good deeds and kind actions simply out of our human resources. It is no accident that this chapter in St Luke begins with love, love even to the extent of loving one's enemies and praying for them, as we do when we say, 'Forgive us our trespasses as we forgive those who trespass against us.' And the love I am speaking of is the love that comes from God: 'The love of God has been poured into our hearts by the Holy Spirit who is given to us.' It is with this love, which we receive from prayer and the sacraments, that we are able to love others, to think well of them and to speak well of them. It is this same love that enables us to go on loving our neighbour and to help and do good to them and any in need. The love of God active within us can cure a sour and a bitter heart. It is the same love of God that empowers us to live the Christian way of life.

Ninth Sunday of the Year

1 Kings 8:41-43; Ps 116: Gal 1:1, 2, 6-10; Lk 7:1-10.

When we are confronted with a miracle story in the gospels it is sometimes a good thing to stop and ask: What does it mean? What is it saying to us and indeed what was it saying to the people of the time, to whom Jesus was speaking? Why in fact did Jesus work miracles? Was he just going about working miracles to show that he was what was called at the time a 'divine man', a mere wonder-worker? There were a number of such wonder-workers in the world when Jesus lived and on occasion Jesus sharply distinguished himself from them. As we read, most notably in the gospel according to St John, miracles were 'signs', signs of events greater than themselves, signs of Jesus' mission which would come to its climax in his passion, death and resurrection. There is a sense that they were all pointing on to that time.

Miracles were signs by which Jesus evoked faith, even an incipient faith, so that people might be drawn to him and finally make a commitment of faith to him and in him. An example of this is the healing of the woman with the incurable issue of blood. As she trembled before him he said, 'Be of good heart, your faith has saved you', and saved in this context can mean 'saved' as well as 'healed'. This gives us a second clue to the meaning of the miracles which points in the same direction. They were works of divine power for *salvation.* Sent by the Father, Jesus is Saviour, he came to save people, body and soul, and he came to heal our diseases, the diseases of both body and soul, a power that is still available to us in the sacrament of the anointing of the sick when we hear the words, 'May the Lord who frees you from sin *save* you and raise you up.'

In the gospel of today, all these aspects of miracle-working are seen in play. The centurion, an officer in the Roman army, was not a Jew but pagan and well disposed to the Jews. He had contributed to the building of their synagogue. He had heard of Jesus who had spent much time in Capernaum. Now that his beloved servant was dangerously ill, he appealed to Jesus. He had an incipient faith for, almost as if he was in the presence of God, he showed his humility: 'I am not worthy to have you under my roof ... say but the word and let my servant be cured.' Without a personal meeting with Jesus, it seems he had come to faith, a fact that is recognised by Jesus in the most extraordinary manner: 'Not even in Israel have I found faith like this.'

To this Matthew adds in his account of the same incident: 'I tell you that many shall come from east and west to take their place at the feast of the kingdom of heaven' (8:14).

This saying, and the whole incident, is a foreshadowing of the coming of all sorts of people, Jews and pagans, into the kingdom, as they were when the gospels were being written. Those who did come were drawn first by an incipient faith in Jesus 'who had gone about doing good', and they came to full faith in him as Saviour and Son of God when they were baptised and celebrated their first eucharist and so committed themselves to him for life.

As for ourselves, we have never seen Jesus, but we have faith in him and love for him. So that our faith may be strengthened, we ponder on the gospels and particularly the humble faith of the centurion and, as we receive holy communion, let us make our own his prayer: 'Lord, I am not worthy to receive you, but only say the word and I shall be healed.' Let us open our hearts and receive Jesus with faith, humility and love, and then Sunday by Sunday our faith will grow stronger, our love more intense and at the end we shall sit down with the Saviour at the eternal banquet of heaven.

Tenth Sunday of the Year

1 Kings 17:17-24; Ps 29 (in part); Gal 1:1-11; Lk 7:11-17.

In a world that is fraught with calamities and much cruelty, in a world where we have witnessed the shocking killings of students and workers in China, of the murder of innocent people, mothers and young children in former Yugoslavia, and the indescribable killings of an untold number of people in Rwanda, we may well ask, 'Is God at work in the world?' That is a large and difficult question which cannot be answered in a few minutes on a Sunday morning. All I would say is that God was present in the ancient world, he was present in the world of the New Testament and he is present in ours, and when we say he is present we are saying that he is active, even if his action is obscured for a time by events.

God was present in the ancient world when the prophet Elijah, in a time of famine, was fed by the widow, and her son and, by the power of God working through him, was raised from death to life. That at least is how the ancient author of the Elijah-saga described the event.

There is a connecting link between this event and the raising of the son in the gospel account. Elijah gave the son to his mother and we read in the gospel that 'Jesus gave him (the son) to his mother.'

Last week we considered the meaning of miracles and we saw that they were signs to elicit faith. But that is not the whole story. Jesus *loved* people and when they were in distress he wanted to help them. Here, in this story of the raising of the young man, 'the only son of his mother', Jesus' whole heart is moved.[1] There is no previous dialogue, no request for faith, there is an astonishing directness about the whole incident. Jesus sees a widow torn by the sorrow of bereavement; her beloved son is gone, perhaps her only support. Jesus is moved to the depths. He stops the procession and says simply to the dead young man, 'Get up' and immediately he does so and begins to walk and Jesus gives him to his mother. The people rejoice and, perhaps remembering Elijah, they proclaim that God is still with his people.

Jesus loved people. He loved the little children whom he took into his arms and blessed. He loved the twelve-year-old daughter of Jairus and he raised her to life. He loved Lazarus, his friend, and called him forth after four days in the tomb. He looked with love and compassion on the crowds around him and he fed them all. He, the beloved Son of the Father, was making God's love present in the world of his time by words and deeds. His words were deeds, 'Get up', and his deeds were words, evoking the faith and love of those who would listen to him and those who would imitate him in his love.

'God has visited his people', he has not forgotten us, he is still visiting his people. He is here in this eucharist, he is present in different ways in the other sacraments, he is with us in prayer, especially the prayer of the church, for 'Where two or three are gathered together in my name, there I am in the midst of them.'

We may ask how and whether we can make Jesus present to those who suffer, those who are being tortured, those who are being brutally wounded by people who were their neighbours. It is we who make, or can make, Jesus present to them. We have been given a share in that love and with that love we can love them in Christ, who is with us as we pray for them, as we make their plight known, as we give to relieve their suffering, as we protest against the appalling violations of God's love that is incarnated in these poor victimised creatures. Jesus, who is ever-living to make intercession with his Father for them as well as us, unites our feeble prayers to his and makes his love present to all who suffer. 'God has visited his people', God *is* visiting his people. His visitation may be invisible; it is nonetheless real and all will be revealed at the end of time.

1. The translation 'he was sorry for her' is quite inadequate. Jesus' whole heart was moved with pity for her.

Eleventh Sunday of the Year

2 Sam 12:7-10, 17; Ps 31 (in part); Gal 2:16, 19-21; Lk 7:38-85.

Today we are presented with two of the greatest stories of repentance in the whole of the Bible. A man has sinned, a woman
has sinned; the balance is nicely kept. David sinned grievously
and his sin is described. The gospel however refuses to describe
the wrong-doing of the woman.

David lusted after Bathsheba, the wife of Uriah, one of his army
officers. He took her into his own household and made her his
mistress. He compounded his crime by ordering his general, Joab,
to put Uriah in the forefront of the next battle. This he did and
Uriah was killed. Nathan, David's personal prophet, comes to
him and shows him the enormity of his sins and David humbly
acknowledges his sinfulness: 'I have sinned against the Lord',
seemingly to echo the psalm (50/51) which at one time was
thought to be David's prayer of repentance:
   Have mercy on me, God, in your kindness.
   In your compassion blot out my offence.
   O wash me more and more from my guilt
   and cleanse me from my sin.

He has sinned against God: 'Against you, you alone, have I
sinned; what is evil in your sight I have done'; but he goes on to
pray, 'A pure heart create for me, O God, put a steadfast spirit
within me.'

The psalm of the Mass (31/32) provides a link with the gospel:
'You Lord, have forgiven the guilt of my sin.'

The woman of the gospel is not named (and it is generally held
now that she was not the Mary Magdalen named in the gospels
elsewhere). All that we are told is that she was a sinner and a notorious one. It seems that she was a prostitute and, in Jewish
eyes, unclean. Yet Jesus does not reject her but he reads his
host's thoughts. It is in the parable that we get the true interpretation of this incident and for an understanding of it, it is important to get it right.

It has been said in the past that the sinner woman fell in love with Jesus and because 'she had loved greatly' her sins were forgiven. The whole incident has thus been sentimentalised. Or it has been thought that because she loved, shown by her actions towards Jesus, she was saved by her good deeds. That we must not go along those lines is shown by the teaching of St Paul which we find briefly expressed in today's Mass: 'We acknowledge that what makes one righteous is ...faith in Christ.' The sinner had heard of Jesus, perhaps she had seen him talking to people and moving among those who like herself were sinners. However that may be, she comes into the Pharisee's house, as was perfectly permissible, and shows her faith and repentance by her tears, by anointing the feet of Jesus with precious perfume ... What was the meaning of it all?

There were two men in debt, one owing a large sum of money and one owing much less. The debt of both men was remitted and then Jesus puts the question: which one will love the creditor more? The answer, which proves to be the correct answer, is 'The one who was pardoned more'. The woman had sinned greatly, Jesus had forgiven her and she now shows faith and great love in return. Her sins, her many sins, *must have been forgiven her*, or she would not have shown such great love.

It may seem tedious to insist on these details. We have before us one of the great examples of repentance and forgiveness, *both* expressed in terms of love. It is that that is important. The woman was a sinner, a great sinner it seems, she was not a respectable member of human society, she was despised and 'untouchable'. Yet love goes out to her from Jesus, it touches her heart to repentance and she shows her love in return in the only way she knows how.

All of us have sinned in one way or another, and at one time or another, and as we look back over our lives we are probably not very proud of what we have done or failed to do. We, or others we know, may have been so overwhelmed by shame that we and they have been ashamed to declare our sins in confession. If this should have been so then we should reflect on the willingness of Jesus to receive sinners and the love that he has for them.

He did not shrink from the sinful woman and he will not shrink from us. Perhaps we can take away with us the saying of St Paul: 'I live in faith, faith in the Son of God who loved me and sacrificed himself for my sake'.

Twelfth Sunday of the Year

Zech 12:10-11, 13:1; Ps 62; Gal 3:26-29; Lk 9:18-24.

Today in the first reading we are confronted with a difficult and obscure text. It is not certain when the prophet was writing or, by consequence, the circumstances in which he was writing. Then there is the mysterious figure, 'the one they have pierced'.

How then are these difficulties to be cleared up and how can we find answers to our questions?

First we note that the prophet is speaking of the future, possibly the renewal of Israel: 'Over the House of David and the citizens of Jerusalem I will pour out a spirit of kindness and prayer'; and he goes on, 'when the day comes a fountain will be opened for the House of David' to take away sin and impurity. It is in this context that we hear of the 'one they look upon', the 'one whom they have pierced' and they will mourn and weep for him 'as for an only son'. Who was he? It is I think impossible to identify him but he seems to be like the Suffering Servant of the Second Isaiah: 'He was despised and rejected ... he as a man of sorrows, acquainted with grief ... Bearing our sorrows and griefs *he was wounded* for our sins and by his wounds we are healed.' Yet though beaten down by suffering and death he would, as Isaiah says, see his offspring and many would be made righteous, that is, in the terms we use, they will be saved. Zechariah seems to be presenting a figure over whom the people would 'mourn' and who was yet 'a fountain' of new life.

As the Christian church from the beginning has seen the Messiah in the Suffering Servant, so we see in the Pierced One, the Christ of God whom the disciples profess in the gospel of today. For the writer of St John's gospel this was certain. After the death of Jesus on the cross, a soldier pierces his side and John quotes this text: 'They shall look upon him they have pierced.' This understanding of the text is suggested by the gospel of today too. The disciples make their profession of faith in Jesus as Messiah and he foretells his suffering, his death on the cross and his resurrection. He was rejected by the people of his time, after his death his side was pierced by the lance, and he was mourned by the holy woman.

There is indeed another connection between this prophecy and the events of the crucifixion. St John records that after Jesus' side had been pierced there flowed out blood and water. Since the earliest days of the church, these have been understood to be symbols of the sacraments of baptism and the eucharist. As St Paul tells us in the Letter to the Romans, we, as it were, die with Christ in the waters of baptism and, as we are raised from the font, we are made like him in his resurrection, dying to sin and receiving from him a new life that we call grace. St Paul repeats this teaching today. We have been baptised in Christ, we have put on Christ as a garment, and so we are all one in him.

The blood is the eloquent symbol of the eucharist. Our union with Christ effected by baptism has to be sustained, nourished, as it is by the holy eucharist which we celebrate Sunday by Sunday. It is thus that by the water and the blood we are put into direct relationship with the Pierced One, the Messiah and the Son of God.

United with him, it is now for us to live out in our daily lives what he has given us. That is the message of Christ himself: 'If anyone wants to follow me, let him renounce himself and take up his cross everyday and follow me.' This is a hard lesson, per-haps the hardest lesson of the gospel, and there is much that might be said about it. I will take just those two words, 'every day'.

The message in these terms seems to involve two things. 1) There should be an element of self–denial, of restraint in all the good things of this life, in our daily living. There is much that we should like, so much we would like even if it were sinful, and we live in a world where people are grabbing everything from money to sex. As Christians, as followers of Christ, we should at least try to be a little different. 2) If we are to live the Christian life we need to look constantly with faith and love on the Pierced One, on Jesus hanging on the cross. We need to keep him before us day by day for he is not only our model, he is the source of life, the source of strength, of grace and love which enables us to bear the burdens of our daily life and to live for him and with him.

Thirteenth Sunday of the Year

1 Kings 16:19-21; Ps 15 (in part); Gal 5:1, 13-18; Lk 9:51-62.

Long ago in the fifteenth century, a man called Thomas à Kempis wrote a book (in Latin) called *The Imitation of Christ*. Translated into almost every language under the sun, it has been read ever since. In the eighteenth century, the saintly Bishop Richard Challoner translated it again and gave it the title *The Following of Christ*, which arguably is better than 'Imitation'. The following of Christ is what the gospel is about today.

But first we need to take note of the first sentence which marks a turning point in St Luke's gospel. Although he is less than a third of the way through his gospel, all the rest of it is put in the context of Jesus' death and resurrection. Jesus sets his face towards Jerusalem for the last time and, as Luke says, it would be the time of his being 'taken up'. That is, the time of his being raised up on the cross and his return to his Father in heaven. The passion, the death – only after that would come the resurrection; that was what lay ahead. That is what the following of Christ would have to take into account and that is why he uttered those seemingly harsh words to certain would-be followers. As he said to his first disciples early on, they must leave everything if they would follow him. As we heard last week, his followers must be prepared to renounce everything and deny themselves and only then could they be his true followers. When they heard the words about carrying the cross, it called up in their minds the instrument of a horrific death, crucifixion.

For the call of Jesus is absolute, and in that is different from the calling by Elijah of Elisha. Elisha could go and say goodbye to his father – if indeed he did for the story is not clear – because he could take the place of Elijah. But with Jesus this is not so. He is unique. We cannot take his place. The apostles could not take his place, the martyrs, most like him in their death, and even the later great saints, cannot take his place. He was the source of their self-giving. We can be like him or attempt to be like him and that is what the martyrs did and have done throughout the ages, and other saints have lived daily to the limit of their power for Christ and with him.

'To the limit of their power'. But that would not have been possible if the love of Christ had not been working within them. Following Christ is not just some sort of external imitation. It is the fruit of Christ's dwelling within us. As St Paul said, 'I live, no longer I. It is Christ who lives in me.' And Christ lives in us through the Holy Spirit who makes him present to us. If we are led by the Spirit, and allow ourselves to be led by the Spirit, then we shall produce the fruits of the Spirit, love, joy, peace and the rest, as St Paul says in the next verses of today's readings. We can begin to become Christ-like. That is a possibility that lies open to us all and that is what we are destined to become. By baptism we began to live in Christ, his image was imprinted on our souls. and by the holy eucharist we are sustained in union with him to the end of our days.

Is there then anything we can do, must do. What is our part in this deep and almost mystical process of becoming like Christ? First we have to open ourselves, our minds and our hearts, to his coming. We must try to be submissive to his action within us in lowliness of heart, as we pray in the psalm, 'A humbled, contrite heart you will not spurn.' Then, supported by his power, we can offer everything we do to him. That is our Christian calling, that is the vocation of us all, and if we are faithful then we too will be taken up where Jesus is and share his glory that never ends.

has done through the ages. Mission, evangelisation, involves community and sacrament and the aim of all mission is to incorporate into the community all who come through the preaching of the word, so that there shall be visible presence of the word and the saving work of our Lord Jesus Christ. Not yet the completed 'kingdom of God,' the church leads us to that final consummation when there will be a new heaven and a new earth and all will be gathered into Christ.

Fifteenth Sunday of the Year

Deut 30:10-14; Ps 68 (in part); Col 1:15-20; Lk 10:25-37.

Sometimes the gospel message seems so bland, unchallenging. It puts before us impeachable sentiments and we say, 'That's fine', we approve, and then we go away without thinking any more about it. We are in danger of being like the man in the Letter of St James 'who listens to the word and does not obey it'. He, as it were, looks at himself in a mirror, likes what he sees and then goes away and forgets all about the word of God.

So it is with this lovely story of the Good Samaritan. We rather think we are like him, we identify with him and we kid ourselves that we should do as he did.

In fact the parable has a quite stern message. Who or what was a Samaritan? For some centuries there had been a division between the Samaritans and the rest of the Jews. As we should say now, there was a schism between them, a schism that was partly religious, partly racial and partly political. The Samaritans, living north of Jerusalem, had separated themselves from the rest, had set up their own kingdom, had built their own temple and had their own version of the law, the Torah. As we know from St John, they had nothing to do with each other and, at least officially, hated each other. It was a man of these people who approached the wounded man, a Jew, by the roadside, tended him and there and then took him to an inn and paid for his care.

That is the first lesson of the gospel of today. Everyone is our neighbour, even those who are divided from us by religious, racial or political differences.

This makes the parable very contemporary. The world is still full of hatred – we have the example of Northern Ireland always before us – but even those who hate us are our neighbours and, as Jesus says, more than once we must love them. We may agree with that in a general sort of way but let us put this question to ourselves and try honestly to answer it: Suppose that by some impossible chance we had come across a Hitler or a Stalin, lying wounded somewhere, and suppose that we knew they would die unless we helped them in some way. Responsible for the murder of millions of people, they were wicked men and the world would have been a better place if they had been left to die. What would we have done? I leave you to find an answer. The gospel is saying that even these wicked men are our neighbours.

But there are others who are our neighbours, as the psalm of today suggests:
    The poor when they see it will be glad
    and God-seeking hearts will revive;
    for the Lord listens to the needy
    and does not spurn his servants in their chains.

This calls up to our minds a whole vision of the world in which we live. It is one of the bitter ironies of our world that in the midst of plenty there are millions of people in want. They are our neighbours. At home there are the needy, the deprived, the homeless, the disabled and the marginalised. All these evoke our compassion and there has been no want of compassion in our time. We remember the spontaneous giving of money and supplies to the starving in Ethiopia, to the victims of the earth-quake in Armenia, and the strenuous efforts to get food and medical supplies to a war-torn Bosnia. These are but examples of generosity in recent years. Less spectacular are the efforts of Catholic and other organisations not only to meet emergencies but to provide the means of self-support and future indepen-dence. This brings us to the second lesson of the parable.

Compassion is not enough, and you will have noticed that Luke gives his story a certain twist at the end. The lawyer – he might have been a modern politician – asks, 'Who is my neighbour?', expecting the answer, it would seem, 'Everyone is your neighbour.' But Luke goes on remorselessly, 'But who was the neighbour?', and the lawyer is forced to say, 'The one who took pity on him.' Then Jesus says, 'Go and do the same yourself'. Love, compassion, mercy demand *doing*. Mercy is a love that goes out to rescue. It acts and that implies that we all have to act. Vague benevolence is not enough. All of us must be concerned with our 'neighbours' whether they are at home or far away and we need to go on doing so. That is the hard bit, and only if the love of God is active within us can we persevere. That love is in our hearts and the law of love that he enjoins on us today is not beyond our strength or our reach. It is in the power of God's love within us that we can have compassion and mercy for God's poor, and it is in the power of that love that we can go out and rescue those in need: 'Do this and life is yours.'

Sixteenth Sunday of the Year

Gen 18:1-10; Ps 14 (in part); Col 1:24-28; Lk 10:38-42.

I know that this gospel sometimes irritates busy mothers, but before I try and deal with that question, let us consider the messages of the scriptures today. For in fact there are two.

The first is about the virtue of hospitality, of which we have the first example in the story of Abraham and the angelic visitors. Here Abraham is practising one of the most ancient customs known to the human race in all ages and all over the globe. The visitors arrive unexpectedly and immediately Abraham welcomes them, washes the dust of the road off their feet and then asks Sarah to prepare a meal for them. That is welcome, that is hospitality, even if we note that Sarah had to do most of the work. Abraham prepared the calf. All this seems very simple and ordinary. But there is something more here and this visit by the angels has for long centuries been regarded as mysterious. In the Old Testament, the presence of angels was regarded as the presence of God himself; they were messengers making God present. This is the sense of the ancient Russia icon depicting the two angels and Abraham.

This is found even more clearly in the New Testament. Jesus says, as you will remember, 'Anyone who welcomes you welcomes me, and those who welcome me, welcome the one who sent me.' To welcome others, to offer them food and drink and even, if they need them, clothing, is to offer them to Christ who said, 'In as far as you did this to one of the least of my people, you did it to me'.

This is the deepest meaning of hospitality and we can thank God that it is going on all the time. Whenever you welcome someone into your home and give them a cup of tea, you are welcoming Christ, as St Benedict told his monks to do in his Rule.

So we come to the second part of the story of Martha and Mary. All the favour seems to go to her. Martha was busy about many things, about preparing the meal; indeed she was worrying and fretting. Was the meal going to be good enough for the visitor? Would it be ready in time? Meanwhile her sister Mary was sitting at the feet of Jesus listening to his words. Perhaps, as Martha might have said under her breath, 'doing nothing'.

The reason why the gospel irritates busy people is that it seems to make them second class Christians and they protest inwardly: 'We can't all sit down and read the Bible for as long as we like.' Or 'Have we all got to become nuns and monks?'

Let us look at the text carefully. 'Mary has chosen the better part.' The original reads 'Mary has chosen the *good* part', that is, she has chosen something that is good, something that is indeed necessary. All of us need to listen to the word of Jesus and we all need to take time off to do so. Excessive, on-going activity can wear us out and blot out any sense of God and of the presence of God with us. There are certain things that are more important than our daily tasks. If Martha was being criticised for anything, it was not so much for being busy as for fretting and fussing. In any case, later on Martha showed that she had been listening to Jesus. After the death of her brother she makes her profession of faith in Jesus: 'Lord, I believe that you are the Christ, the Son of

God, the one who was to come into the world.' Perhaps she had more than an inkling of this as she welcomed Jesus to her home.

If we understand the gospel in this way, perhaps busy people, especially mothers with small children, will no longer feel irritated. They are on the stretch sometimes for almost twenty–four hours of the day. Little children are very demanding. They have to be cared for, washed and fed and even at night in their little fears and needs they will cry out for their mothers. But then and above all, she is serving Jesus in the persons of the little ones. Her life may well be stressful and at this point we might recall the message about hospitality. Others not so burdened could offer to take care of the children for a day, or part of a day, so that the mother can relax. She, like us, may then be able to reflect a little on the words of Peter to Jesus: 'You have the message of eternal life.' In listening to his word, as we do or should do whenever we have the opportunity, and praying, we are all being Marys and, by helping others as well, we are combining Martha and Mary in ourselves.

Seventeenth Sunday of the Year

Gen 18:20-32; Ps 137 (in part); Col 2:12-16; Lk 11:1-13.

What, you may say, yet another sermon about prayer? Well, yes, that is the obvious sense of the scriptures today and as people often have difficulties about prayer, especially the prayer of petition which is so much the theme of the readings, it will, I think, will be useful and I hope helpful to say something about the matter today.

First, let us remember that there are different kinds of prayer, and it is important to do so, as the prayer of petition is best seen against the background of a kind of prayer that takes us out of ourselves and directs us to God. This is the prayer of praise and thanksgiving, as in the psalm: 'I will thank you, Lord, with all my heart ... I will adore before your holy temple.' This reminds us of the lovely prayer of the Gloria in the Mass: 'We praise you, we bless you, we glorify you, we give you thanks for your great glory …'. And it is important to note that the first phrase of our Lord's prayer is, 'Father, may your name be held holy'. That is, 'May your name be held in reverence', and by us; or simply 'Holy is your name', because God is the All-holy One. Then there is the public Prayer of the Church, the Divine Office, when the local Christian community gathers together for prayer, to sing for example Vespers or Evening Prayer, which consists of both praise and petition. Through the Prayer of the Church, when we are united with Christ, we give acceptable worship to God. It is a great pity that it has disappeared from our parish life.

Thirdly, there is private or personal prayer, when we speak to God in our own words, or simply stay still, thinking about God, reflecting on his great and unfailing love for us shown in the life, teaching and passion and death of our Lord Jesus Christ. It is the sort of prayer that keeps our faith alive and enables us to live with Christ day by day.

All these forms of prayer combine praise and thanksgiving with petition or asking prayer, and it is with this that the gospel and the reading from Genesis are chiefly, and, one might say, urgently concerned. But it is precisely this prayer of petition that gives people most trouble. People say, 'I have prayed for this or that for years and my prayers have never been answered', or, 'I have prayed that so-and-so may get better … may be converted … but she or he is not or does not.' What then is the answer to these and similar questions?

The first answer comes out of the gospel itself. The total meaning of the Lord's Prayer is that it is an expression of complete trust in God, the Father who loves us. The prayer of petition is supremely the prayer of faith, one would say almost blind faith, but it is a faith that is based on the goodness of God who cares for us and knows all our needs.

The second answer will be found in those other words of Jesus: 'Ask and it will be given to you: search and you will find; knock and the door will be opened to you …' These words, which can be paralleled in other parts of the gospels, are absolute. Whether we know it or not, sincere prayer is always answered: 'The one who asks receives; the one who searches always finds'. No prayer addressed to God goes unanswered even if we do not know how it is answered.

But it must be true prayer and this brings us to the heart of the matter. I have used the word 'faith' but that is just another way of saying that we must have complete submission to the will of God, as is indicated in Matthew's version of the Lord's prayer: 'Your will be done'. When we are asking God for anything, we are not trying to change his mind, we are not trying to push him to give what he doesn't want to give. We are not praying, 'My will be done', we are not trying to impose our wills on God, but precisely the opposite. We are submitting ourselves to him, we are fitting ourselves into his vast and loving purpose for the good of the whole human race. Which is just another way of saying that we are trying to do his will for ourselves but also for others.

Finally, let us remember that, as Christians and members of the church, we are always praying with and through Christ, as so many of the prayers of the liturgy show us. What is more, we are consciously putting ourselves with Christ in the agony in the garden. There he prayed again and again, 'Father, not my will but yours be done.' In our prayer we are enfolding our wills in his. We are praying with him, in union with him, and how should such a prayer not be answered? As we read in the Letter to the Hebrews, 'His power to save is utterly certain, since he is living for ever to intercede for all who come to God through him.' Praying with Jesus is the heart of Christian prayer and, if our will is set with his, then we can pray with the fullest confidence, with tranquility and peace of mind. We are in the hands of God, and with Julian of Norwich we can say, 'All shall be well, all manner of things shall be well, all shall be very well.'

Eighteenth Sunday of the Year

Ecc 1:2, 21-25; Ps 89 (in part); Col 3:1-5, 9-11; Lk 12:13-21.

It is sometimes said that 'money is the root of all evils', and there are those who think it is a quotation from scripture. What the scripture says is, 'The love of money is the root of all evils' (1 Tim 6:10), and the quotation continues, 'and there are some who, pursuing it, have wandered away from the faith, and given their souls any number of wounds.' Or, as another translation has it, 'pierced their hearts with many pangs'. Evidently the *love* of money is dangerous and can do great harm to those who pursue it and to others who suffer from their depredations. In recent years we have heard a great deal about the love or lust for money, not only on the part of individuals but by large corporations and institutions of the City who have heaped up enormous wealth which has become concentrated in the hands of the few. It is not for me to attempt a description, or much less an analysis, of the situation that this lust for wealth has created but there are those who can judge who think that much of our economic distress now is the result of that behaviour.

The rich farmer of the gospel, if a tycoon, seems to have been an honest tycoon. He and his workers have worked hard, they have gathered in so great a harvest that the barns are not big enough to contain the yield. Regardless of the future and forgetting that abundant harvests do not occur every year, the farmer has vast new barns built and thinks that he will have enough for many years to come. What is worse, he thinks this happy situation can go on forever. 'Eat, drink and be merry,' he says to himself. What he has he will go on possessing and enjoying for many years to come. The future is a long way off and he need not worry about it. He has forgotten that one's life is not made secure by what one owns. We can heap up riches (or some can), we can multiply our possessions, we can go after the latest gadget, and above all we can become to so attached to what we have that we think we can find security in them. That is the great mistake, and it is that radical error that the preacher is pointing out today: 'Vanity of vanities, all is vanity.' All these things, all this wealth is as nothing when we leave this world. All possessions are transient things and as one grows old one realises that this is so. If we live long, we find that gradually things are stripped from us. Movement is restricted, we cannot do this or that, we cannot eat this or that, we become dependent on others and whatever little wealth we may have had gradually dwindles in one way or another.

That may seem a gloomy picture. But in fact it is the kindness of God who is gently teaching us not to rely on material goods. He is gently teaching us that there is something of infinitely greater worth that does last for ever. 'Where your treasure is, there is your heart also', and the treasure is God himself, the infinitely generous God who offers us a permanent happiness with himself: 'Think of the love that the Father has lavished on us by letting us be called God's children ... we are indeed God's children but what we are to be in the future has not yet been revealed; all we know is that, when it is revealed, we shall be like him because we shall se him as he really is' (1 Jn 3:1, 2), and seeing him, we shall be filled with an indescribable joy.

Does the gospel suggest anything we can do, any line of action that would be appropriate and indeed necessary if we are to try and live out the saying 'Where your treasure is there is your heart also'? We might take a hint from the psalm, 'Make us know the shortness of our life that we may gain wisdom of heart. ' 'Wisdom of heart', in this context, is the sense we have that, however long our life may be, it yet will come to an end. Then we shall encounter God who lives for ever. As we grow into old age, let us pray that we may less and less be attached to the things of this world and so be ready to come into the presence of God, casting all our care on him, knowing that he will hold us up and keep us close to him for all eternity.

Nineteenth Sunday of the Year

Wis 18:6-9; Ps 32 (in part); Heb 11:1, 2, 8-19; Lk 12:32-48.

Sometimes the scriptures are clear and sometimes they are not, and there is no harm in admitting that we do not always understand them. It is the same for the preacher. When they are hard to understand he has to search the scriptures and find out what they are saying. So today. What, we may ask, is the author of the Book of Wisdom talking about? Let us see.

'That night had been foretold to our ancestors.' The 'night' was the night of the first Passover, when God through Moses told the Israelites to prepare a meal of roast lamb and bitter herbs on the eve of their deliverance from the captivity in Egypt. They were to eat in haste, with their clothes girded up as for the journey that would begin next morning. This meal was the first Passover, the sign of the passing of God over Egypt and the sign of the passage of the Israelites into the desert. The Passover meal was to be the memorial of the Lord's presence with his people and later, in the desert, it was connected with the covenant God made with his people: He would be their God and they would be his people if they accepted his laws and commandments, the way of life of the chosen people of God. Moses took the blood of the lamb and sprinkled it over the people saying, 'This is the blood of the covenant.' The Passover was kept every year at about what we call Easter time. God had visited his people and this they were to remember throughout the ages.

In the gospel, Jesus recalls that visitation of God with the words, 'See that you are dressed for action ...' like the Israelites of old. There is to be another visitation of God: 'Be like men waiting for their master to return from the wedding feast ...' What was this wedding feast? In the New Testament it is, in the first place, a symbol of the eucharist and, as we know, later Jesus would gather together his disciples at Passover time and at the Last Supper he would say a prayer of blessing over the bread and offer it to them, 'This is my body that will be given up for you'; this is myself to be given up for you. Likewise, over the cup of wine he said, 'This is the blood of the new covenant, shed for you', for the taking away of sins. This is my life poured out for you, as it was next day on the cross. Jesus is the Paschal Lamb, the Passover Lamb, and in his self-offering he establishes a new covenant, a new union with his people, a covenant that transcends the old for it is the gift of God himself to us, and the source of eternal life.

Like the old covenant, it was to be a perpetual memorial of the action of God for his people, an action that we call salvation, and it is a memorial that effects that action and presence among us every time we celebrate it: 'Do this in memory (or as a memorial) of me.'

God came to his people in various ways in the Old Testament. Jesus, the Son of God, came in the flesh to save the people and he comes to us every time we celebrate the eucharist. But the gospel seems to be referring to a time in the future, perhaps in a long distant future: 'You must stand ready, because the Son of Man is coming at an hour you do not expect.' When would this be? Jesus does not say, and in the gospel of Mark he says that no one knows, neither the angels in heaven nor the Son (Mk 13:32). What immediately lay before him was his contests with the Jewish leaders and, as he realised, their growing hostility. He saw ever more clearly that they would bring him to his death. But constantly, and especially in St John's gospel, he refers to the time after his death and resurrection when he says he will be with his disciples, and presumably with those who attach them- selves to them: 'I will not leave you orphans.' He will send the Holy Spirit who will make him, Jesus, present to them.

The Lord came, the Lord will come again, the Lord comes to us here and now. He is present in our prayers, he is present in his word, he is present in the eucharist, and if we welcome him now that will be the best preparation for his coming in glory at the end of time. Then we shall sit down with him at the eternal banquet of which the eucharist is the foreshadowing and the promise: 'Blessed are those who are called to the wedding feast of the Lamb' (Apoc 19:9).

Twentieth Sunday of the Year

Jer 38:4-6, 8-10; Ps 39 (in part); Heb 12:1-4; Lk 12:49-53.

The scriptures today speak of acceptance and rejection, accept- ance of the word of God and rejection of it, acceptance of Christ by faith and the awful consequence of rejecting him. So we have set before us two figures, the figure of Jeremiah, so often seen as a type of Christ, and Jesus himself who utters the anguished words, 'I have come to bring fire to the earth and how I wish it were blazing already. There is a baptism I must still receive and how great is my distress until it is over.'

Jeremiah, speaking on the brink of invasion and captivity, has been exhorting the authorities of Jerusalem to listen to God's word that he has been commissioned to proclaim. They must reject the false hope of deliverance by the Egyptians and they must accept God's assurance that, if they trust in him, they will avoid at least the worst effects of invasion and captivity. We see the results of his preaching. He is thrust down the well and left there to die.

Jesus too has been in conflict with the Jewish authorities, he has severely criticised them for substituting external observance of the law for a response to God from the heart: 'Unless your virtue is greater than that of the scribes and Pharisees, you cannot enter the kingdom of heaven.' Jesus is becoming aware that the tension between them and himself is growing, and yet he has a mission to fulfil that will have painful consequences both for himself and those who follow him. So first he expresses his ardent desire that his mission should be accomplished, 'I have come to bring fire to the earth ...' He is speaking of the Holy Spirit who will come upon his disciples and will spark off their ardent preaching of Christ and him crucified. He is speaking of the scandal of the cross which will be a stumbling block to the Jews and folly to the Gentiles. He is speaking of his own painful death, the baptism he must receive by which he will inaugurate the new age, the messianic age when the fire of the Holy Spirit will touch their hearts and prompt them to accept Christ in faith. A little later he speaks of the reading of the signs of the times. The people can read the signs of the weather, when a cloud looms up they know that rain is coming, but they cannot read the most important sign of all, his presence among them and his word.

As holy Simeon had said, 'this Child is set for the fall and rise of many'. He will be a sign of contradiction, a sign that will be rejected – as he was. Many however would come to accept him, both of his own people as of the Gentiles. They would accept him as the true Messiah sent by God, as indeed the Son of God who would bring salvation, reconciliation and peace. That was his Father's purpose and that was Jesus' ardent desire. Those who accept him, those who will commit themselves to him in faith will, as St John says, be made children of God, united to the Father through the Son by the power of the Holy Spirit.

But there remain those terrible words, 'Do not suppose that I am here to bring peace on earth' ... father will be divided against son and mother against daughter, and so on. What do these words mean? As I have said, Jesus is speaking of the scandal of the cross which will divide, he is thinking of the time after his death and resurrection when his disciples will proclaim the Christ and him crucified, and then there will be those who accept the crucified Christ and those who will reject him. And so it has gone on throughout history. Quite beyond the desire or intention of Jesus, he would become the cause of division.

Such division can be in our own hearts too. We can be half-hearted about believing Christ, of serving him, and this sets off conflict within us. If that by any chance should be so, let us turn to the reading of the Letter to the Hebrews: 'Let us not lose sight of Jesus who leads us in our faith.' He is leading us into an ever deeper faith if we will let him, if we open our hearts to him. He is our model, our help and our salvation: 'For the sake of the joy which was still in the future (the resurrection), he endured the cross, disregarding the shamefulness of it, and from now on has taken his place at the right of God's throne' where, as we read in the same letter, he is always interceding for us.

We can take courage too from some other words of the same writer who snatches victory out of defeat: 'Think of the way he stood *such opposition* from sinners and then you will not give up for want of courage.' Yes, there are times when we must oppose the world so that we can be with Jesus.

Twenty-first Sunday of the Year

Is 66:18-21; Ps 116; Heb 12:5-7, 11-13; Lk 13:22-30.

It has been said, and it is felt by many today, that one of the difficulties about Christianity is that it is so particular. We are asked
to believe, they say, that God made known his teachings and his
commandments to a small, obscure people called Israelites living on a small piece of land that had been trampled by the troops
of all the empires of the ancient world. Worse, he chose to communicate his message through a Jew of that race, even if he and
his followers claimed that he was the Son of God. Against the
background of the vastness of the universe and the length of its
history, such a procedure and such a claim seems improbable. It
is what is compendiously called 'the scandal of particularity'.

Against that, it can be said that all we know of God shows us
that he deals in particularities to work out his plan which is
worldwide and indeed cosmic, embracing heaven and earth. He
chose one people as the vehicle of his message, he chose one
man, his own Son, the Christ and son of Mary, to reveal himself
and his teachings, and this man, Jesus Christ, hung on the cross
for the salvation of the whole world: 'And I, when I am lifted up,
will draw everyone to myself.'

But if God chose one people, they learnt only gradually that they
were chosen to be the instrument of God for the proclamation of
the word to the peoples of the world. This is expressed in the
passage from Isaiah, which is perhaps the most universalist passage in the whole of the Old Testament. After the seventy years
of exile, and now after the first efforts of the Jews to rebuild
Jerusalem and the holy Temple, there comes the voice of the
prophet: 'The Lord says this: I am coming to gather the nations
of every language.' The message seems a foreshadowing of
Pentecost. Not only that, not only will the message go forth
throughout the Roman Empire, from east to west, but the pagan
converts will bring 'all the brothers' from the nations and will
themselves be made priests and levites in the restored and new
Jerusalem.

This seems to be echoed by the very words of Jesus himself: 'They will come from east and west, from north and south, and take their places at the feast of the kingdom of God.'

This we feel is wonderful, we are exhalted by the vision of the peoples of the world streaming into the kingdom. God, through his Son Jesus, through the prophets and now through the church, calls and invites everyone into his kingdom. But are there no conditions, no conditions at all? It is here that the tension between particularity and universalism becomes acute. If we would enter the kingdom then we have to enter by the 'narrow door' and that narrow door is faith, a personal faith, a committing and committed faith in Jesus, who at the same time is the universal Saviour of the human race. It is not good enough to say, 'Oh, yes, we knew him. We said "Hello" to him in the street. We even had a meal with him and he spoke to us. He was very nice.' We need to recall those words of Jesus to be found in another place: 'It is not anyone who says to me "Lord, Lord" who will enter the kingdom ...' What is required is that we should be ready and willing to 'do the will of the Father in heaven' and the will of the Father is that we should accept his Son Jesus and live by all he has told us to do.

But what of those outside? What of those who would like to believe and find it difficult, or, as they would say, impossible to do so? For them we must have the utmost compassion; we must not only pray for them but we must examine our own ways of acting and speaking. Are we a bit exclusive, thinking that we are in the right club? All is well with us and we are not too keen on seeing outsiders come in? Are our ways of speaking about our own attachment to the church, and about religious doctrine or Catholic ways, off-putting? A touch arrogant? Do we care whether our discourse about religion is comprehensible to those outside? To pose these questions is to pose a greater one. Are we, is the church as a whole, really communicating with a world for which the jargon of religion is literally incomprehensible? That in turn poses the question: what should we be doing to make the church and its teaching attractive and comprehensible to those without knowledge of, or faith in, the Christian revelation? This is the great problem that faces Christians and the church in this post-Christian, industrialised west. If people are once more to come streaming into the kingdom, these questions will have to be answered.

Twenty-second Sunday of the Year

Ecclus 3:17-20, 28, 29; Ps 67 (in part); Heb 12:18, 19, 22-24; Lk 14:1, 7-14.

This gospel is not just about good manners, about not pushing yourself forward, about waiting to be given your place at table by your host. No doubt, we all need to 'mind our manners' in these free and easy days when anything seems to go. But it is not the business of the gospel to teach good manners though we can see that good manners are the result of a deeper, inner attitude.

The first thing to note is that what Jesus is saying is a parable and he told parables to make us think, to challenge us. As so often when Pharisees are mentioned, there is a certain undercurrent. They were rather satisfied with themselves, they kept the law more perfectly than others and, as the gospel story shows, they expected to have the best places at table – rather like certain prelates and priests of a later age! Jesus however is saying, Wait to be asked, wait to be given. Salvation, grace, are the totally free gift of God; there is no way of getting it other than by receiving it from God through Jesus Christ. Let us recall the words of St John: 'Think of the love that the Father has lavished upon us'; he has made us his children, he will make us like him when, by his grace, we meet him at the end of our lives.

If we look at the parable in another way that is suggested by the first reading, what is being referred to is what we call humility: 'The greater you are, the more you should behave humbly.' Humility, that is the inner virtue from which come good manners. Humility, a word which comes from *humus*, the ground; we put ourselves at ground level vis à vis others. Or perhaps we can say, we respect others, recognise their worth rather than thinking of our own. Understandably, then, all the spiritual writers regard humility as the ground and foundation of the spiritual life. It was so important to St Benedict that he discerned twelve degrees of humility. I will not detail them to you now, though they are very well worth considering.

Still, I do not think this goes to the heart of Jesus' teaching in the parable. It is possible, and no doubt very usual, to think of humility simply in terms of our relations with other people. It is, however, the fundamental virtue because it is the basis for our relationship with God. What does that mean? In the biblical phrase, 'Walking humbly before God', it means that we stand before him in an attitude of reception. All comes from him, our very existence, our salvation, grace, our status as Christians, all the love that has been lavished upon us from the beginning of our existence until now. 'Walking humbly before God' means listening to God's word as we hear it in church or reading it at home. It means pondering on God's word and seeking its meaning for our lives. No doubt we need guidance and that we get in a general way from the church. 'Walking humbly before God' means praying to him and listening to him in prayer. It can mean simply silence, being before God, in his presence, reflecting on the words, 'Be still, and know that I am God.'

If all this seems merely passive, too passive, we should remember that it is in these ways that we assimilate, take to ourselves and make our own, God's word and God's grace. It is by these that we in fact live as Christians and they are the source of every kind of Christians activity we may undertake.

And Christian action is what is suggested by the last paragraph of the gospel. As God has freely given us his grace and love with a boundless generosity, so Jesus urges us to give as freely as we have been given. Do not entertain just your relatives and friends. Invite the poor, the crippled, the lame, and the blind, for in doing so you are becoming a channel to others of the grace and love you have so abundantly received.

Twenty-third Sunday of the Year

Wis 9:13-18; Ps 89 (in part); Letter to Philemon; Lk 14:25-33.

The words of the first sentence of the gospel today are perhaps the most frightening of any we hear. 'If anyone comes to me without hating his father and mother ...' Can these be the words of Jesus? Are they not in contradiction of those other words of

his, so often repeated, 'Love one another'? Then again, they do
not seem to have anything to do with the second and longer part
of the gospel, about building towers and going to war. There *is* a
connection and it is to be found in the word 'disciple' at the end
of the first sentence. We will reflect on these two parts separately
first and then see how they are connected.

First, let us think about the harsh words of Jesus. As I remember
saying to you before, the language Jesus spoke, Aramaic, liked
very strong contrasts. Everything was either black or white.
There was nothing that we call a comparative and Matthew in
his gospel brings in a comparative; if anyone loves father or
mother *more than* Jesus he is not worthy to follow him. That, I
suggest, is how we should understand these harsh words as
recorded by Luke. As the Bible says in many places, as the books
of spirituality have said for centuries, God must be the object of
our love, he is the supreme object of love, we must love God
with all our hearts, mind and strength. If we do, or if we try to,
then we can love others in God, with the love he plants in our
hearts.

This is especially true of discipleship, the following of Christ,
which is what the gospel of today is all about. In our easy-going
way we all like to think that we are followers of Christ. We believe the Catholic faith, we say our prayers, we come to Mass,
we try and live our lives according to his teachings which are
communicated to us by the church. But what does this cost us?
Has it come a matter of routine? And what happens when things
go wrong? Do we moan and groan and perhaps say, 'I can't go
on'? It is just at that point that we should realise that we are
being asked to pay the cost of discipleship. The Christian life, or
rather the Way of Christ, is not always easy and for some it is
very painful, almost a crucifixion. It is then that we must cling to
Christ, uniting ourselves and our pain with him and his suffering, the suffering he took on himself on our behalf. By his very
suffering we are granted the strength to bear ours, whatever it
may be.

Understandably when we were young and when we decided to
follow Christ (as we did, or we would not be here today), we did

not think of these things; in the terms of the gospel, we did not sit down and count the cost. To echo the words of the Book of Wisdom, we did not recognise or did not recognise fully that 'this perishable body presses down the soul and that this tent of clay weighs down the teeming mind.' We are human, all too human, and it takes time to recognise our weaknesses and our faults. Nonetheless Jesus calls us, urges us to follow him who is the light, and if we remain faithful he will enlighten us, enabling us to see the meaning of our dismay or suffering, and supporting us with his grace and love. Like the man thinking of building a tower, we sit down and 'count the cost', that is, we review our life and our situation, and, calling upon our Saviour, we determine to go on. Come what may, we continue to follow Christ, we give ourselves to him in prayer, and above all in the celebration of the eucharist. In doing so, we are with Jesus Christ and he is with us, and perhaps with the psalmist we shall be able to sing, 'In the morning fill me with your love, and I shall exult and rejoice all the days of my life'.

Twenty-fourth Sunday of the Year

Ex 32:7-11, 13, 14; Ps 50 (in part); 1 Tim 1:12-17; Lk 15:1-12.

Today the lectionary seems to give us too much; three parables together and four if we count the words and actions of the elder son as separate from the parable of the Prodigal. Extended commentary on all of them would be out of place, and we have to look for a theme that binds the first reading, the psalm and all three parables together.

The passage from Exodus marks a crucial turning point in the story of the Israelites in the wilderness. Moses their leader has been in the mountain communing with God and receiving from him the Way of Life, the Law called the Ten Commandments. The Israelites have apostasised and provoked the wrath of God. At this point Moses shows that he is not only the leader, but also the mediator. He pleads urgently for the people, knowing full well their wickedness; he 'reminds' God of the promises he had made to Abraham, Isaac and Jacob and he obtains God's forgiveness for the people. But they, they had to repent and do penance. Though written much later, we can put the prayer of the psalm on their lips: 'Have mercy on me, God, in your kindness, In your compassion blot out my offence ...'

The response, however, leads us to the gospel: 'I will leave this place and go to my father.'

Luke wrote his gospel with great care and artistry, and it is no accident that he prefaced the three parables with the first sentence of this chapter. The tax–gatherers, the 'sinners', the ritually unclean, the riff-raff, swarmed around him and he welcomed them – to the scandal of the smug and self-satisfied. Whether these 'sinners' repented or not we do not know, but it seems to be hinted that they did by the first parable. Jesus appears as the Shepherd and he goes beyond welcoming sinners. He goes out to them, he acts, he intervenes. He finds the errant sheep, brings it home gently on his shoulders and proclaims, 'Rejoice ... there will be more rejoicing in heaven over one repentant sinner than over the virtuous ninety-nine who have no need of repentance.' He is like the housewife who will turn the house upside down to find the lost coin. He is like the father in the third parable who looks anxiously for his lost son and goes out, rushes towards him and hardly listens to his confession and words of repentance. He embrances him, kisses him and takes him home to celebrate. His son, who seemed dead, has come to life, he was lost and now is found.

These images of Christ as friend of sinners, as shepherd, as housewife and father, touch our hearts and the words of the gospel are a great consolation to us. Whatever our sins may be, they tell us that Jesus is close to us, that he loves us, in spite of our sins, and that he is always ready to offer us the grace of repentance and forgiveness if we turn to him. Repentance and forgiveness are like the two sides of the same coin; both come from God through Jesus Christ our Saviour.

Our Saviour? He may be seen in some parts of the New Testament like Moses, a mediator with God, but only for a time and only by way of intercession. And although he mourned and

lamented the sins of his stiff-necked people, he could do no
more. I have said that Jesus acted, that he intervened, he is the
One Mediator between God and the human race who gave himself as a ransom for our sins, as an offering and sacrifice to take
our sins away. When, like sheep, we had gone astray he took on
himself our sins, our griefs, our wretchedness and, in the almost
too graphic phrase of St Paul, Jesus the Sinless One became sin
for our sake so that we might become the goodness, the holiness
of God. As a criminal hanging on the cross, he has drawn innumerable people to himself.

These considerations may seem to take us far away from the
gospel, but they are necessary. The redeeming work of Jesus in
his passion, death and resurrection, is the source of mercy, repentance, forgiveness and sanctification by which we are saved
and become the very holiness of God.

Twenty-fifth Sunday of the Year

Amos 8:4-7; Ps 112 (in part); 1 Tim 2:1-8; Lk 16:1-13.

It is probable that, when we think of the moral life, we think first
about personal morality, about what I must do as a priest, as a
husband or wife and so on. That is right and proper. We are
thinking about our response to God; it is what we call examina-
tion of conscience. But there is a social morality, a morality that
concerns the society in which we live, for a society without
morality is corrupt. Both Amos and the gospel prompt us to
think of this matter today.

Amos, the farmer, a countryman, called by God, goes from his
own area to preach to the well-to-do people of the Northern kingdom of Israel and he denounces not only unjust wealth used to
oppress the poor but also fraudulence: 'By lowering the bushel,
raising the shekel, by swindling and tampering with the scales,
we can buy up the poor for money ...' Put 'wheeling and dealing' and 'working the market' for 'raising the value of the shekel
and tempering with the scales' and you make Amos seem very
modern.

When we listened to the gospel we may have thought that it was saying the opposite. The steward is being praised for his trickery and dishonesty. Or so, at first sight, it seems. So we have to find out what the parable is really about.

The steward was a responsible officer, in charge of the master's finances. He was paid no salary but was allowed to take a commission on what he sold. What he does in the parable is to give up his commission to the merchants so that they would befriend him when he was chucked out by his master. His dishonesty happened before and that is why he was dismissed. He was not being praised because of his crooked dealings with the merchants, but because he had made arrangements (shall we call them?) for his future. In other words, the parable is about seeking the kingdom of God and to do so with the prudence of what Luke elsewhere calls 'the children of this world'.

Then comes the last sentences of the gospel that are only loosely connected with the parable, and they lead us to think of social morality, social justice.

As we have heard, the sayings are about money, which in the original is called Mammon. It is called 'tainted' because it is dangerous, and misuse of it can lead to all sorts of evils. As we read in the Letter to Timothy (1:6, 10), 'The love of money is the root of all evils'. Note that the text says not that 'money is the root of evil' but that 'the love of money' is and, in our day, there seems to have been a lust for money and even more money. This was characteristic of the 1980s when there were those people we called The Young Upwardly Mobiles (Yuppies), whose one aim in life seems to have been the making of ever more and more money.

One thing that has prompted this lust for money is that we live in a society that can be described as a consumer-waste society. Objects are not meant to last. When 'used' or broken, or even when people have got tired of them, they are just thrown away, and this leads to more and more spending. One consequence of this is that there are difficulties of disposing of the waste and, if it is toxic, it becomes detrimental to people's health and to the environment.

But the gospel also speaks of honesty and dishonesty and it seems to me that one of the worst features of our society, and indeed of the international financial world, is that, as we hear month by month, there are vast dealings involving millions of pounds that are often dubious and increasingly fraudulent. This would seem to indicate that there is dishonesty on a global scale.

I am aware that you may think this has nothing to do with us, nothing to do with people who have high mortgages, nothing to do with the old and the poor who have not enough to live on. But as we view our situation, we see that more and more wealth is going to fewer and fewer, more and more people are getting rich and more and more are getting poorer, not only in this country but in those countries we call the Third World.

Is there anything we can do, anything we ought to do? If these matters seem remote from us, if they are even difficult to understand, yet we should keep them in mind, we should try to understand them as well as we can. By being concerned, and by our own life and behaviour, by being scrupulous about whatever dealings we are involved in – even the paying of our bills promptly – we can begin to create a moral atmosphere in which dishonesty and fraudulent dealings are shown to be wrong and to be disapproved of. Long years ago the City of London, then the centre of the financial world, was regarded as the most trustworthy and honest financial institution in the world. That was because there remained enough of the Christian, i.e. the gospel ethic, to prompt men to be honest and to do the right and just thing.

If my suggestions seem impracticable and useless, let us remember that, in the past, the Christian church did change society and, with the help of God, it can do so again.

Twenty-sixth Sunday of the Year

Amos 6:1, 4-7; Ps 145 (in part); 1 Tim 6:11-16; Lk 16:19-31.

I wonder if you can guess what is the main message of the gospel today? It looks as if it is a message about the terrors of hell which it paints in very vivid colours. Or it might be simply a denunciation of a heartless rich man. This last fits in very well with Luke's gospel for, over and over again, he shows that he is the evangelist of the poor and oppressed. And we should not think that it is a matter of sour grapes on Luke's part. He was an educated gentleman and wrote good Greek. But when he is giving his version of the Beatitudes he writes: 'Blessed are you who are poor', and not as Matthew, 'Blessed are the poor in spirit!' In the same place he says of the rich, 'Woe to you who are rich; you are having your consolation now.' Lastly, Luke is the only one to record this parable about a rich man and a poor man, with evident sympathy for the poor man.

But we should remember that it is a parable and the vivid picture language about hell is just that, not a photo of it. And parables anyway are not usually simply denunciations. No, Luke gives his message right at the end: 'If they will not listen either to Moses or to the prophets, they will not be convinced even if someone should rise from the dead.' What Jesus was doing was to take an old story that was current among the Jews and use it for his own purpose.

What he was saying to his audience was that they were refusing to listen to the word of God as it has been proclaimed by Moses and the prophets through the centuries, and were deaf to the definitive word of God that was coming to them through the Messiah sent by God. They were blind and could not see that he was the Messiah and they were rejecting the word of God through which alone they could come to faith and salvation.

This applies not only to the people Jesus was speaking to, but it may well be relevant to the people of our time and indeed to people of all times. If we ask what it was and what it is that keeps people from hearing God's word and responding to it, the searing denunciation of Amos gives us one answer. In vivid and frightening language, he describes the heartless rich lolling on soft divans, eating of the fat of the land and drinking choice wines and bawling out their drunken songs. And all this when there was a threat of invasion and the poor were probably lying at their gates.

Amos, in his rough way, was saying that luxury, self-indulgence and contempt of the poor, blinded and deafened them to the word of God so that they would not, and indeed could not, take in the word of the prophet who was God's messenger.

Applying the message of Amos and the parable more generally, we can say that the selfish use of wealth, combined with an indifference to the poor, the disabled and the weaker members of society, blinds people to spiritual values and pervents them from hearing the word of God which alone can raise them out of their spiritual torpor.

Although there is no one here rolling in riches, the parable has a message for us too. We live in a very materialistic society and perhaps we too can be tempted, without knowing it, to over-value material things that are thrust at us by the publicity merchants who spend millions a year trying to persuade us to buy things we do not want and perhaps do not need.

What is even worse, and harder to contend with, is that we live in a world that does not seem to care about religion, God or faith, a world that makes up its own morals without reference to God or even to the natural law. We can be unconsciously affected by all this too. And the remedy, or at least the prophylactic? This is to be found in the main message of the parable. We must listen to the word of God and respond to it and live by it. And if you ask, when do I hear the word of God?, I answer, every time you come to Mass when, as today, the gospel may disturb you and make you think. That is what it is for. You hear the word of God when you attend to the church's official teaching on the great truths of the faith. You hear the word of God when you read the Bible at home – and alas, how few do! The word of God comes to you in your private prayer, for through prayer and worship God is leading us into the truth and to himself.

Today we might make our own the words of St Peter: 'Lord, to whom should we go? You have the message of eternal life.'

Twenty-seventh Sunday of the Year

Hab 1:2-3, 2:2-4; Ps 94 (in part); 2 Tim 1:6-8, 13-14; Lk 17:5-10.

As we can gather from the first reading, from the second and from the gospel, the principal message today is about faith.

Although the word 'faith' is very familiar to us, perhaps we do not always realise that it has three meanings which, in the end, coincide.

1) We speak of faith, as we do in the Creeds, and there it means the content of our faith. It is what is sometimes called the 'articles of the Creed'.

2) It means faith in us, our act of believing what God has revealed to us in the scriptures and is taught us by the church. It is what we call 'the act of faith' which is a gift from God. But it goes beyond expressions of belief in forms of words, however important. The first (and last) object of faith is God himself who has spoken to us and given us a kind of knowledge, about the Holy Trinity for instance, that we could not know unless he had revealed it. At its deepest, however, it means an adherence to God himself as the Revealer.

3) This brings us to another kind of faith that is closely united to that faith I have just spoken of. It is our approach to God, prompted by grace, by which we entrust ourselves to God, giving ourselves to him, or, as we say nowadays, committing ourselves and our whole life to him. That is what the prophet is speaking of when he says, 'The upright (or righteous) man will live by his faithfulness.' He was speaking at a time of great danger, Israel was in peril, invasion threatened and God seemed remote. So the prophet cries out, 'How long, Lord, am I to cry for help?', and the answer comes that the danger will only be for a time. If the prophet and the people trust in God he will rescue them. In this sense, faith is a response to the faithfulness of God who will always be with us, however dark the situation may seem. In fact one of the great themes of the Bible is the faithfulness of God to his people. He binds himself to us if we respond in faith to him. This is illustrated most vividly by the coming of our Lord Jesus

Christ who revealed God, and his unfailing love for us in his own person and life. On the cross he gave himself for us that we might come to the Father and be united with him.

The message of the gospel today is that it is this kind of faith that we must have. In deliberately exaggerated terms, or hyperbole, Jesus tells us that we can do things that seems impossible. Matthew indeed in his gospel tells us that 'Nothing will be impossible for you'. If that seems unlikely, let us remember that when saints worked miracles they were doing so by the power of God who was working through their faith-trust in him.

So first – we realise that faith, whether it means the act of faith or the trusting-committing faith, is not static. It is meant to grow and, with the disciples, we can and should pray, 'Increase our faith.'

Secondly, we can see also that faith is basic to our Christian life. As I have said, it is a gift from God, it is faith that first enables us to move towards God and it is only because he calls us that we can do so. In technical terms, it is faith that first justifies us and changes us from non-Christians into Christians, from sinners to people who become pleasing to God, people who are thus put on the way to holiness which God wants of all of us. Of ourselves we can do nothing to 'win' faith. Grace, faith, salvation, are all gift and that is why Jesus tells us to say today, 'We are merely servants; we have done no more than our duty.' All is from God and it is only through his goodness that we can be even his servants.

How then can we increase our faith, how can we work along with God to help it to grow within us? In baptism we received the gift of faith, and all our Christian education was intended to nurture our faith and make it grow. It can grow and I believe it does as we listen and take to heart the word of God as we hear it every Sunday. We grow in faith as we receive Jesus in holy communion, and we grow in faith as we pray during the week. So let it be our aim, through our religious practice, to develop our faith with the help of Jesus and the Holy Spirit so that, when we come to die, the faith-knowledge we have in this life will be transformed into the light of glory when we shall see God face to face.

Twenty-eighth Sunday of the Year

2 Kings 5:14-17; Ps 97 (in part); 2 Tim 2:8-13; Lk 17:11-19.

There is more than one way of reading the gospel story of today. If we take it with the first reading, the healing of the pagan Naaman, and the psalm that follows, it is telling us that God's saving mercy was not confined to the chosen people of Israel nor yet to members of the church. But the point about thanksgiving is made very strongly. Naaman offers a present in thanks for his healing. Elisha refuses it, but Naaman asks that he may take away earth with him to offer sacrifice, a sacrifice of thanksgiving to God who has healed him.

Then, when we come to consider the gospel, we remember that although Mark and Matthew record the healing of the Samaritan, only Luke mentions the thanksgiving of the Samaritan, the 'foreigner', one who was not of the chosen people of Israel. It seems then that today we should think about thanksgiving or gratitude.

We all know how difficult it is to express our gratitude for a kindness or a gift. My car, say, has broken down on the road and some kind traveller has rescued me, has taken me and my car to a garage and afterwards has taken me home. My words of thanks or anything I offer him are, I know, totally inadequate to express my gratitude.

It is the same when we try and say 'thank you' to God. Our words seem thin, often I cannot find any at all, but we shall find them in the scriptures, especially in the psalms. There is one that begins, 'My soul give thanks to the Lord, all my being bless his holy name. My soul give thanks to the Lord and never forget all his blessings' (102). There is the psalm of today, 'Sing a new song to the Lord …', which is a hymn of thanksgiving for healing and indeed for salvation. There is expressed in exultant length in another psalm (135) when we give thanks to God for all he has done for us throughout the ages: 'Give thanks to the Lord for he is good, for his great love is without end.'

These and many other words are helpful because they remind

us of what God has done for us and suggest something of what
he is. He is good, he is love, he is love towards us, his love is ever
faithful, it never fails and never will fail as long as we live and as
long as the world lasts.

The psalms, the scriptures, remind us that we owe our very existence to God. He drew us out of nothing, and our existence is the
first sign and proof of his love. Perhaps we don't think of this,
perhaps we have become a little sophisticated. We are born of
our parents and of a long line of people going back into the distant past. But at our origin and at the origin of everything there
is God, the giver of all good gifts.

To God we owe the fact that we are Christians. As the psalm of
today has it: 'All the ends of the earth have seen the salvation of
our God.' It is God's saving mercy that has made us Christians:
'God loved the world so much that he gave his only Son' so that
we might have a life that is eternal. Salvation, reconciliation,
grace, may not say much to us but they are all gifts of God's love
towards us. Once, said Paul, you (the human race) were alienated
from God by sin but, he goes on, 'you who used to be so far apart
have been brought close, by the blood of Jesus Christ'. The
whole purpose of Christ's redeeming work is that we should be
united to the Father in an embrace of love, to live with Jesus and
the Holy Spirit, to be members of the family of God.

If we reflect on these matters from time to time, then we shall rejoice to say 'thank you' to God in the words of the psalm: 'My soul
give thanks to the Lord, all my being bless his holy name.'

Even so, our words as individuals may seem feeble, so God
through his Son has put into our hands the *thanksgiving*, the eucharist, at the dynamic heart of which is the Thanksgiving
Prayer when we unite our thanksgiving and self-offering to
Christ, or rather he unites them to his self-offering, so that with
him and through him we give thanks to the Father at the
prompting of the Holy Spirit. This is not only words, it is an action, the greatest action we can ever perform and it is acceptable
to God because Jesus is every-living to make intercession for us.
So then, let us attend to the words at the beginning of the

Eucharistic Prayer: 'Let us give thanks to the Lord our God. It is right to give him thanks and praise.' That is what we are going to do in a few minutes, and we can repeat,, with a new sense of reality: 'My soul give thanks to the Lord, all my being bless his holy name.'

Twenty-ninth Sunday of the Year

Ex 17:8-13; Ps 120; 2 Tim 3:14-4:2; Lk 18:1-8.

Some Sundays ago, we listened to a gospel passage about petitionary prayer: 'Ask and you will receive, seek and you will find …' The message is indeed repeated today but with certain differences. Here there is a very heavy emphasis on perseverance in prayer, perseverance against what seem to be impossible odds. The hard-hearted judge (who by the way is not an image of God) refuses to do his duty, he seems to be an insurmountable obstacle to the granting of the widow's just plea for her rights. He is the very antithesis of what in Jewish culture a judge should be; he was required to defend and protect the orphan and the widow. But she persists, she 'kept on coming to him', and out of fear of what might happen to him (the Greek word could be translated 'give him a black eye'), he gives way.

Yet it is just this kind of prayer, prayer over the months or years when nothing seems to happen, that gives us trouble. Nothing is more difficult than to go on praying when there seems to be no answer. Nothing is more heart-rending than to see a mother praying for a sick child, with, say, leukaemia, and it never seems to get better. There is indeed a mystery here. As the scripture says, God's ways are not our ways, and sometimes we are faced with the mystery of God whom we can never wholly comprehend. But the last sentence of today's gospel, which at first sight seem discouraging, brings in another and an essential element of the prayer of petition. That is faith. As we read in the Letter of St James, 'the prayer of faith will save the sick person', and about this we need to remember that there are two aspects. St James was speaking of the prayer of the church. The mother is not alone; her prayer becomes the prayer of the church of which she is a member and, in the eucharist Sunday by Sunday, the church prays for the sick, joining her intercession to the mighty prayer of Jesus who is always interceding for us before the throne of his Father. And the prayer of faith is a prayer with a profound trust in God and his infinite goodness.

But from time to time there is light in darkness. Some few years ago now, four people were exonerated and released from prison. This was the result of ceaseless petitions, the result of approaches by highly placed people, led by Cardinal Hume, to have the case reviewed. And all through those years there had been people who were praying that justice would be done. The whole story was very complex and it is not my intention to liken the judge or judges to the unjust judge of the parable. They could only judge on the evidence put before them and we now know that some of it was withheld. Still, it is an illustration of how God can work through a highly complex set of circumstances and this should encourage us in the difficult matter of the prayer of petition.

Can we, however, throw some light on the mystery of God, can we come to some understanding of his ways? The woman was a widow and she cried out, perhaps with tears, and there was another widow who had lost her only son and the gospel tells us that Jesus' heart went out to her. If God is to some extent unknowable, Jesus knew the mind of his Father: 'No one knows the Father except the Son and the one to whom the Son chooses to reveal him.' Jesus is the image of God, he is the revelation of God and as we watch him in his earthly life in the pages of the gospel we find that he is full of mercy and compassion. He loved people, he forgave sinners, he healed the sick, he raised the only son to life as he raised the daughter of Jairus. And this was God acting in this world.

If then, as St Paul urges, we have 'the mind of Christ', then we shall see that God is not remote, he is with us, Immanuel, he is still reconciling the world to himself, he is still forgiving, still healing, and always in answer to our prayers and the prayer of the whole church. This is the foundation of the 'prayer of faith', the prayer of trust, trust in the goodness and infinite generosity of God who is with us in all our ways: 'The Lord will guard you from evil ... He will guard your going and coming both now and for ever.'

Thirtieth Sunday of the Year

Ecclus 35:12-14, 16-19; Ps 33 (in part); 2 Tim 4:6-8, 16-18; Lk 18:9-14.

What was wrong with the Pharisee? According to his lights he was a good man. He observed the Jewish law, he worshipped regularly in Temple and synagogue, he did not defraud anyone, he fasted twice in the week, he paid a tenth of all his possessions and he was not an adulterer.

There were two things that were wrong. First, he despised, looked down on, the tax-gatherer standing at the back of the Temple. He was a wretch, a sinner, and the Pharisee implied that he had committed all the sins that he himself had not committed. The Pharisee set himself over the tax-gatherer, he was better than he, he was proud.

Secondly, he was self-satisfied, pleased with himself, as we say, he was smug. He was telling God what a good man he was. He considered that he was right with God, righteous, but he did not realise that he was being self-righteous. He was thinking of himself rather than God; as the text of the gospel says, he was praying to himself. As we learn from elsewhere in the gospels, the Pharisees were deaf to the word of God coming to them from Christ. They are called stubborn, stiff-necked and hard-hearted. They closed their hearts to the message of the kingdom that was being announced to them.

What a contrast with the tax-gatherer! He too was a Jew, he was one of the hated class who exploited their own people. He did a deal with the Roman authorities and worked for them. He paid them the sum of the taxes imposed on an area and then felt free to extract from the people as much as he could wring out of them to recoup his outlay and make a good profit. Whether he committed the other sins the Pharisee hinted that he did, we do not know. All we know is that, with bowed head and knocking his breast, he acknowledged to God that he was a sinner: 'God be merciful to me, a sinner.' As the gospel tells us, he humbled himself before God and that is why he could go home at rights with God whereas the Pharisee did not.

That is the message of the gospel today. But, simple though it is, it makes us think, as all parables are intended to do. And the first question we might ask is, Is there anything of the Pharisee in me? Are there any people I am inclined to despise? There are many dreadful things going on in our society nowadays. There are those homeless young people who have run away from their families, sometimes with good reason. They fall into the hands of drug-pushers and themselves become addicted. Pimps get hold of them and lead them into prostitution. Criminals draw them into the ways of crime and they end up in prison, which does little or nothing to rehabilitate them so that there is a downward spiral into worse crime. Are we inclined to think of them with contempt? Do we say, if only to ourselves, 'Serves them right'? Let us remember that they, like us, are all children of God and that he loves them as he loves us. Are we to condemn them to the outer darkness? They too can repent, sometimes in their own peculiar ways. It is known that some Catholic prostitutes pin a picture of the Sacred Heart to their walls with its prayer underneath, 'Lord, have mercy'. Without knowing it, they are echoing the prayer of the tax-gatherer.

However, it is unlikely that we have anything of the Pharisee in us. Most of us are not satisfied with ourselves. Week by week in the penitential act of the Mass we acknowledge that we are sinners and need the grace of God. From time to time, I hope, we make use of the sacrament of penance when we confess our sins and seek God's pardon, perhaps praying the words of the psalm, 'A humbled, contrite heart, O God, you will not spurn.'

But that word 'humbled' leads us to something radical, something of the greatest importance. The Pharisee was a Jew and as a Jew he had received the Law, he had listened to the prophets; he ought to have been well aware that he owed all his religion and his devotion to God. His great error was that he seemed to have thought he was *self*-justified. We must not make that error.

All that we are as Christians, we owe to the infinite generosity of God. As the apostle says, 'We cannot do anything (for our salvation) of ourselves as of ourselves. Our sufficiency comes from God.' So if there is any good in our lives, any achievement, we owe it to God through the saving work of Jesus Christ who suffered, died and rose again that we might be able to enter his kingdom. That is why we should be humble before God and that is why we can and should say with the sinner of the gospel, 'God be merciful to me, a sinner.' Then the grace and love of God will flow into us and we shall be at rights with God as the tax-gatherer was.

Thirty-first Sunday of the Year

Wis 11:22-12:2; Ps 144 (in part); 1 Thess 1:11-2:2: Lk 19:1-10.

Last Sunday we heard about another tax-gatherer whose humble and contrite heart was pleasing to God, and we learned what these tax-gatherers were and why they were regarded with contempt by the Jews and treated as outcasts. Today we are presented with a tax-gatherer who was wealthy and possibly an even greater sinner. So now can we concentrate on what is the special message of the gospel? It is a story of conversion.

Prompted by we know not what, which seems like mere curiosity, Zacchaeus wants to see Jesus, simply to see him. What kind of man was he? Zacchaeus was a little man and to see him he shinned up a tree and, probably to his great surprise, Jesus stops and speaks to him. He is going to come to his house. That is the first movement of Jesus towards him. There was the usual criticism. Jesus was consorting with sinners but no one took any notice. Then, as if it were the first response to Jesus' presence, Zacchaeus confesses his crimes, he rejects his past and promises to make reparation for all his wrong-doing.

It is at this point that comes the great word of Jesus, 'Today salvation has come to this house.' Though the man was an outcast, untouchable, he was yet a son of Abraham and Jesus had come into the world 'to seek out and save what was lost'.

'Today salvation has come to this house.' Salvation, a word we are very familiar with but we do not always reflect on its meaning or on what it reveals to us of God himself.

Its meaning is first hinted at in the first reading: 'You (God) are merciful to all ... you spare all things ... Lord lover of life ... little by little you correct those who offend, you admonish and remind them how they have sinned so that they may abstain from sin and trust in you, Lord.'

So even in the Old Testament we learn that God is a God of mercy, as also the psalm tells us: 'The Lord is kind and full of compassion, slow to anger, abounding in love.' But this mercy of God is revealed to us in full only in the New Testament and the one word that describes it is *salvation*. Mercy has been defined as a love that goes out to rescue those who are in danger or in some kind of need. The scriptures tell us that was precisely what God did and what his love is: 'God so loved the world as to give his only Son ...', or again, 'God loved us with so great a love that when we were in our sins he did not spare his own Son and gave him up for us all.'

We can think of God's mercy as a mighty downrush of his love to human beings who were (and are) desperately in need of being rescued from the plight they were in: alienated from God by the ancestral sin, and by their own sins cut off from him and totally unable to be united with him.

That is something of what salvation means but it is not all. The saving love of God was made present in the world and to human beings when Jesus took up our human nature, the unforgettable sign of God's ceaseless love for us. It was shown forth in fact by his life, by his word and by his approaching sinners and granting them forgiveness. But it was revealed above all when he entered his passion, when he suffered and when he hung on the cross. Even at that moment and in his agony he showed his merciful love when he said to the thief, 'Today you will be with me in paradise.' All this was the supreme sign and sacrament of God's love for us and its power is with us today if only we will turn to him in repentance as Zacchaeus did. The very presence of Jesus was the sign of his mercy and love and his mercy went out to the tax-gatherer and converted him, turned him to God.

Though Jesus is hidden from our sight under the veils of bread and wine he is still with us, still reaching out to us, still wishing to draw us to himself. But like Zacchaeus, we must listen to his word, take ourselves in hand and, as we receive him in holy communion, we must turn to him heart and soul.

'Today salvation has come to this house'. This gospel is often read at the dedication of a church and its meaning is that God in Christ comes to take possession of it. The church is God's house, it is a sign and symbol of his presence among us, and it must be treated with reverence and respect. At Mass, and whenever we come into church, we are in the presence of God in a very special way and it would be well if we remembered this.

'Today salvation has come to this house' and here, in God's house, his saving love and mercy are always going out to us. Let us open our hearts to receive him.

Thirty-second Sunday of the Year

2 Macc 7:1-2, 9-14; Ps 16 (in part); 2 Thess 2:16-3:5; Lk 20:27-38.

'This corruptible must put on incorruptibility and this mortal must put on immortality ...' These words of St Paul have rung down the centuries in funeral Masses and memorial services and they have lifted up hearts and given assurances and comfort to countless numbers of Christians.

It may be, of course, that the words pass over the minds of some with little understanding and it may even be that the doctrine of the resurrection of the dead does not mean much to them. But they are magnificent words that deserve to be taken seriously. No doubt all sorts of difficulties arise in our minds when we consider the resurrection of the dead, but let us put them aside for the moment, for the church wants us to think about the matter today.

In the Old Testament times, the Jews came only slowly to an understanding of life after death, but here in the passage from Maccabees the seven brothers and their mother give splendid testimony to their faith in the resurrection of the body. Then in the gospel Jesus, cutting through the casuistry of the Saducees, proclaims the resurrection of the dead. Those who are faithful believe that they are 'children of the resurrection' because they are children of God; as they have shared Christ's life in this world so will they share risen life in the next.

That in fact gives us a clue to an understanding of this mystery which, in this life, we can never hope fully to grasp. Jesus shows up the materialistic notions of the Saducees and tells them that in the completed kingdom there will be no marriage or giving in marriage. It will no longer be necessary for we shall enter a new kind of life which he compares to that of the angels.

But it is again St Paul who carries us a further step in understanding (1 Cor 15:45-50). 'As this earthly man (i.e. Adam) was, so are we on earth; and as the heavenly man was (i.e. Christ), so are we in heaven.' In other words, the resurrection of Christ is the model of our own. He had a human nature and a body like ours, he lived a fully human life, he underwent the suffering of the passion and a cruel death, but on the third day he rose again and appeared to his disciples. He was bodily present though his body was transformed and at first the disciples did not recognise him. There was something puzzlingly different about him; he was the Jesus they knew but somehow not. In scriptural terms, his was a glorified body. The glory, the light of God, was shining on him and through him, he was transfigured. Gradually the disciples came to see that he was the same Christ and they asked to touch his body.

To put the matter more briefly: St Paul said on more than one occasion that, if in this life we have suffered with Christ, we shall be made like him in the resurrection. That is our faith, and that is the faith of the church as we profess it in the Creed. But difficulties remain and people ask, and have asked for many centuries, various questions.

Some of them are coloured by over materialistic views, as in the Middle Ages when people tried to imagine what will happen. There are all those gruesome paintings and sculptures of half-alive corpses struggling out of their graves only to be forked into hell. Nowadays other people have more radical concerns: How can a body blown to bits be raised? It is a difficult question. All that can be said in a homily is that body and soul are so intertwined that they cry out for each other. But the body made of matter, which Paul calls corruptible, changing as it does through life so it can be said that 'the amount of matter' at the point of death is not of over-riding importance. If, as we believe, God created the human race in the beginning and sustains it from moment to moment, he can do something similar when we die.

To this we can add (from our side) that there is in us a desire for God and a desire for wholeness, and if the eternal life that we are promised did not include our bodies we would remain eternally unhappy and frustrated. In fact the seed of immortality is planted in us at baptism, it is nourished in us throughout our lives by the holy eucharist, and the body and blood of Christ have, since the earliest days of the church, been called the medicine of immortality. That seed of immortality is destined to grow and be transformed into the light of glory when the glory of Christ's risen body will shine on us and in us. Thus transformed in body and soul, we shall live in indescribable joy for ever. That is what awaits us, and that is why St Paul's words can give us assurance and comfort.

Thirty-third Sunday of the Year

Mal 3:19-20; Ps 97 (in part); 2 Thess 3:7-12; Lk 21:5-19.

The second coming of the Lord, the Last Day – these are not topics we readily turn our minds to. In the past, the Last Day was presented as a judgement, an event of terror, a time of shame when the whole human race will be arraigned before God and all our secret sins will be revealed. Or if we turned to the theological manuals or the catechism, we found there the four last things ever to be remembered: death, judgement, hell and heaven. Well, we know that death will come to us all. Hell remains a possibility – if we turn from God – and we hope for heaven. No doubt we do need to remember these things, but they are not what the scriptures are about today. The Day of the Lord is the subject-matter of the scriptures we have heard, as it is of the first part of Advent which is approaching, and I think we ought to try and see what the scriptures are saying to us today. Not all is clear, for we are faced with a mystery which will be revealed only at the end of time. Meanwhile we are given glimpses of what is to come and they are intended to encourage us and not terrify us.

In all the first three gospels, we have long or longish discourses about the Day of the Lord or the coming of the Lord at the end of time. If we are to understand them, there are I think three things to be kept in mind. First, the evangelists saw the eventual capture of Jerusalem by the Romans in 70 AD as a kind of example of what will happen in some unpredictable and unpredicted future ('No one knows the day or the hour') when the Lord will come again. Secondly, they are using traditional and conventional language much of which comes from the Old Testament, as today when we hear Malachi saying, 'The day is coming now, burning like a furnace and all the arrogant and evil doers will be like stubble.' Many of the Old Testament writers saw the end of the world as a great conflagration; yet others, as suggested in the gospel, described great cosmic events, signs in the sky and stars falling out of it. There were to be wars and rumours of wars and nation fighting against nation, and we find some of this language in St Luke's gospel today. But we need to remember that this is no more than picture language, it is not to be taken literally.

So, thirdly, if we are to come to a deeper understanding of the event, we have to turn to the sayings of the New Testament. In the gospels we find this: 'Then they will see the Son of Man coming ... with great power and glory', and when he does, 'stand erect, hold your head high, because your liberation is at hand'. This will be a climactic moment, our salvation will be complete, we shall be finally liberated from all that the binds us to earth, and our joy will be full. There is no terror here – at least for those who have tried to serve the Lord. The second coming will be a glorious event. There and then there will be a final manifestation, a revelation that Jesus is in fact the Lord of the world and we shall begin to understand the whole loving purpose of God's saving work throughout the history of the human race. Then, Jesus said, many mysteries will be revealed, mysteries that are now hidden from our understanding. It will be the triumph of God in Jesus Christ and we shall enter with him into the joy of eternity.

This is the fundamental theme of the New Testament, as it is of the liturgy, for every week in the Mass we hear the words, 'We wait in joyful hope for the coming of our Saviour, Jesus Christ', which is echoed in the psalm we have sung today, 'With trumpets and the sound of horns, acclaim the King the Lord.'

That is what is promised, but it will not be out of place to remind you that we must remain faithful to God in our daily life, for the Second Coming concerns not just some far distant future but our day-to-day living. As St John's gospel makes very clear, it is the choices we make here and now, the decisions we make for Christ or against him, that are of eternal consequence. That means in practice that we try and live out the gospel day by day and, if we do, we shall hear the words of the Lord, 'Come, blessed by my Father, and take for your heritage the kingdom prepared for you since the foundation of the world.'

The Feast of Christ the King

1 Sam 5:1-3; Ps 121 (in part); Col 1:12-2; Lk 23:35-43.

'Almighty and merciful God, you break the power of evil and make all things new in your Son, Jesus Christ, the King of the universe ...'

We have said these words or heard them many times and we may have asked ourselves: Are they true? Has evil been broken? Has anything been made new?

A few years ago we witnessed extraordinary events in Eastern Europe. There was the Velvet Revolution in Czechoslovakia, there were the crowds of people who filled the church of St Nikolas in Berlin and then with lighted candles in their hands flooded into the streets defying the police who were afraid to shoot. Then came down the Berlin Wall and the two Germanies began to be united. Finally, the great and cruel Soviet Empire, which had endured for more than seventy years, crumbled into confusion. Poland and Hungary had already liberated themselves and Eastern Europe was free. All this was totally unexpected, the face of Eastern Europe and Russia has been changed, communism has withered away.

But you may ask, has this any relevance to the Christian message? Was it not just the uprising of oppressed people? In a way, yes, but it is well to recall that for many years we had prayed for the conversion of the Soviet Union, for the liberation of so many Christians and others, who had been spied on and ruthlessly punished by a police state. While we have to be careful about seeing answers to prayers in events, I do not think it is too much to say that what has happened is owed to the prayer of the church, the prayers and sufferings of countless Christian people for more than fifty years. We can I think say that God has broken the power of evil.

Nor were these happenings irrelevant to the feast we celebrate today. When Pius XI instituted the feast in 1925, he was aware of the growing power of totalitarian and heathen states and of the increasing secularisation of society. His purpose was to encourage Christians to take their part in the social life of their time and to bring before their minds that Jesus Christ is Lord, the Lord of heaven and earth. In a way he was continuing the work of John the Seer, the author of the Book of Revelation, who proclaimed Jesus as Lord of lords and King of kings, to give courage to the Christians of the Roman Empire.

In his way too, St Paul tells us today what his Lordship means. Before all time the Word was with the Father and at some unknown moment in the distant past 'all things were created through him and for him', and even now he holds all things together. He is Lord because, with his Father, he is Creator. As the psalm (23) says, 'The Lord's is the earth and it fulness, the world and all its peoples.'

But what sort of Lordship is it? Though all things belong to him, he is yet described as the first-born from the dead. When he shed his blood and died for us on the cross, he reconciled all human beings and all things to his Father. His suffering and the blood and the death were expressions of his redeeming love for us and it was through that love and self-giving in sacrifice that he established 'a kingdom of holiness and grace, a kingdom of justice, love and peace'. At the very moment that he established his kingdom he reconciled the sinner on the cross: 'Today you will be with me in paradise.'

There is, I think, a twofold message in all this. If Christ's ways remain hidden from us, he is still Lord, he is still in ultimate control. And he can draw good out of evil as he has done, through his followers on earth, in recent months and years.

Secondly, we must note that his kingdom is a kingdom of justice, peace and love. He does not compel or force; he invites, he urges us and seeks our willing response. In the intolerable conditions in which the people of the communist empire existed, many made their response through commitment to Christ, through suffering and death – as did that young Polish priest who was brutally murdered by the secret police. But in asking for our response, Jesus is also asking us to co-operate with him in bringing his kingdom into existence in the day to day life of nations and communities. That is our task, but that is also our high vocation and, if the circumstances of our society seem to be less brutal than those countries that suffered so appallingly, there is still much to do in our own. All of us, at least, must bear witness to Christian moral standards by our daily living and do what we can to re-Christianise our society which once regarded itself as Christian.

Homilies for certain Feasts

Whitsunday or Pentecost

I sometimes wonder what people make of Whitsunday or Pentecost. It may seem just like one of the greater feasts such as Corpus Christi or the Sacred Heart. It is much more than these, and the peculiarly English name for it, Whitsunday, gives us the first clue that it is different. It is related to Easter, the celebration of the resurrection, but also the time when catechumens were baptised (and of course still are) during the vigil. Whitsunday, or White Sunday, was the second great day of baptism in the early church and the word 'White' recalls the white robe with which the newly baptised were clothed after their baptism.

The Greek word *Pentecost* may not say much to us, but it provides the second clue to an understanding of the feast. It means the fiftieth day after Easter when we celebrated the passion, death and resurrection of our Lord Jesus Christ. During the fifty days of Eastertime we have been celebrating just that, and now are celebrating what the liturgy calls 'the completion' of Christ's saving work for us and for our salvation. But what do we mean by 'completion'? Was not the saving work of Jesus all complete? Indeed it was. He offered himself in sacrifice and died for us once and for all. But what he did has to be brought to us, as Jesus said before he died: 'It is good for your own good that I am going because unless I go, the Advocate (the Holy Spirit) will not come to you; but if I go I will send him to you.' Jesus sent and sends his Holy Spirit into our hearts and lives to make effective the redeeming work that he began on the cross. All this is summed up in the words of the Preface: 'Today you sent the Holy Spirit on those marked out to be your children by sharing in the life of your only Son, and so you brought the paschal mystery to its completion.' The passion, death and resurrection of Christ and the sending of the Holy Spirit are so many phases of the action of God to draw the human race out of sin and to make it possible for us 'to share the divine life' of the only Son of God.

All through the last Sundays of the fifty days we have been hearing of the promise of the Spirit: 'I shall ask the Father, and he will give you another Advocate to be with you for ever …', and now on the first Pentecost Sunday we hear of the dramatic descent of the Holy Spirit on the first Christian community, the church.

What is important here is not the description of the details. What is important is that this was the first public manifestation of the coming of the Spirit on the church and the consequences of it. The first consequence was the proclamation of the good news of salvation to the world, and the second was that this was prompted by the Spirit of Truth who guides the church throughout the ages. In a sense, the church, indwelt by the Holy Spirit, is completing the saving work of Christ, though it must be emphasised that the church is totally dependent on him. The truth the church has to communicate is God's word, not its own. The sacraments by which we are empowered to live the Christian life are Christ's and it is he who is active in them through the ministry of the church.

Indeed, the whole church, as St Paul suggests, is the body of Christ and he is active in it through his Holy Spirit: 'In the Spirit we were all baptised, Jews as well as Greeks, slaves as well as citizens, and one Spirit was given to us all to drink.' 'Given to drink' for, as Jesus said, 'If anyone is thirsty let him some to me' … for 'as the scripture says, from his breast shall flow living water.' And St John explains, Jesus 'was speaking of the Spirit which those who believe in him were to receive.' Water was and is the symbol of the Holy Spirit within us and in the whole church.

St Paul goes on to tell us that the same Spirit is given to all in different ways. We receive him for special 'missions' and special tasks and ministries, but all the gifts of the Spirit are given for the upbuilding of the church. So we come to see the church not simply as an institution but as the living body of Jesus Christ with at its heart the Holy Spirit, who, as we profess in the Creed, is the giver of life, Christ's life whereby we are able to live as Christians.

For the Holy Spirit is not only in the church; he is in each one of us also, as the hymn written by an Englishman, Stephen Langton, reminds us. The Holy Spirit, Lord of life, is the soul's delightful guest, he gives us refreshing peace, peace with God and others. He is our comfort in toil, he heals our wounds, restores our strength and washes away the guilt of sin.

So on this Pentecost Sunday we can pray:

Bend the stubborn heart and will,
Melt the frozen, warm the chill,
Guide the steps that go astray.

The Feast of the Holy Trinity: Year A

Ex 34:4-6, 8, 9; Ps Dan 3:52-56; 2 Cor 13:11-13; Jn 3:16-18.

It shocks some people when they hear that God is a mystery that we can never wholly comprehend. He is so great that he is beyond our capacity to define. As we learnt long ago, God is infinite and we are finite, limited, and the limited and the finite cannot grasp the infinite. But God in his mercy gradually revealed himself to the people if Israel. At first they thought of him as a tribal God, a God just for themselves. They thought of him as terrible and even vengeful but throughout the Old Testament God revealed himself, revealed that he was something, or rather someone, very different from what they had imagined. Here in today's passage from Exodus, he reveals that he is 'a God of tenderness and compassion, slow to anger, rich in kindness and faithfulness', and he shows this in two ways. He was the God of mercy and he would show that he was, first by rescuing the people from the slavery of Egypt and then, later on, making a pact, a covenant, with them, a covenant that if they were obedient to the law they would be his people and he would be their God. This was an expression of his love for them, a love that was so great that the later prophets and psalmists called it a marriage, a love pact, between God and his people.

As the centuries went by, the people realised ever more clearly that the God who had revealed himself to them was one, the one true God, and they professed this in their twice-daily prayer: 'Hear, O Israel, the Lord is one Lord, and you shall love the Lord your God with all your heart and with all your soul and with all your might ...' (Deut 6:4-7). This was their faith, this was a noble expression of faith, this they profoundly believed and they saw it as separating them from all the surrounding pagans of their time.

It was in this faith that the disciples, and all who followed Jesus, had been brought up, and it is not surprising or to their discredit that they found it difficult at first to accept that Jesus was the Son of God. If was only after the resurrection that they came to full faith in Jesus Christ as the only Son of God. And they had yet more to learn. Several times before his passion, Jesus had told them of a Holy Spirit who would come upon them and be with them always. This Holy Spirit they received after the resurrection, and at Pentecost and in the power of the Spirit, they began to proclaim the good news of salvation. In his first sermon, after receiving the Spirit at Pentecost, Peter evoked all three persons of the Holy Trinity: 'God raised this man Jesus to life, and all of us are witnesses to that. Now raised to the heights by God's right hand, he has received from the Father the Holy Spirit, who was promised, and what you see and hear is the outpouring of that Holy Spirit.' It was in this way that the apostles and their disciples, the first Christians, came to know and believe that God is Father, Son and Holy Spirit.

But was that the whole extent of the revelation of God? For St John, and indeed for St Paul, the Holy Trinity is the revelation of the love that God *is* and the love he has for us: 'God loved the world so much that he gave his only Son so that everyone who believes in him may not be lost but have eternal life.' This reveals to us the astonishing generosity of God. The almighty God 'who dwells in unapproachable light', is yet the God who is open to us, who, as it were, goes out from himself towards us to give himself to us in his beloved Son. 'God is love', said John, 'God's love for us was revealed when God sent into the world his only Son so that we could have life through him; this is the love I mean: not our love for God but God's love for us when he sent his Son to be the sacrifice that takes our sins away' (1 Jn 4:7-10).

God takes the initiative, as he has done since the beginning of time, he approaches us, he gives his Son to us and for us, and he and his Son send the Holy Spirit into our lives and hearts so that we can respond to love with love.

It is for this reason that today, and perhaps daily, we respond with the prophet: 'To you glory and praise for evermore', while praying also that the grace of our Lord Jesus Christ and the love of God and the communion of the Holy Spirit may be with us all for ever.

The Feast of the Holy Trinity: Year B

Deut 4:32-34, 39-40; Ps 32 (in part); Rom 8:14-17; Mt 28:16-20.

It is perhaps necessary to say that the doctrine of the Holy Trinity was not revealed in the Old Testament. It was revealed by Jesus in the New Testament, who constantly spoke of his Father, and innumerable texts speak of him as the Son of God, 'eternally begotten of the Father', and from him we hear of the sending of the Spirit who will come upon the church at Pentecost to inspire its actions and its teaching. The feast of today is not just the celebration of the doctrine but an important reminder to us of how God has approached his people through the ages and what he has done for them.

This is the sense of the first reading from Deuteronomy. In solemn and moving tones, the writer tells of God as creator of the world and the human race, and marvels at the power of God's word that brought the world and ourselves into existence. That same word was heard by the Israelites gathered at the foot of Mount Sinai when God spoke 'from the heart of the fire'. He made his presence known to them in the centuries that followed; but that was not all. When we hear those words, 'Keep his (God's) law and his commandments', the writer was reminding the people of the covenant that God had made with his people in the desert. Through Moses he gave the Torah, the law, which was a whole way of life, and if the people kept the commandments they would be his people and he would be their God. He bound these people to himself by a covenant that the psalms and the prophets described as a love pact. If they were faithful he would be with them always. This is hinted at in the psalm: 'The word of the Lord is faithful and all his works to be trusted ... The Lord looks on those who revere him, on those who hope in his love.' For the God of the Old Testament loved his people and held them together as a people until coming of the his Son, Jesus Christ.

With him began a new era, a new age. It was he who revealed his Father: 'Philip, the one who has seen me has seen the Father.' It is through Jesus that we know what God is like, and it was through his life, his teaching, his miracles and his passion, death and resurrection that we know God, though great and almighty, is a *God for us*. God, who gives himself to us through and in his Son, made and makes that divine love present in the world and present in us. For the Holy Trinity is not a remote doctrine of concern only to the theologians. It is the vital centre of our Christian life, as St Paul tells us today. All of us who are moved by the Holy Spirit are sons and daughters of God. We are not slaves, the Holy Spirit is dwelling in our hearts so that with Jesus, the Son of God, we can cry out 'Abba', Dear Father, expressing our love to him who loves us. Jesus himself taught us this when he said 'If anyone loves me he will keep my word and my Father will love him and we shall come to him and make our home with him' (Jn 14:23).

God, Father, Son and Holy Spirit, are with us, dwelling in us and only grave sin can dispel that holy presence. As the gospel of today reminds us, that indwelling began with our baptism when, in the name of the Father, Son and Holy Spirit, the water was poured over us and we became sons and daughters of God and brothers and sisters of Jesus Christ, the only Son of the Father. Because of this we are heirs with him of the eternal life.

What then can be our response to the great mystery we celebrate today? As we reflect on it and realise that it intimately concerns our Christian living, we cannot but give praise and thanks, as indeed the liturgy of the day invites us to do: 'Blessed be God the Father and his only-begotten Son and the Holy Spirit: for he has shown that he loves us.' Again, before the gospel we sing 'Alleluia ... Glory be to the Father, and to the Son and to the Holy Spirit, the God who is, who was, and who is to come.' But above all in the Mass, in the Eucharistic Prayer in particular, we give praise and thanks to the Father, through his Son and at the prompting of the Holy Spirit. This is brought to a splendid conclusion when we say Amen to the eucharistic prayer: 'Through him (Jesus Christ), with him, in him, in the unity of the Holy Spirit, all honour an glory is yours, Almighty Father, for ever and ever.'

The Feast of the Holy Trinity: Year C

Prov 8:22-31; Ps 8 (in part); Rom 5:1-5; Jn 16:12-15.

It is possible that when we hear the words 'the doctrine of the Holy Trinity', we turn away our minds. Perhaps that is on account of the way we were taught long ago: 'Three in one and one in three.' It seemed like a piece of holy mathematics that was without relevance to our Christian life. Then later, when we were taught about 'the proofs for the existence of God', we were tempted to think of him as a solitary being, remote and unapproachable. This and much else of the kind we put 'in parentheses' and in our prayer and devotion turned to our Lord Jesus Christ. This was understandable but regrettable. We no doubt did not realise that we were omitting from our practice the central doctrine and reality of the Christian faith.

The scriptures show us a way into some understanding of the Holy Trinity, though we should always remember that it is the ultimate mystery which we can never wholly comprehend. This way was the way of the disciples of Jesus and of the first Christians. Knowledge, understanding and faith in Jesus Christ as not only the Messiah but as the Son of God was the way they came to see the Father in a new way. In the Old Testament, which they knew so well, they heard of God as Father but they also heard Jesus speak to his Father in the familiar and affectionate term 'Abba' which is the word that might have been used by a child of its father. Dimly at first they realised that there was a special relationship between Jesus and the God they had believed in and worshipped since ever they could remember. They also knew the passage from the Book of Proverbs which has been read today, a passage which is not without obscurity but one in which they discerned that special relationship: 'Wisdom cries aloud ... From everlasting I was firmly set, from the beginning, before earth came into being ...' and this ill-defined 'person' was 'ever at play in his presence', eternal like God. But this eternal One was also 'at play everywhere in his world, delighting to be with the sons of men.' In his gospel, St John took over this and other Old Testament passages about Wisdom and identified it with Jesus, the begotten of the Father, his only Son who in the fullness of time became man: 'The Word was made flesh and lived among us.'

It was from Jesus, the Son of God, that the disciples learnt of the Holy Spirit who is united with himself: 'All he tells you will be taken from what is mine', and it is this Holy Spirit whom Jesus will send after he has gone. He will lead them into the complete truth, he will be with them, he will not leave them orphans, for the Holy Spirit will make the Risen Lord present to them in all their preaching and in their sufferings.

But as St Paul tells us today, the Holy Spirit did not remain outside them: 'The love of God has been poured into our hearts by the Holy Spirit who has been given us.' This is reinforced and expanded by St John. Speaking to his disciples before his passion he say, 'On that day you will understand that I am in the Father and you in me and I in you. Anybody who receives my commandments and keeps them will be the one who loves me and anyone who loves me will be loved by my Father ... and my Father will love him and we shall come to him and make our home with him' (Jn 14:20-23).

So the Holy Trinity is not just a doctrine, not just some academic teaching that we have to know. It is a reality, the deepest reality of our Christian life. God is with us, God is within us, God, Father, Son and Holy Spirit, are active within us, sharing their divine life with us and making it possible for us to lead a Christian life and to aspire to that complete union with God when we shall see him face to face and will be made like him.

The Feast of the Body and Blood of Christ

It may seem strange that an act of worship, this feast, should celebrate what is in itself an act of worship. But that very strangeness should lead us to deeper thought, a deeper understanding of the feast.

The holy eucharist appears first as a sacred and a very solemn meal. On the night before he died, Jesus took some bread and said over it, 'This is my body which will be broken for you. Take and eat.' Then, 'This is my body which will be poured out for you. Take and drink.' He concluded, 'Do this for a memorial of me.' Jesus was not only giving himself *to* his disciples but *for* them: the body broken, the blood shed, as they would be next day.

The eucharist appears as a meal among the first Christians. There was teaching, there was prayer and there was 'the breaking of the bread' (Acts 2:42). Within less than twenty-five years after our Lord's resurrection, St Paul 'handed on' to his converts at Corinth the tradition he had received from Peter and James, the brother of the Lord. For them and for Paul, it was a meal with the deepest meaning, a unique meal: 'The cup of blessing', the cup over which Jesus had said the prayer of blessing, 'is a communion with the blood of Christ', and the bread that is broken 'is a communion with the body of Christ', and that communion is so real, so actual, that the assembly becomes one body, the body (mystical) of Christ. Wholly consonant with this is the teaching of St John which he expresses in his own way: 'The one who eats my flesh and drinks my blood lives in me and I live in him.' We, the whole church, are 'oned' with Christ by the holy eucharist which we celebrate in obedience to the word of the Lord, 'Do this for a memorial of me.'

In the rite of baptism we say, 'This is our faith, this is the faith of the church,' and we could do well to repeat these words whenever we celebrate the eucharist. For in so doing we are responding to the teaching of Christ in so much of the sixth chapter of St John where Jesus teaches emphatically that faith in himself is the indispensable condition of receiving him in the eucharist: 'I tell you most solemnly, everybody who believes has eternal life. I am the bread of life ... this is the bread that comes down from heaven so that a man may eat it and never die. I am the bread that comes down from heaven.'

This faith, our response to Christ, is set forth in the Eucharistic Prayer. Echoing Christ, we say, 'Let us give thanks to the Lord our God', and the priest continues, 'Father, it is our duty and our salvation always and everywhere to give you thanks through our Lord Jesus Christ.' Then the priest, representing Christ, says his words over the bread and wine repeating the injunction 'Do this for a memorial of me.' After this, the prayer of thanksgiving continues and in this part of the prayer we celebrate the memory of Christ, recalling his passion, death, resurrection and ascension and offer 'the holy and perfect sacrifice (which is now), the bread of life and the cup of salvation.' Through the making of the memorial, the Christ of the passion, death and resurrection is made present among us. Through this sacramental sacrifice the redeeming work of Jesus is made effective among us by the Holy Spirit who makes us 'one body, one spirit in Christ'. As we pray on Maundy Thursday, 'As often we celebrate this memorial sacrifice, the work of our redemption is accomplished' within us.

When, then, we come to receive holy communion, it is this Christ, the redeeming Christ, the Christ who suffered, died and rose again for us, whom we receive and who by the power of the Holy Spirit is active within us, for 'all who share in the body and blood of Christ' are 'brought together in unity by the Holy Spirit'.

These are a few glimpses of the great Mystery of Faith that is the eucharist, and as we ponder on it, it should evoke from us a great reverence, a reverence that should be with us as we celebrate it and as we receive into ourselves the Lord who suffered, died and rose again for us so that we could offer ourselves and our lives with him and become, indeed and in truth, one with him.

24 June: The Birthday of John the Baptist

As John appears in the gospel accounts, he seems to be a transient figure. He is no more than a voice, a voice crying in the
wilderness. He must decrease and pass away and the One he is
proclaiming must increase. He is not a prophet like those of the
Old Testament. Yet he is like Jeremiah, formed in the womb and
before the birth dedicated, consecrated to the Lord. Like Elijah
he resists kings and queens and wanders in the desert wearing
the garb of a prophet and eating the food the desert provided.
Like Samson he kept the Nazirite vow, going unshaven and
with hair uncut and never taking strong drink. He seems to sum
up so much of the Old Testament, yet in a way he is not *of* it. As
Jesus said of him, 'Of all the children born of woman, greater
than John the Baptist has never been seen ...', and 'it was toward
John that all the prophecies of the prophets and of the law were
leading ...'. He is unique, he is 'much more than a prophet'; he is
above all 'the messenger', the one sent by God 'to prepare the
way before him'. He is the forerunner of the Messiah and, to prepare the way for him, he calls the people to repentance, 'Repent,
for the kingdom of heaven is at hand.' Yet, another paradox,
'The least in the kingdom of heaven is greater than he.' He prepared for the kingdom, he proclaimed the kingdom, but the
kingdom had not yet come and would not come until Jesus the
Lord had suffered, died and risen again and so inaugurated the
kingdom which we can be sure John entered by virtue of his
martyrdom.

He was a transient figure, he was not the bridge between the old
order and the new. What then was his role? To find out what his
role was we have to turn to the gospel of St John. He was not the
light, he was a witness to the light who enlightens all in the
world who will come to the light. He baptised with water but
there was one, already standing among his hearers, who would
baptise with the Spirit and with fire, and he, John, was not worthy to do the work of a slave and untie the Messiah's sandals.
And then comes the climax. He is with his own disciples and he
sees Jesus coming towards him and he cries out, 'Look, there is
the Lamb of God who takes away the sin of the world ... I saw

the Spirit coming down from heaven and resting on him' and 'the man on whom the Spirit came down is the Chosen One of God', and John was his witness.

The next day Jesus passed by again and John was standing with two of his disciples and he repeated, 'Look, there is the Lamb of God' and the two disciples followed him. Andrew, then Simon Peter and Philip and Nathaniel, followed Jesus. They said, 'We have found the Messiah', the Messiah, the Chosen One of God, the Lamb who takes away the sin of the world, and they remained with him. In a sense, John's work was over. He would have his own faith confirmed when he was perhaps already in Herod's prison and was told by his disciples that the Messiah, the Christ, was already at work, healing the sick, the blind, the deaf, the dumb and the crippled and even raising the dead to life. Above all, he was preaching the good news of salvation to the poor, the neglected, the marginalised, as the prophet had foretold. All that remained for John was to die and this he did, heroically.

In the many paintings and sculptures of John the Baptist, he is often represented as standing with his finger pointing away from himself to Christ and that, it seems to me, is his eternal role but also his role for us. John is telling us now that Jesus is the Lamb of God who takes away the sin of the world, the Lamb who takes away our sins now if we will approach him and confess our sins to him. He is the Messiah, the Chosen One of God, who still proclaims the good news to us, and John is still saying to us, as he said to his disciples, 'Look, he is coming, he is here. Follow him, listen to him.' He is the Saviour of the world.

The Feast of St Peter and St Paul

Acts 12:1-11; Ps 33 (in part); 2 Tim 4:6-8, 17, 18; Mt 16:13-19.

There are those who do not like the idea of an institutional church and, perhaps through an excess of legislation, even Catholics are becoming cool to the institution. It is thought that it suppresses the Spirit and takes away freedom. Each of us can read the Bible, each of us can approach Christ as we will, we can get along very well on our own.

But the church is not just any sort of institution; it is much more than an institution. As St Paul teaches us, the church is the living body of Jesus Christ, indwelt by the Holy Spirit and, said St Paul, where the Spirit is, there is freedom. The Spirit-filled church can liberate us from ourselves and perhaps from our superficiality, from our all-too-personal and narrow notions, enabling us to go to God.

Institution is not a foreign body imposed on a 'spiritual' church. Right from the beginning we find that it had structures. In Christ's promise to Peter we see that he gave him authority to rule over a community, that is, the church (*ecclesia*). Jesus gave him the keys of the kingdom, on him he will build his church; as we say now, he gave him the power of jurisdiction.

But also he was 'a fisher of men', like Paul he was a preacher, he proclaimed the good news of salvation not only in the Middle East but also in Rome. Like Paul too he was given charismatic gifts of healing and he was happy and ready to acknowledge the movement of the Spirit even outside the usual order (Acts 10:44-46). He was not rigid in his views; he accepted correction from Paul (Gal 2:11-14), as he had previously accepted a severe rebuke from Jesus (Mt 16:23).

For his part, Paul was given charismatic gifts but could insist on his authority, as he does with some force in that same Letter to the Galatians (1:6-9), where he says that his gospel was given to him by Christ and that it must be accepted by all. He was keenly aware of the movement of the Holy Spirit in the church and yet he established the church in many parts of the Roman world and appointed overseers like Timothy and Titus as rulers of the people.

In fact, both institutions and dynamic 'spiritual' action are essential to the life of the church. Without institution it would dissolve into a vague religiosity, and without the Spirit it would become no more than any other secular institution. Both institution and dynamism are, as it were, personified in Peter and Paul and thanks to both the church is able to carry out its mission.

Today, then, as we celebrate the feast of St Peter and St Paul, we can thank God that through Christ he has given us such a church and that, without any merit of our own, we belong to the one, holy, Catholic and apostolic church which we are about to profess in the Creed. Here we have sound doctrine and the constant impulse of the Holy Spirit which prompts us to bear witness to the faith that Jesus delivered to his church in the beginning.

With thankful hearts then we sing today:
    Rejoice, O Rome, this day; thy walls they once did sign
    With princely blood, who now their glory share with thee.
    What city's vesture flows with crimson deep as thine?
    What beauty else has earth that may compare with thee?

Rome is the symbol of the whole Church and the focus of unity for all.

6 August: The Transfiguration of the Lord

Dan 7:9, 10, 13, 14; Ps 96 (in part); 2 Pet 1:16-19.
Gospel: Year A, Mt 17:1-9; Year B, Mk 9:2-10; Year C, Lk 9:28-36.

The Transfiguration is so stupendous an event that we hardly know what to make of it. This is not surprising since the disciples were themselves overcome by it. Here was their Master, their friend, whom they had followed for some months, suddenly transformed in such a way that he seemed to be entirely different from the one they had known. But very quickly they realised that they were in the presence of the all-holy God whom they had worshipped from their youth. They saw the brilliance of the divine light shining through Jesus; they almost thought that they were in heaven and wanted to stay there for ever: 'Let us make three tents, one for you, one for Moses and one for Elijah.' But that was not the message and we have to find out what the message was, both for them and for ourselves.

The Transfiguration is set in the gospels between two fore-tellings of the passion and death of Christ, and according to a long tradition of interpretation, the purpose of the Transfiguration was to strengthen the faith of the disciples for the day when they would be faced with his degradation in his passion, when they would see him 'as a worm and no man, despised ... a man of sorrows, acquainted with grief', the day when he would die as a condemned criminal. As we know, the purpose was hardly successful. They all ran away.

What, then, is the message of today, and especially for ourselves? This is first suggested by the Opening Prayer: 'As we listen to the voice of your Son, help us to become heirs to eternal life.' This is put in more concrete fashion in a sentence of 2 Peter 1:4 (which might well have been included in the Mass of today): 'In making these gifts, God has given us the guarantee of something very great and wonderful to come: through them we shall be able *to share the divine nature* and to escape the corruption of the world ...' That is what the Transfiguration foretells, that is what it promises. This is the thought that is taken up by the Preface of the Mass, which in turn is quoting St Leo the Great: We and the whole church are destined to share the glory of Christ, 'His glory shone from a body like our own to show that the church, which is the body of Christ, would one day share his glory.'

This is taken a step further in the Prayer after Communion: 'May the food we receive from heaven change us into his image', the image of Christ. That echoes St Paul when he wrote, 'That same glory, coming from the Lord who is the Spirit, transforms us into his very likeness, in an ever greater degree of glory' (2 Cor 3:18). The transfigured Christ is transforming us here and now, as he will do at the end of our lives: 'The Lord Jesus Christ will transfigure these lowly bodies of ours into copies of his glorious body. He will do that by the same power with which he can subdue the whole universe' (Phil 3:21). That is what we are destined for. It is almost unbelievable: we shall be made like Christ and our poor bodies, our whole being, will be permeated by the indescribable glory of God.

Yet, on the way to that consummation, life for most of us is difficult. We are weak in our endeavours, we are aware that as Christians, and even perhaps as human beings, we do not make a good job of our life. We most of us encounter disappointments, events may send us into the depths. But all the time, if we are faithful, the power of the Risen Christ is with us, at work in us, transforming us, transforming us through the very troubles that afflict us. This should give us confidence, a confidence that comes from Jesus himself as we obey the injunction of the gospel: 'This is my Son, the Chosen One, the beloved. *Listen to him.*' As we listen to Jesus and his word and make it our own, as in our troubles we look to him, as we try and follow him in our daily living and pray to him, he will be bearing us up, supporting us through all our tribulations, right on to the end when the glory of Christ will shine on us and we shall be made like God because we shall see him face to face.

Footnote: I have provided homilies on the Transfiguration for the Second Sunday of Lent for Years A, B, C, 22, 38, 53 in my Journey through Lent, *Kevin Mayhew, 1989.*

The Assumption of the Blessed Virgin Mary

(The Mass of the Day)
Apoc 11:19, 12:1-6, 12; Ps 44 (in part); 1 Cor 16:20-26; Lk 1:39-56.

It is difficult to *imagine* the Assumption of the Blessed Virgin into heaven, and we feel impelled to seek its deeper meaning. What actually happened we cannot know, but if we ask, 'What does it mean?', I think we can get somewhere near an answer.

There are many pictures of the assumption, both old and newer, and most of them present the apostles gathered round a bed and looking upwards at the ascending body of Mary. There is one, and one alone, that impresses if only because it does not attempt to describe the ascent. It is by Blessed Fra Angelico, a Dominican, who painted a picture of dazzling simplicity. The background is gold, in the centre is a seated figure of Christ, golden also, but with a little colour; kneeling before him, slightly to one side is Mary, also in gold, and Christ is raising a crown which he is going to put on her head. The picture may have been inspired by a verse of the psalm we sing in the Mass today: 'On your right stands the Queen in gold of Ophir.' As Fra Angelico read it in

Latin, Mary stands *in vestito deaurato*, 'in a golden robe'.

Although the picture is some five hundred years old, it gleams with light which seems to shine out of it, and yet it is a scene of the utmost simplicity. What seems to be important is that it has caught the meaning of the assumption very well. Its message is that the assumption of Mary was her *exaltation*, if you like her glory, as is suggested by the Opening Prayer: 'May we see heaven as our final goal and come to share her (Mary's) glory.' This too is suggested, perhaps surprisingly, by the passage from St Paul which is first about the death and resurrection of Christ and then about the consequences: 'Christ as the first-fruits and then, after the coming of Christ, those who belong to him.' The apostle sees those who have been redeemed by his passion, death and resurrection, streaming behind him in a great procession towards the glory of God which will radiate their whole being. First among these is Mary, the Mother of Jesus, who in her lifetime, by her faith and total dedication ('Let it be to me according to your word'), is the model of Christians who would make the pilgrimage from this world to the next.

This is the theme of the Preface of the day. Mary's departure to heaven was the 'beginning and the pattern of the church in its perfection, and a sign of hope and comfort for your people on their pilgrim way'. What was given to her in perfection will be given to all who are faithful to God in this life. We too will be transformed as Mary was by the glory of God and we shall be with him body and soul, as she is. So with her today we can sing, 'My soul glorifies the Lord, my spirit rejoices in God, my Saviour.'

But if we can rejoice in anticipation of what awaits us, we have first to make the pilgrimage, as the mysterious passage from the Apocalypse tells us. As the Preface says, Mary is the model or pattern of the church, but in this passage it is the church that is in view. The church gives birth to Christians by baptism, as Mary gave birth to Jesus so long before, and as the Mother and Child were harassed at birth, so was the church. Jesus lived and suffered and died and was taken up to heaven but the church enters the toils. The Dragon, the Satan, the Adversary of God is in conflict with the church, ever trying to subvert it and, for the author of the Apocalypse, this was the secular power, the one with 'seven heads and ten horns', the Roman Empire of the day. This has continued and at times the conflict has been bitter and very damaging to the life of the church. But ultimate victory is promised: 'Victory and power and empire for ever have been won by our God, and all authority for his Christ.'

What has happened and what is happening to the church also happens to us who are its members. We too have our trials, our temptations and our failures; from time to time, we may be in the toils, and as we approach the end of our lives we may experience fear. Let us lift up our hearts then to Mary, glorious with the glory of God. What God has given her, he will give to us if we are faithful to the end.

The Feast of All Saints

Apoc 7:2-4, 9-14; Ps 23 (in part); 1 Jn 3:1-3; Mt 5:1-12.

It is difficult to grasp the breadth and the depth of this feast. It shines with the glory of heaven and invites us into it, and it seems to embrace the whole of the human race, 'those who have gone before us marked with the sign of faith.' It is of this that the author of the Apocalypse is speaking, so first let us follow his thought.

He has had a series of visions of the realm of the blessed, the realm we call heaven. But that is not all. In the light of his visions he sees the unfolding of history and God's purpose of salvation under the lordship of the Lamb, the Son of God. First, in this perspective he sees the church of his own time which had already suffered persecution. Peter and dozens of others had been put to a cruel death in Rome, Paul had suffered death just outside Rome, James the apostle had been put to death in Jerusalem and Stephen had been stoned to death. He sees their death as martyrdom, as victory and not defeat, a victory owed to the Lamb in the power of whose own sacrificial death they were able to lay down their lives for him. As the writer of the Apocalypse put it:

'These are the people who have been through the great persecution, and because they have washed their robes white in the blood of the Lamb, they now stand in front of God's throne and serve day and night in the sanctuary.'

Then the vision of the Seer turns to the future and he sees in anticipation the innumerable multitudes – the hundred and forty-four thousand means that – who will live and die for Christ, and because of that the angelic hosts will sing, 'Praise and glory and wisdom and thanksgiving and honour and power and strength to our God for ever and ever, Amen.' For it is by God's power that they are able to give their lives for him.

The mind of the Seer is that, though the church on earth may be persecuted and its members suffer, as it has done since the beginning, yet Jesus the Lord is always with it but its victory over evil can only be seen, and perhaps not in this world, in the light of heaven. The message of the Apocalypse is that we can trust in the Lord Jesus and that meanwhile, and however hard the going may be for ourselves and for others, we must not give up hope.

But how, at the level of their own living, did the martyrs and the other saints achieve their victory? For an answer we turn to the beatitudes.

They, the holy ones of God, have been detached from the things of this world. They were poor in spirit, open to God and ready to do his will. They have mourned with those who suffer, they have been merciful in their judgements of others, they have been peace-makers, always seeking to reconcile people with people and all with God. They have been pure in heart, without evil intentions and with their eye set on God. They have hungered and thirsted for what is right, for God's justice, for God's plan of salvation in the lives of men and women through the centuries, and in one way or another, whether by martyrdom or by spending their lives for it, they have suffered in his cause. For all this the kingdom of heaven is theirs.

As the scripture suggests, we cannot know how many of them there are, but we should remember and take comfort from the thought that all, canonised saints included, were ordinary men and women like ourselves; the only difference was that they were totally dedicated to God.

We all of us are called to the same destiny, called to be saints, as St Paul said. We have received that same gift: 'God's love has been lavished on us.' By baptism we were made children of God, by confirmation God's love was established within us, in this eucharist God's love is poured into our hearts again and again by the Holy Spirit, and by our prayer we are held in the love of God. By our lives, by our generous self-giving to others, by faithfulness to Christ, we bear witness to him so that we are in a sense all martyrs, witnesses to Christ when we mourn with the sorrowful, when we show mercy and love to those in need and by seeking justice and peace in our stricken world.

Then, if we have tried to live by the beatitudes, at the end God in his glory and beauty will be revealed to us. We shall see him face to face and seeing him we shall be made like him, God-like.

That is what is promised and, with the help of Mary and all the saints, let us strive for it.